TAROT
D'AMOUR

TAROT D'AMOUR

Find Love, Sex, and Romance in the Cards

KOOCH DANIELS
&
VICTOR DANIELS

WEISERBOOKS
Boston, MA/York Beach, ME

First published in 2003 by
Red Wheel/Weiser, LLC
York Beach, ME
With offices at:
368 Congress Street
Boston, MA 02210
www.redwheelweiser.com

Chakra figure on page 56 by Pieter Weltevrede used by permission
of the artist.

Chakra figure on page 58 by Jodi Carr used by permission of the
artist.

Library of Congress Cataloging-in-Publication Data

Daniels, Kooch N.
  Tarot d'Amour : find love, sex, and romance in the cards / Kooch
N. Daniels and Victor Daniels.
        p. cm.
Includes bibliographical references.
  ISBN 1-57863-292-7 (pbk. : alk. paper)
  1. Tarot. I. Daniels, Victor. II. Title.
  BF1879.T2 D35 2003
  133.3'2424--dc21

                                                        2002156319

Typeset in Bembo

Printed in Canada

TCP

10 09 08 07 06 05 04 03
 8 7 6 5 4 3 2 1

CONTENTS

ACKNOWLEDGMENTS

We are deeply indebted to the many teachers, colleagues, friends, and others who have contributed generously in diverse ways to this project, and without whom it would be less than it is. We especially wish to thank Jean Stein whose sexual savvy inspired our vision of sex, love, and the tarot, our agent Bob Silverstein of Quicksilver Books who kept us going when we were ready to give up, publisher Jan Johnson of Red Wheel/Weiser who gave the book a home, editor Jill Rogers who shepherded the book through the production process, our longtime spiritual teachers, and the good Faire People of the Northern California Renaissance Faire. The many others who have in some way influenced this book are too numerous to mention, but you know who you are. We'd like to give a special thanks to our daughter Tara, who assisted our editing process when we came to an impasse or our brains turned into mush. We are grateful to our spiritual family and intimate family, especially Lila, for their inspiration and support.

We also appreciate the many authors who throughout the past several decades have been our guides in shaping our understanding of tarot, and whose insights and wisdom filter through our personal understanding of the mystical arts and this book.

INTRODUCTION

Among the broken pillars of Apollo's temple at Delphi, a small, unobtrusive, rectangular hole opens into a dark subterranean space beneath the floor. In ancient times, braving hardship and hunger, travelers would come to this remote spot to ask questions of the oracle whose voice emerged from that small opening. The oracle seldom gave clear-cut answers. More often, it offered enigmatic responses that provoked the inquirer to think more deeply about his or her question.

In a sense, the Delphic Oracle, the most celebrated oracle in Western history, was an ancestor of the tarot, which is another kind of oracle that has spread far and wide. Like Delphi, the tarot offers insightful advice but leaves questioners with the ultimate responsibility for their decisions and actions. The tarot does not tell you exactly what to do, but rather illuminates the internal and external forces in a situation. It guides you toward a broader understanding of possibilities, deeper reflection, and, with a little luck, better judgment. Out of these may emerge unanticipated paths of growth and transformation.

The tarot is like a mirror that reflects the love, joy, pain, and struggles of life. Since its symbolism connects you with realities that live deep within your psyche, its cards can help you truly listen to your inner self, connecting you to an infinite well of wisdom that brings new perspectives to old dilemmas. When you contemplate the symbols shown on each card, you open your mind to look deeper within yourself and broaden your awareness of how you connect with the world around you. The tarot can help you take an important step toward a fuller understanding of your emotional life, and more effective action in your intimate encounters.

Whether you're new to the tarot, a longtime student of it, or somewhere in-between, you can benefit from our interpretations, card spreads, and commentaries to learn how to find greater adventure, clarity, and personal balance. Whether you do readings for yourself or for others, you'll sort out your emotions, and have more fun in the bedroom.

The tarot is a storybook of universal wisdom that consists of 78 playing cards divided between 22 major arcana cards and 56 minor arcana cards. The picture on each card connects you with a universal experience such as birth, initiation, transformation, and death. The cards portray romantic, psychological, financial, tangible, and spiritual dimensions of life. Mind, matter, and spirit can be explored in depth with the help of the tarot. In this book, we focus on romantic, sexual, emotional, and psychological concerns. It is written for love junkies, and everyone who enjoys learning more about their feelings. In these pages, you'll discover the potential truth of your own, or another's, romantic nature through our detailed explanations of the cards and their emotional meanings. You'll find playful possibilities for your lovemaking pleasures, and opportunities to move toward greater self-awareness and understanding of your specific situation. You'll open to new ways of thinking, feeling, and acting, and begin to find more enjoyment in things you already do.

No tarot card or spread will have exactly the same meaning for any two people. If you find that some of our interpretations fit your experiences and some don't, use just the information that makes sense to you. Ultimately, each person decodes the meaning of a card's symbols in terms of his or her own life situation, experience, and inclinations, and every person's interpretations are uniquely his or her own. We offer suggestions on how to interpret a card, but your own insights as you respond to the cards are the crucial catalyst for expanding your comprehension of the tarot and awareness of its implications.

Your own interpretations of the cards, and your ability to use them to live well will evolve as you continue on your life's path. Our intent is to offer you a lantern that will illumine your own inner truths, and those of others.

This book focuses explicitly on love, emotions, sexuality, romance, and the relationships in which all these occur. Love and its complexities dominate much of our life's journey. We can't, however, draw a simple line that separates our love life from the rest of our existence. Currents of emotions, the mysteries and magic of relationships, the forbidden fruits of love, and the many faces of Eros often get tangled up with ambition, money, children, power struggles, insecurity, envy, anger, greed, and personal identity. And yes, sex. When sexuality gets mixed up with any of the above, often it works yet another transformation. Things that seemed relatively simple suddenly become very complicated—sometimes in a difficult way, sometimes in a delightful one, and sometimes both at once. At other times, our emotions can make complications fall away, leaving exquisite simplicity. The cards can clarify our feelings and directions in ways that help us move through our dilemmas. They can be a direct channel into the human psyche and a reservoir of infinite wisdom.

Even if you're just interested in studying the cards, and not in doing readings with them, the message of each card can increase your understanding of your own consciousness and situation by inspiring deep reflection. The cards may communicate with you by answering your questions and offering you greater clarity, or, they may create more questions for you to ponder. They often serve to *illuminate* events of which you are only dimly or unconsciously aware, *affect* what occurs by opening up new directions of personal development you didn't even know existed, and *predict* by portraying configurations of forces and events that have meaning to you and implications for your future. Sometimes, by illuminating a situation and predicting where the forces at play seem to lead, a reading can inspire or frighten you into taking action that affects the way events unfold.

A mysterious wisdom can emerge from the unexpected turns we find in the tarot cards and their combinations. The ways in which they are juxtaposed in reply to our questions can loosen or break up our accustomed ways of thinking about ourselves, presenting ourselves, and meeting others. They can make us think deeply and creatively about our relationships and inspire new ways of connecting. They can lift us out of old ruts and habits, tap the wellsprings of our aliveness, and illuminate new possibilities and directions. We may discover that we are more than we dreamed we could be. We may find, to our surprise, that another person is quite different than we knew or thought he or she was. We can approach life in ways that we might never have considered if we'd remained locked in our old habits of thinking and acting.

PART I

THE ART OF READING

CHAPTER 1

GETTING STARTED

It [the tarot] is a monumental and unique work . . . strong and simple like the architecture of the pyramids, consequently long-lasting like them; it is a book which, as it speaks, makes us think; and surely one of the finest things which antiquity has left to us.

—ELIPHAS LÉVY, AS CITED BY OSWALD WIRTH
IN *TAROT OF THE MAGICIANS*

Your personal connection with the cards is the key to unveiling their mysteries. The more you study them, the more they tell you and the deeper you are drawn into the depths of your own psyche.

Just studying a book—even this one—won't teach you the magic of the tarot. You have to get to know the cards on a familiar, personal level—treating them like good friends with whom you can converse about matters great and small, and sometimes share your deepest secrets. Some cards help you feel better about yourself and your life, some cause you to question particular attitudes and actions, some help you use your mind more effectively, and some help you open up to your feelings, intuition, and hidden potential. When you share your hopes and fears with the cards, often they answer back, sometimes in surprising ways.

If you don't already have a deck, now's the time to get one. Metaphysical bookstores usually have a variety of demonstration sets that you can look through in your search for a deck that's right for you. Exploring various sets and comparing their colors, styles, and stances will help you find one you especially like. The more you enjoy looking at your deck, the more interested you'll be in studying it, and the more quickly you'll become acquainted with it. In turn, the more time you spend playing with the cards, the faster you'll learn how each card communicates with you about mind, body, heart, and soul.

Students sometimes ask if it's OK to use someone else's deck. This question is best answered by your own intuition. When you look at cards that others have used, ask yourself how they feel. Do you get a good feeling from them, or do they feel strange? If you feel good using them, they'll work for you. If you feel weird about using someone else's cards, they probably won't work in a positive way.

Using Your Cards

Whether you're a psychologist, sorcerer, yogini, or soccer mom, when you first begin to use your cards, you may want to think about your relationship with them and your purpose for using them. Whether you plan to use them for personal inquiry or for doing readings for others, you'll want to create a special bond between you and your cards. Your personal ritual to connect with them can be large or small, uniquely your own, or something borrowed from a spiritual tradition, like doing a Native American chant to communicate with the Great Spirit. You may want to use candles, incense, or aromatherapy to make an offering to the spirit who will be your inner guide as you ponder the cards' messages. Before I begin to use a new deck, I say a prayer and ask the goddess of esoterica and magic to shine her light to help me see the meaning of the cards clearly.

The first question I present to a new deck of cards is: "Will you work for me?" I need to know if the cards and I will be able to communicate. If the first card contains positive images, I assume the answer is yes. In time, it will become obvious whether a deck will work for you, because you'll find yourself either using your cards often or putting them in a drawer behind something you deem more important.

Whatever method you choose for initiating your cards, we recommend tucking them under your pillow for a night to let them rest under your dreaming, subconscious mind. This can enliven your relationship with the cards and improve your chances for a meaningful connection with them.

Putting your deck in a silk cloth or wooden box will protect your cards, and perhaps invite you to play with them. Covering your cards can also protect them from unnecessary worldly energy so they'll work better for you.

The Structure of the Tarot

The tarot is divided into two parts: 22 major arcana cards and 56 minor arcana cards divided into four suits. The major, or greater, arcana is allegorical, illustrated in the language of symbols. It describes various passages a person may take during the earthly journey. Love/hate, pleasure/pain, problems/resolutions, death/rebirth, and other transitions are visually depicted through a symbolic dialogue that can best be understood when you balance your conscious rational understanding with your unconscious intuitive understanding. The more you feel, as well as think, about a card's symbolic content, the more it will tell you.

The minor arcana, or lesser trumps, are represented in four suits: cups, swords, pentacles, and wands. Each suit corresponds to one of the four ancient elements and to an essential dimension of life. Cups are linked to the element of water and with emotional matters. Swords, representing the element of air, are connected with various kinds of mental energy. Wands, linked to the element of fire, are the creative, enterprising passions. Pentacles, or the element of earth, correspond with activity on the material plane, especially career and finances. Each suit consists of cards numbered 1 through 10, and four court cards: a king, a queen, a knight, and a page.

The Major Arcana: Storybook of Life

The major arcana, or major trumps, are a pictorial storybook of human consciousness. They depict the most important symbols in the tarot, illustrating pivotal stages in life's unfolding journey. They are considered so vital that some readers choose to do readings using them alone, without the minor arcana cards. They are numbered from 1, The Magician, to 21, The World. A card numbered zero, The Fool, can be placed at either the beginning or the end of their sequence.

The symbols in the major cards illustrate the gamut of life's experiences. Birth and death, pleasure and pain, heroes and villains, lovers and hermits, success and challenge, and evolution and transformation are represented in powerful images that reflect polarities that we all face as we swim through the myriad currents in the river of life. Spiritually, their substance has been correlated with unlocking the mysteries of the wisdom of the soul, but it is worldly concerns, relationships, and loves that lead most people to consult the cards. Fortunately, the symbols speak to both heart and soul. Just as tantric yogis embrace their passion as they walk their spiritual path, the cards can focus equally on enlightenment or lust, and cast light on whatever concern a person is questioning. The major arcana interpretations given here focus specifically on examining the cards for answers to queries about love, partnerships, emotions, and sexual dilemmas and opportunities.

0 The Fool: Fun-loving, funny, carefree, high-spirited, adventurous, willing to play in the moment, vulnerable, and truth seeking

Reversed card: Mentally aloof, gullible, noncommittal

I The Magician: Has sex appeal, intelligence, creativity, and charm; may analyze emotions and be critical of feelings, but desires love

Reversed card: Overly analytical, nervous, impatient, sometimes lost in mental vortexes

II The High Priestess: Not aware of her attractiveness, dutiful, truthful, idealistic about romance, sensitive to emotional stimuli

Reversed card: Easily infatuated, emotionally distant, insecure, dogmatic

III The Empress: Loves affection; enjoys romance, wine, music, and fun; passionate, loving, nurturing; understanding of partner's needs

Reversed card: Schemer; obsession with emotions; demanding, egocentric

IV The Emperor: Responsible for his commitments, supportive; enjoys physical passion and debate; observant, powerful, respected, armored

Reversed Card: Domineering, obsessed with sex, insensitive, egocentric

V The Hierophant: Philosophical about love; intolerant of indiscretions; tries to control passion, may be emotionally reserved; often a healer

Reversed card: Possessive, blindly dogmatic, argumentative, unbending

VI The Lovers: Questioning; loves romance, enjoys flattery and flirting, but devoted when in love; moves quickly toward consummating passion

Reversed card: Indecisive, arrogant, ambivalent

VII The Chariot: Fast-moving, ambivalent about commitments, sees the value of staying single, but wants to enjoy the fruits of passion, playful when in love

Reversed card: Unforgiving, melancholic, holds on to the past

VIII Strength: Catlike; sees through you; persevering, usually gets his/her way; likes to get lots of attention; may be passionate and fiery or quiet and inward

Reversed card: Dominating, needy, afraid to show vulnerability

IX The Hermit: Independent; attracted to love, but shy of going after it; has fear of intimacy, but strong need for acceptance and love

Reversed card: Controlling, critical, emotionally introverted

X Wheel of Fortune: Flexible toward change; the wheel of romance turns toward the new, bringing improvement and greater enjoyment in love

Reversed card: Doubting, status-seeking, undependable

XI Justice: Looks at consequences of actions; can get caught up in guilt; mediator, peacemaker; may spoil partner with strong sentiments and caretaking

Reversed card: Judgmental, lacks trust, indecisive, easily hurt

XII Hanged Man: Sees things from unusual perspectives, needs emotional space, doesn't make promises unless they can be kept, doesn't open the heart easily

Reversed card: Hungup on emotions, unrealistically idealistic, inflexible

XIII Death: Loves teasing, sex, and physical pleasures; intensely emotional; can be secretive about feelings; able to detach and start anew, transformative

Reversed card: Overly sensitive; cynical, vengeful; moody if things don't go right

XIV Temperance: Inwardly strong, emotionally centered; reconciles opposites; generous, optimistic; works toward self-improvement, enjoys freedom

Reversed card: Undemonstrative, insensitive to feelings, impulsive

XV The Devil: Energetic, passionate, lustful, strongly sexual; struggles with temptations; plays devil's advocate; dutiful, serious, intolerant

Reversed card: Pessimistic; low self-esteem; sometimes dishonest, or too clever for his or her own good

XVI The Tower: Intense forces of nature; turbulent emotional currents; resistance to change; confronting challenge, facing the inevitable

Reversed card: Lack of compassion; confrontational; sabotages love

*XVII **The Star:*** Cheerfulness, hope, inward peace; optimistic about love and willing to go the extra mile to make it happen; a sense of perspective

Reversed card: Unforgiving, head in the clouds, insisting that things be other than they are

*XVIII **The Moon:*** Romantic, sensitive to natural and personal rhythms; passive, reflective, dreamy; willing to pursue love no matter what the challenges

Reversed card: Moody, holds on to the past, overbearing

*XIX **The Sun:*** Openhearted, happy, extraverted, energetic, independent; doesn't waste time when opportunities for love arise; creative in the bedroom

Reversed card: Fiery; runs from conflicts; gloomy

*XX **Judgement:*** Keeps promises, bonds deeply; subtly demanding or insatiable when it comes to romance; searches for emotional depths, spiritual

Reversed card: Unpredictable; loses sense of self in others; easily infatuated

*XXI **The World:*** Focused intentions, altered awareness, expansiveness; opening the heart; intimacy; going beyond limitations, responsibility for commitments

Reversed card: Deflated sense of self; lacking perspective; stagnant emotions

The Minor Arcana: Windows on a Wider World

Images in the minor arcana reflect currents and eddies in the river of life. Each suit represents a different dimension of existence and examines events through a distinct lens. When a lesser trump (minor arcana) card appears in your spread, it points to the earthly play of natural forces in spiritual, psychological, emotional, and physical realms. By contemplating the universal qualities found in these cards, we can see new dimensions of reality come alive—qualities that speak to us all, regardless of our religion or culture. The minor arcana expand the compass of the tarot beyond the dimensions represented in the major arcana. The central theme of each suit works with the symbols found on the individual minor arcana cards to deepen your understanding. Table 1 (see page 13) gives a summary of correspondences and themes of the four suits of the minor arcana.

Table 1. Correspondences for the Minor Arcana.

Suit	Element	Sign	Purpose	Realm	Affects	Sexual Link	Anatomical Influence	Season
Wands	Fire	Aries, Leo, Sagittarius	Doing and creating	Inner spirit	Will/desire, enterprise	Attraction, passion	Digestion, hunger, sleep	Spring
Cups	Water	Cancer, Scorpio, Pisces	Feeling and intuiting	Emotions	World of sensing	Sensuality	Semen, blood, fat, urine, mucus	Summer
Swords	Air	Gemini, Libra, Aquarius	Thinking, challenging	Mind	World of ideas, intellectual pursuits	Seduction	Circulatory, lymph, endocrine, and nervous systems	Winter
Pentacles	Earth	Taurus, Virgo, Capricorn	Touching and grounding	Body	Material concerns, physical realities, financial world	Copulation	Bones, flesh, skin, hair	Autumn

The Suit of Wands

Key Associations
Element: Fire
Esoteric maxim: To achieve
Realm: Inner spirit
Desire: Enterprise

Wands are linked with the element fire, which appears in forms that range from the warmth of affection to the heat of passion. It can point to the intensity of desire, the ardor of love, or even a fanatical obsession of someone blinded by love, lust, or longing. This suit parallels the feelings deep inside you when you recognize your life mate, or when you have a heated debate that kindles friction in your mind. The challenge is to turn that friction into useful lessons rather than lingering and poisonous resentments. Connect with its power, and your creative spirit can swing into action. The forceful energy associated with wands can appear in such diverse forms as emotional quests, financial ambition, spiritual pursuits, and passionate concerns about life's directions, challenges, and rewards. When no wand cards appear in a spread, it can indicate a need for greater focus or for defining goals.

The three astrological sun signs linked with this suit are Aries the ram, the first sign of the zodiac, which is ruled by Mars; Leo the lion, the royalty of the stars, which is ruled by the Sun; and Sagittarius the archer, ruled by Jupiter. They share the fiery qualities of enthusiasm for living, vitality of mind and body, a potent, willful nature, and thirst for wisdom.

Positive Attributes: Willpower; stimulating, exhilarating, creative, exciting; expansive radiance, warmth, passion, high energy, power, ingenuity; productive, affectionate.

Negative Attributes: Hotheadedness, insensitivity; control or power trips, manipulation, provocativeness, egocentricity, restlessness, overzealousness.

The Suit of Cups

Key Associations
Element: Water
Esoteric maxim: To know
Realm: Emotions
Desire: Experience

The dominion of this suit is the emotions and the world of romance. Linked with the element water, it suggests the ability to go with the flow, to feel tides of emotions on deep levels, to dive into the heart of concerns, to be sensitive, reflective, and empathic, and to intuit unspoken and subconscious realities. Drink from the cup of love and your heart is never empty! Hold the chalice of the divine and your mind is never without hope. Deeply understanding the realm symbolized by cups involves moving from love as infatuation and personal gratification to love as mutual giving and appreciation of the gift of infinite joy that a heart connection can bring. Sexual realities are significant when discussing cups, for the physical joys of the body are most often tasted when someone drinks from the juicy cup of love.

The lack of cups in a spread can indicate disconnectedness from feelings or lack of emotional concern. On the wheel of the zodiac, the Sun signs that correspond to cups are Pisces the fish, ruled by Jupiter and Neptune; Cancer the crab, ruled by the Moon; and Scorpio the scorpion, ruled by Mars and Pluto. These watery personalities are often described as intensely emotional, sensitive, caring, psychic, and good in bed.

Positive Attributes: Emotional; depth of feeling, penetrating insight; empathy, sensitivity, sensuality, intuition; dreams, memories, the subconscious, sexually passionate.

Negative Attributes: Jealousy, possessiveness, insecurity, loneliness, complicated emotions; fools around flirtatiously; self-indulging, too fluctuating, moody, or changeable.

The Suit of Swords

Key Associations
Element: Air
Esoteric maxim: To dare
Realm: Intellect
Desire: Equilibrium

Swords represent the element air, the intellect, the construction of ideas, fanciful flights of insight, foresight, logical perceptions, critical thinking, and conscious wisdom. When discussing this suit, ideas, like seeds blowing in the wind, are the key to interpreting its meaning. Whether they're rational or intuitive, serious or somber, spiritual or romantic, thoughts play a central role when an abundance of swords appears in your spread. Decision-making about romance and lovemaking, choosing between or among alternatives, and determining love's direction fall under the symbolic canopy of swords. When you take a sword in hand, you wield power, and this suit is a metaphor for the strength of thoughts, words, and visions. The cutting edge of the blade symbolizes the power of ideas. When swords dominate a spread, the mind rules—except in those cases where they point to a lack of thoughtfulness and a need to think more carefully about a matter.

Swords are associated with the zodiac signs of Aquarius the water bearer, coruled by Uranus and Jupiter; Gemini the twins, ruled by Mercury, and Libra the balance, ruled by Venus. Natives of these sun signs often display analytical and creative thinking, mental dexterity, and versatility in the realm of contemplation. Their ideas can be capable of soaring above the mundane, refreshing like a breeze on a hot summer day, or, if negative, chilling like the sharp winds of a winter storm howling across a barren plain.

Positive Attributes: Mental forces, swift thinking, keen ideas, logic, wisdom, clear perceptions; discriminating, persuasive; the cutting sword of truth; utilizes potential.

Negative Attributes: Ignorance, vulnerability, lack of discrimination; difficulty making decisions; biases or dogmas stronger than reason; self-righteousness; flighty, teasing.

The Suit of Pentacles

Key Associations
Element: Earth
Esoteric maxim: To survive
Realm: Physical reality
Desire: Security

Pentacles, linked with the element earth, are connected with physical matter, finances, worldly obligations, grounded ideas, and diverse realms of material reality. Environmental concerns, real estate, and the tangible transformation of dreams into reality are related to this suit. Whenever the heart and emotions are being questioned and a pentacle appears, look at the practical side of the romantic situation. What pragmatic implications and elements—overt or beneath the surface—need to be considered? For instance, if you're considering marriage, where would you live? Would your family or your partner's help you get a loan to buy a house?

"Keep your feet on the ground!" can be considered the catch phrase for this suit which is linked with earthly measurements, practical hardheadedness, bodily sensations, and carnal desires. Physical needs, financial security, and concrete realities are a major focus, along with such questions as who pays the bills, what the harvest of your efforts is likely to be, and where your financial ambition lies. Your home, office, store, or any other tangible building, neighborhood, or other physical location may be involved when this suit appears in a spread.

Signs of the zodiac linked with pentacles are Capricorn the goat, ruled by Saturn; Taurus the bull, ruled by Venus; and Virgo the virgin, ruled by Mercury. Natives of these signs are said to be down-to-earth, pragmatic, good with money, and forceful in their professional world. When pentacles abound in your spread, money, status from career accomplishment, security needs, or financial situations linked with love concerns may be connected to the question you have asked or the issues that you need to address.

Positive Attributes: Physical gratification, body awareness, practicality, being grounded, stability, security, tangible realities, possessions, money matters, realism in romance.

Negative Attributes: Being overly materialistic or too worried about money; lack of sentiment; insecurity, impracticality, codependence; too focused on the physical.

The Suits and the Elements

The four classical elements, the foundation of all cards, embody intrinsic forces of nature. Whether these forces are compatible depends on the situation, the mood of the moment, and how the elemental properties interact. If you have enough water, you can put out a fire. Air, on the other hand, fans burning flames.

Looking at how elemental energies interact can help you make sense of minor arcana cards when you see different suits in a spread together. You can think about their associations in terms of a kind of relationship that could come into existence, one that exists and may or may not continue, or that doesn't have the potential to exist.

Alternatively, you can look at what the combinations of elements in a spread say about the relationships among different sides of yourself and how these may complement or conflict with one another, or what it says about someone else for whom you're doing a reading. Table 2 summarizes the elemental correspondences of each suit in the minor arcana.

Table 2. Elemental Correspondences for the Minor Arcana.

Suit	Element	Correspondence
Wands	Fire	Wands and swords (air): sizzle with the heat of desire. Wands and cups (water): create steamy emotions. Wands and pentacles (earth): ground the will. Wands and wands (fire): stoke fires of passion.
Cups	Water	Cups and swords (air): reflect the depths of insight. Cups and wands (fire): ignite the flow of lust. Cups and pentacles (earth): provide emotional foundation. Cups and cups (water): inspire high or low tides of emotion.
Swords	Air	Swords and wands (fire): generate heat and desire. Swords and cups (water): inspire intensity, which can be good or bad. Swords and pentacles (earth): combine contemplation with practicality. Swords and swords (air): express passionate playfulness (especially with ideas) or dry rationality.
Pentacles	Earth	Pentacles and swords (air): indicate realistic understanding. Pentacles and cups (water): mix strength with feeling. Pentacles and wands (fire): generate prosperous opportunity. Pentacles and pentacles (earth): create tangible reality.

The Court Cards

The court cards portray powerful possibilities, noble intentions, and royal personalities. While giving a reading, it's useful to examine each of the different possible meanings of a court card and explore which aspects apply to the situation being discussed. Table 3 explains some of the most obvious meanings of the court cards. This is, of course, just a beginning. Your discussion of each court card in relation to its corresponding suit and element will amplify its possible meanings.

Table 3. Court Card Correspondences.

Card	Correspondence
King	adult male; masculine power; active; leader
Queen	adult female; feminine power; passive; authority
Knight	male or female; awakening of power; active or passive; militant, warrior, crusader, activist
Page	young or young-minded male or female; learning about power; active or passive; student, apprentice

Court cards can represent aspects of your situation or environment, other specific people, or parts of yourself as mirrored in their symbolic images. As you look at the specific masculine or feminine qualities they embody (while remembering that "masculine" and "feminine" often belong in quotation marks because qualities of each kind find various forms of expression in both men and women), keep in mind the basic qualities of the suit of the court card you're reading.

Traditionally, the king is masculine, the queen is feminine, and the knight and page are viewed as being of either gender. Because every person has both feminine and masculine qualities, the king can also characterize the strong, active, task-oriented, or assertive side of a woman and the queen can portray the nurturing, reflective, gentle, or passive nature of a man.

If you use astrology in your tarot readings, you can think about court cards in relation to their Sun-sign correspondences. Court cards in the suit of wands are discussed in relation to the fire signs Aries, Leo, and Sagittarius. A king, queen, knight, or page of swords represents the element air and the Sun signs Gemini, Libra, or Aquarius that are linked to it. Court cards in the suit of pentacles correspond to the element earth and its associated Sun signs, Taurus, Virgo, or Capricorn, while the nobility of the suit of cups share character with the watery signs of Cancer, Scorpio, and Pisces.

The queen of pentacles selected in an upright card position, for example, might reflect a down-to-earth woman who wants to be in charge, perhaps like the personality type often associated with Taurus, the bull, who tends to charge ahead. Because this sign is linked with Venus, she may be inclined to be sensuously romantic, amorously affectionate, and a potent sexual playmate. Or perhaps you'll intuit that the person who is represented by this card reflects the qualities of a Virgo, someone open-minded yet discriminating and cautious emotionally. Capricorn, another earth sign, is also linked to this queen, so you can consider whether qualities such as seriousness, emotional integrity, and a strong sense of ethics add meaning to your interpretation. Look at the connections and qualities attributed to the elements and their corresponding Sun signs to discern how they may contribute to understanding this card.

When they refer to specific people, court cards may need to include qualities associated with more than one suit or element. For example, when interpreting the king of cups you may find that the watery person represented by the card also has fiery wand attributes such as a hot temper or fierce motivation. It's up to you to determine how specific correlations can or can't be used with a given person and situation.

As always, let your intuition guide you in creating interpretive links. Be open-minded in your description of court card personalities because there aren't any purely fire/wand people, or earth/pentacle people, or air/sword, or water/cup people. When an astrologer reads a horoscope, he or she looks at the combination of all the planets and their constellations in relation to a person. People are more diverse than their Sun sign, which depicts only one element and one aspect of the ethereal map of their psyche.

Likewise, every good psychologist knows that the application of psychological concepts has to be sketched out in shades of gray rather than trying to stuff real people into tightly drawn conceptual boxes. Anyone who tries to pigeonhole a person into being all one thing and none of another is sure to miss the mark.

Thinking about the court cards in relation to suits, elements, and Sun signs gives you a springboard to dive into a reading. When you've grasped the implications of how all these interact, the oracle of your inner mind will find the best way to use or not use the information. And there will be times when your better judgment tells you not to say everything you think, see, or imagine.

CHAPTER 2

TRANSFORMATION AND SEXUALITY

Spiritual lovemaking transcends all other sexual experience.
Viewing sexual intimacy as sacred may well be the beginning
to rebalancing the female and male energies of the Earth.
—SIRONA KNIGHT, *MOONFLOWER*

The tarot helps us recognize the themes of transformation that dominate our sexual and emotional relationships. How these themes unfold and connect for you depends on how the cards relate to your issues and dilemmas, or those of the person for whom you're reading. As you work with your cards, you'll identify troublesome issues and intriguing possibilities concerning love's journey. Whether you're seeking friendship, looking for love, casually or seriously dating, involved in a committed relationship or marriage, or struggling with one that's on the rocks, the tarot can help you recognize what's most important in your life.

Lessons on the Path of Life and Love

Here are ten themes of transformation that the tarot can help you recognize and apply to your experiences.

1. Finding your own way. We can learn to accept each other as we are, without trying to change each other to fit preconceptions and misperceptions. Trying to force change on another is a recipe for ongoing trouble. Instead, try to change how you are with your partner, which may, in turn, cause him or her to act differently with you.

2. Living your life as if it's an intriguing adventure. Give yourself permission to focus on what you presently have that contributes to your well-being instead of dwelling on fears, negativity, or doubt. This can make all the difference between feeling good or feeling bad. Your situation may need to be changed, but your state of mind can make these changes exciting or difficult, depending on your outlook.

3. Freeing others from blame for your problems. None of us likes being the object of ridicule or reproach. If you and another person are having problems, you each contribute to the situation (even if you're deaf and blind to your part of what you're doing). You're each 50 percent responsible for your relationship. Blaming the other person may make you temporarily feel better, but it's likely to make your relationship worse.

4. Learning to express both your love and your power. The desire for power over another is often a second-rate substitute for expressing love when we are afraid our caring won't be reciprocated. Happiness intensifies when you give your friendship in a way that involves mutual communication and caring, or you give love in a way that involves mutual passion and satisfaction. One-way relationships that demand much and give little are usually dead-end streets.

5. Taking charge of your own attitudes and feelings. Some of our suffering is inevitable, but with negative thinking, we ourselves create the rest of it. We can learn to create joy, happiness, and pleasure instead. Positive thinking and the ability to transform our attitudes with skills such as "positive reframing"—reinterpreting a situation or event you view as negative so that your focus shifts to something in the situation that can be seen as positive—are available to anyone who wants freedom from feeling helpless and seeing every glass as half empty rather than half full.

6. Learning to form various kinds of relationships. There are a number of different kinds of short-term, long-term, and permanent relationships. Choose to develop those that fit your needs and allow them to evolve into something else when your needs change. One size and style does not fit all in relationships any more than in clothes or shoes.

7. Drawing nourishment from both your senses and your depths. Life lived well draws fully on your sensory contact with the world. This includes the sounds you hear, the scenes you see, and the fragrances you smell, as well as the movement, tension, and relaxation of your body. We are physical beings.

At the same time, consult your dreams, daydreams, drawings, writings, and the powerful, evocative images of the tarot cards. These can provide powerful keys to insights, needs, and inclinations that can help you confront and transcend troublesome habits and obsolete ideas about how you "should" be living.

8. Encouraging intimacy and satisfying lovemaking through good communication. Communication includes learning to see, hear, and sometimes intuit what's going on with others—and within ourselves. It includes learning to say and point out clearly what's going on around us. Also, it includes developing the ability to sense the best moment and method to make our statement or our move, as well as when it's wise to avoid either saying or doing certain things.

9. Bringing closure to old, unfinished conflicts or complexes. Being here now means meeting someone without transferring your unfinished business from past relationships—whether with parents, friends, or lovers—onto that person. If you're seeing your friend or lover only dimly through a projection screen of your past traumas, troubles, or glorifications, then you need to work those through in counseling, therapy, or relationship coaching. You also need to be honest with your friend or lover about what you're trying to get through in order to be truly with that person, in the present. And he or she may need to allow you room to do that.

10. Invoking the magic of love through mutual respect. This entails no coercion, no exploitation, no deception, and no self-deception. It means honoring the other person's uniqueness and inclinations and also his or her fears and inhibitions, moving as gently or passionately as is appropriate.

In the best relationships, the line between giving and receiving may blur into a synergy in which you receive in giving and give in receiving, and there is no clear boundary between the two. To develop and express respect of this kind may require that you let go of old role expectations that impede it.

Sex and Spirituality

The sacredness of sex is a central focus of this book. Sex is a natural function. Necessary for procreation, it is usually quite enjoyable when both parties are willing participants. In fact, sexuality is not only natural and a potential source of great pleasure, but it can be profoundly blissful, and even deeply spiritual. It can embody a

- 23 -

communion between two people and the divine spirit of life that animates all beings.

Our approach to sexuality is connected with the tantric path that includes sharpening your mind/body awareness and learning to open your heart. "Tantra teaches you to revere your sexual partner and to transform the act of sex into a sacrament of love," declares Nitya Lacroix in *The Art of Tantric Sex*.

In modern Western societies, "foreplay" is widely regarded as just a prelude to intercourse. In both tantric and Taoist practices, however, the point of foreplay is to prolong all the lovemaking—the touching, caressing, and teasing that are part of the experience. This prolonged ecstasy deepens partners' joy, increases their interpersonal sensitivity, and enriches their souls.

Loving and respecting our bodies and striving to experience greater sexual pleasure does not mean acting in ways that are likely to have unwanted consequences—for you or for anyone else. Awareness includes recognition of possible future effects of present actions.

Since lovemaking is part of most people's lives anyway, we do well to perceive and experience it in a way that is respectful, beautiful, affirming, and enriching, rather than in a way that is insensitive, hard, judgmental and degrading. In the following pages, we explore how to make sex more fun and enjoyable and invite you to do the same.

CHAPTER 3

INTERPRETING THE CARDS: EIGHT SOURCES OF ILLUMINATION

Reading the Tarot symbolically rather than literally doesn't predict a given future; rather, it offers us opportunities to participate in the creation of a new and unpredictable future.
—SALLIE NICHOLS, *JUNG AND THE TAROT*

The tarot is a tool to help you look into your soul and into the souls of others. It helps you see the potential for love waiting within and the forces that threaten it. It can also enhance your ability to find love, by showing you how to make better use of your personal strengths and your less-developed qualities. You can use the cards to help you find a new lover (or even lovers), or to deepen and enrich your relationship.

When you look at a card, examine its various components, and free-associate ideas with them as well as with the whole card. When you put all your thoughts and feelings about a card together, you'll have discerned what it means to you. Aspects that can help you decipher a card's significance are:

- Title
- Symbols
- Numbers
- Astrology
- Archetypes
- Colors
- Gender
- Reversal

You can use as many of these as you wish to help you interpret a card, and you can emphasize whichever of them you like. For instance, if you're really into mythology or astrology, you may want to put extra emphasis on those aspects. If not, you can do excellent readings without discussing them at all. As you practice, you'll find which aspects resonate with your own inclinations, and develop your own interpretative style. When you read the cards, anything that gives you a clue for doing insightful interpretations is fair play. You can use the resources you have and the tools you're familiar with to start exploring the meanings of the cards. For instance, you can apply tantra, the Kabbalah, the Tao, the Medicine Wheel, and any other spiritual and transpersonal teachings to help make card interpretations. The more willing you are to trust your own insight, intuition, and awareness, the faster you'll progress. If you're a beginner, you can start out by using just one or two of the items that follow.

Titles

Each of the 78 tarot cards has a title that suggests something about its meaning. The themes summed up in the titles reflect different aspects of human nature and activity.

The following list of major arcana titles was recorded by the London-based occult fraternity the Hermetic Order of the Golden Dawn in the early 1900's:

I The Magician	XII The Hanged Man
II The High Priestess	XIII Death
III The Empress	XIV Temperance
IV The Emperor	XV The Devil
V The Hierophant	XVI The Tower
VI The Lovers	XVII The Star
VII The Chariot	XVIII The Moon
VIII Strength	XIX The Sun
IX The Hermit	XX Judgement
X Wheel of Fortune	XXI The World
XI Justice	0 The Fool

Let's use The Sun as an example of searching for a card's message just by considering its name. Begin by free-associating with your understanding of the sun. What does it mean to you? When I think of the sun, I feel warm, happy, positive thoughts. The Sun, the closest star to Earth, is the center of our universe. Its radiant rays encourage growth, healing, and regeneration. On the zodiac wheel, the Sun rules Leo. In our bodies, it represents a channel of positive energy that dances in polarity with negative lunar energy going up the spine. When I interpret The Sun card, I use all these associations to describe its meaning. You will use your own associations.

Often, people unfamiliar with the tarot become anxious when the Death card appears. Their fear stems from the name of the card, which makes them think immediately that they or someone close to them will soon die. It's important to remember, however, that the potential for physical death is only one aspect of this card. Symbolically, death is the falling away of an old habit, way of thinking, or life circumstance that allows a rebirth of spirit and leads to a vital period of growth and transition. An old reality or pattern dies, and a new one emerges. When you interpret this title, keep in mind that it can point to a time of enriching transformations and energizing new and potent directions.

Children have a harder time grasping a metaphorical meaning than adults do, and because they tend to understand things literally, the Death card can be very upsetting for them when it appears. In readings for children, I usually remove this card from the deck.

The title of each of the 56 minor arcana cards also contains clues to its meaning, but the titles are enigmatic unless you're familiar with the qualities associated with the four suits (Cups, Swords, Wands, and Pentacles) and the ten numbers. Once you can respond to each suit in relation to its associated attributes, the minor arcana meanings also become more apparent through their titles.

Symbols

A symbol can be a name or picture that's part of everyday life, or it can be more esoteric. It may imply something specific, like a heart that represents love, a skull and crossbones that indicates poison, or something more abstract. When you study the tarot, you'll increase your understanding of the unspoken language of symbols.

The tarot carries us into a symbolic realm rich in possibilities. When we open our minds to the signs and symbols in these cards, we expand our awareness of the universal, nonverbal language found in the collective unconscious of humanity. The symbol of an arrow, for example, transcends time, nation, and culture. Our own understanding of an arrow mirrors that of people who lived a thousand years ago: a shaft shot from a bow, a potentially lethal weapon that has the power to point toward and hit a target.

When you look at an arrow on a tarot card, your personal association will reflect your own background or experience. You may take it as a sign that Cupid is ready to strike, or draw on your knowledge that an arrow represents the zodiac sign of Sagittarius. Depending on the symbols around it, an arrow may seem passionate in one context, and aggressive in another.

Your associations will tell a story that gives meaning to your reading. Every symbol, whether a coin, a bird, or a path, contains several, or even many, possible messages. Your ability to interpret symbols and apply them to the psychological realities and life situation of the person for whom you're reading is one of your most important tools for card divination. The better your grasp of the language of symbols, and the more fully you let your imagination, intuition, and awareness guide your insights, the faster and more deeply you'll be able to convey the meanings found within each card.

A good way to interpret tarot symbols is to free-associate ideas with the picture—and/or let your client do so. Keep things simple. Let your mind and feelings be open and relaxed, play with ideas, and let the card or one of its symbols trigger one word or phrase after another. Describe what you see, hear, or feel on as many different levels as you feel appropriate. Use your senses. Taste, smell, touch, and kinesthetically sense inside your body what each symbol is about and how you're responding to its message. What you *feel* about each symbol connects you with its deepest significance. The impact of symbols is felt inwardly, and frequently it's on a subconscious level that they're recognized and intuitively understood.

As you practice, try thinking about symbols in relation to the different planes of manifestation represented by the four elements: earth, air, fire, and water. Earth corresponds to the material, physical plane, which includes the financial world. Air is associated with the mental plane, or psychological aspects of life. Fire is linked with passion, creativity, and the inner spirit. Water is connected with the emotions, intuition, and deepest feelings about life. These four realms encompass much of what people will ask you, and probably much of what concerns you.

But beware of getting locked in too tightly to the cards' usual symbolic meanings. Once I did a reading for a jovial, down-to-earth gentleman whose cards were filled with swords. Nothing he said suggested that he was lost in his mind, or that he needed to clarify his thinking. He turned out to be a surgeon, and the swords were a literal representation of the precise cutting that filled his daily work.

The more you're willing to use your own interpretations and intuition instead of relying on a book for the meaning of the symbols, the more skilled you'll become. To give good readings, you'll need to use your own insight.

Symbols don't have a fixed or single interpretation. For instance, you may interpret the wheel on the Wheel of Fortune card in relation to Christian thought, and others may offer alchemical, Buddhist, Hindu, or strictly personal explanations. And all may be right. The symbolic content of each card reflects the subjective viewpoint of the person who's discussing it. When you open your mind to unveil the mysteries of tarot, you're opening a door to the world of symbolic creation.

Numbers

Every card, except the court cards, has a number as well as a title. Numbers offer another way to grasp the meaning of each card. You can include simple numerology (the meaning of numbers in relation to human behavior) in your interpretation of each card.

When you put the central theme of a card's suit and the symbols shown on the card together with the qualities of its number, you immediately know something about any minor arcana card you pick up. This makes interpretation easier than if you had to learn about each card individually with no guiding principles to connect them. Once you've assimilated this section and have a feel for the qualities that go with each suit, you'll have some understanding of the minor cards even without remembering all of the comments in chapter 7 about every card in each suit.

Suppose, for instance, that you use this method to interpret the Ace of Cups. Use information about the suit of cups, and add what you learn about the qualities attributed to the number one. Cups relates to feelings, emotions, sensuality, and intuition. Number one is linked to the power of masculine, positive energy, radiance, leadership, and great potential. Combining these sources of information yields a picture of powerful, positive emotional energy with a potential to radiate strong feelings. Just knowing something about the number and the suit tells you enough for a basic interpretation.

With the major arcana, if a card bears a number between one and nine, you may interpret its numeric vibration as equal to its assigned number. For example, The Magician and all aces are interpreted as the number one. However, if a card's number is higher than the number nine, then it must be reduced to a single digit between one and nine. To find the card's single digit, add the numbers together. For instance, since the Wheel of Fortune bears the number 10, you add the one and the zero together (1 + 0 = 1).

Likewise, The Devil card is number 15, so you add the one and the five to yield six (1 + 5 = 6). Thus, The Devil card has a number-six vibration. (Interestingly, The Devil is numerologically equivalent to The Lovers card and the numerical vibration of the planet Venus, which is associated with the Goddess of Love and Pan, the horned god of seduction and playfulness.)

By looking at the numerical vibration of each card, you obtain a different key to understanding behavior and compatibility. Table 4 gives a summary of the cards' numeric correspondences that can help you clarify each card's numeric significance.

Table 4. Numerological Correspondences of the Major Arcana.

Card Number	Major Arcana Card	Numerical Value
Ace & Ten	The Magician, Wheel of Fortune, The Sun	1
Two	The High Priestess, Justice, Judgement	2
Three	The Empress, The Hanged Man, The World	3
Four	The Emperor, Death	4
Five	The Hierophant, Temperance	5
Six	The Lovers, The Devil	6
Seven	The Chariot, The Tower	7
Eight	Strength, The Star	8
Nine	The Hermit, The Moon	9
Zero	The Fool	0

There are many associations with numbers in both Eastern and Western numerological traditions. If you're a student of numbers, stay with your own system and use its correlations to examine your own life in relation to numbers and analyze your associations with them. Your own insight into a number's potential meaning will carry the most weight. For example, if two is my favorite number, I'll interpret twos as auspicious, pointing to probable good fortune when they appear in my readings. The following interpretations are offered only as a guide.

1: Beginnings, Potential, Creativity, and Power

One, the first number, has a phallic quality. It leads the way as the seed or source for new opportunity and original beginnings. Because it correlates with masculine power, it's associated with yang, positive energy, light, radiance, leadership, authority, and rulership. It often points to people who are freethinking, self-sufficient, ambitious, and wise. When a number one type personality is in love, it's an all-or-nothing affair in which sex and affection are prominent. This person likes people, is outgoing, and will take center stage, for the limelight is his or her natural environment. It may refer to the first bloom of a new relationship, or to the achievement of a true sense of unity by a couple or family.

Negative qualities associated with this number are insensitivity, selfishness, and giving more criticism than one is willing to take. It can refer to an egocentric approach to a relationship ("I'm Number One") in which either you or your partner are unwilling to meet the other's needs or respect his or her individuality and directions.

2: Polarity—Splitting Apart and Coming Together

Two is associated with the feminine, receptive, Shakti, or *yoni* (derived from the Sanskrit *yonih,* signifying womb, abode, source) energy. Women's issues, motherly concerns, sisterly love, emotional and intuitive perception, and choosing between different alternatives are qualities associated with this yin (the feminine complement of yang) number of duality. Two is the number of intuition and the ability to see into the subconscious—qualities associated with the High Priestess. It shows the potential for a relationship, as one and one equals two, a couple, the pairing of two people whose hearts open to enable the development of a relationship. The opposite of number-one energy traits, the two personality is inward, feeling, sensitive, open to messages from the unconscious self, and prone to experiencing highs and lows like the ebb and flow of the ocean's tides.

Two's negative qualities include worry, moodiness, and getting involved head over heels before the time is right. Two can also point to getting stuck in your feelings, in power struggles, or in polar-opposite views about a situation.

3: New Dimensions

Three is linked with ambition, scholarly ideas, philosophy, unity, and love's fortune. These attributes are keys to understanding the personality of this numeric vibration, which is adaptable and expansive. When you see the number three, it often indicates good times, high-spirited, inspirational moments, and fertile abundance.

Three's disposition is outgoing, optimistic, generous, good at making friends, flirtatious in courtship, and energetic in bed. Adventurous by nature, these numeric types try to go many places and enjoy a wide variety of experiences. Controlling passion is not one of their strong points, and talking too much usually comes easily to them. Interest in mystical traditions opens the spiritual dimension in many three relationships.

Although customarily an auspicious number, three can forecast downward turns and havoc when desires, aspirations, or ideals have no basis in reality. Wanting to go too far, too fast, and to test all limits can get in the way of sensitive and enduring encounters if the number three vibration is off-key. A triad in love can be troubling or exciting, but in either case, it's seldom a stable situation.

4: Steady Progress

Four is connected with laying a foundation and taking slow-but-steady steps up the ladder of romance or of life pursuits. However, since it is also a symbol of natural instincts, the unexpected, teenage energy, rebellion, the eccentric, nonconformity, and revolution, its vibration is anything but calm. Excitement is this number's rhythmic inheritance, and outbursts of emotions go hand-in-hand with it. Forceful and wild, the four vibration is hard to domesticate or tame, for opposition and noncommitment are among its characteristics. If you have a worthy cause, the large-hearted number four personality will often take the lead in helping spread your word. If you like the idea of foursomes in bed, flirting with your own gender, kinky sex, or playful sadomasochism, this number is for you.

When the four vibration moves the wrong way, everything that seems strong can fall apart. Foolishly taking love for granted is associated with this number, and so is the challenge of learning the hard way.

The shadow side of four is immobility, a commitment to keeping things the same even when they need to change. Four is the number of intolerant self-righteousness and acting without sensitivity to others' emotions. This side of four may have a hard time adapting to change. A four who is expressing this side may resist trying anything new in bed, and may be impervious to any of a partner's feelings that don't fit his or her own ideas about how things should be.

5: Thoughtfulness and Lyricism

Five is associated with the intellect, quick thinking, wit, education, communication, youthful vitality, and travel. Staying organized, keeping systematic records, writing a personal journal, paying attention to detail, and analyzing things critically are linked with this mercurial number.

People with this numeric vibration speak from the heart to deliver strong, inviting lyrics that carry emotional power, making them attractive partners for lovers who look for deep communication. For a number five, sitting and thinking without physical movement contributes to restlessness and hyperactive nervous thought. Miscommunication and tension around commitments can accompany the number five when it's upside down in a card reading. A personal solution is to cultivate focus and patience. Within a relationship, it's important to develop procedures for problem solving, rather than resorting to manipulation or insults. The art of disagreeing without becoming offensive is a lesson that fives often have to struggle to master.

6: Passion

When pleasure is too tempting to ignore, the sex—I mean the six—doesn't always cater to common sense. Connected with the Goddess of Love and the *Kama Sutra* (the ancient Indian text on the art of making love), the number six can't get away from its link to passionate sensations, heated mating rituals, erotic foreplay, and succulent lovemaking. Having fun, going out on blind dates, making wonderful wild love for hours, and renting XXX-rated videos to find out if there's anything new to be discovered are all characteristic of a number six personality.

Doing everything possible to win love, not taking no for an answer when there's a chance of success, and being persistent are all part of the winning disposition associated with the slow-but-sure success that often accompanies the aspirations of a number six person. Six is also a number of compromise, as it is linked with a dislike of arguments and a tendency to avoid confrontation. On the other hand, if conflicts are not buried and avoided, six is a good number for finding resolution and reconciliation of opposing inclinations, since pleasure and good times have a higher priority than disagreement.

7: Mysticism, Dreams, and Intuition

Seven indicates awareness through expansion of consciousness using some sort of intuitive or sensory process. Many people consider this a lucky number. It is connected with altered states of consciousness as well as winning at love. It is also linked with mysticism, tantric philosophy and the seven chakras, dreams, and psychic realities such as intuitive readings or spiritual healings. When seven turns up in your reading, it may mean that consulting your dreams will help you answer your question. Since it's also connected with fantasy, foggy illusions, the water's depth, addictions, and compulsions, this numeric vibration can be challenging to the practical or logical mind. Writing poetic verse, giving roses, and interpreting dreams are part of the natural domain of a number seven personality, who can become mentally restless while lost in his or her own mind trying to figure out what's real and what's illusion.

Because secrets are associated with this number, seven can also indicate distorted information or a lack of crucial data. An overactive imagination, a mistrust of emotions, and an unwillingness to be practical or to commit are qualities sometimes found with the number seven.

8: Limits and Responsibility

Learning is a key word for this number, which often indicates high energy and intense encounters. When such struggles with circumstances or with yourself are approached with a positive attitude, power, wisdom, and a release of creativity or active energy can emerge.

Karma, authority figures, conformity, restrictions, meditation, and visualizations are all associated with the number eight. Working hard and taking responsibility seriously are personality traits connected with it. So are goal-directed thought, following through on your intentions, perseverance, and concern with the passing of time. When you pull cards with this number, it's a reminder that your own actions and choices play a major part in almost everything that happens to you. It can be a message to stop blaming others for what happens in your life and fully recognize your role in creating your reality.

Taking life too seriously, worry, and heavy feelings can accompany this number. It often points to the need for contemplation, patience, and pause, to get a clear sense of where you are now and what you truly want before moving forward. When a card shows an eight lying horizontally, as in The Magician or the Strength cards in the Waite deck, it becomes a symbol of infinity, representing eternal life and unlimited possibilities.

9: Energy and Action

Don't plan on sitting still if this number is placed in your spread. Linked with martial arts, the aggressor, offensive and defensive positions, courage, assertiveness, independence, fiery thought, heated passion, stamina in lovemaking, and finding hidden reserves of strength to meet a challenge, this numeric vibration is the antithesis of sloth, weakness, or fear. Taking action and charging forward are the instincts of someone who has nine energy. Because it's the last digit in the numerical sequence, it corresponds with finding resolution, endings, cleaning out the psychic closet, getting rid of what doesn't fit, and moving in a new direction. It's a magical number associated with tantric ritual, initiation, and delicious sex.

Making a bad exit and leaving matters unfinished are negative attributes of this number. Being too dominating, angry, or sexually aggressive while overlooking other people's needs, sensitivities, and responses also linked with the nine's blunt edge. This can cause trouble in relationships.

If you and your partner slip into power struggles in which one or both of you are more committed to winning or to being "right" and having the other be "wrong" than to finding mutually acceptable resolutions, you need to ask, "Is there a way I can get what I want without having to be the winner and have the other person be the loser?" If the answer to that question is no for both of you, and neither of you is willing to work on changing that pattern, the outlook for the relationship is poor. Being obsessed with your ideas about how things are and ought to be, or clinging to old expectations of yourself and each other leaves little room for growth. If this "locked-in" quality becomes stultifying enough, one of you may feel driven to break out of the relationship, and the completion aspect of the number nine will turn the Wheel of Life.

0: Emptiness and Infinite Possibility

There is just one card given the number zero in the tarot. It is The Fool, the only card given the privilege of being placed either at the beginning or the end of the major arcana sequence. This card may suggest that the possibilities in a person or relationship add up to a big zero, or conversely that an openness, awareness, and receptivity make all things possible. Symbolically, the zero is described as the cosmic egg, or seed, from which numeric existence is birthed. By itself, it means nothing, but when joined with other numbers, it has infinite possibilities. It is considered neutral, neither positive nor negative, odd nor even, yet it is friendly with all other numbers. Although empty by itself, this numeric vibration is said to love company, and to expand the dimensions of any number it joins.

10: Return to One

The qualities of the Wheel of Fortune and the minor arcana cards numbered 10 are like the qualities of one, since you add the one and the zero to yield one $(0 + 1 = 1)$. Since ten follows nine, it also indicates that the old has come to an end, and in our reflections on it, we see a time for new beginnings. Yet it is also more than a one, for we arrive at ten after going through all the pain and joy, the bliss and suffering, of one through nine. As we embark on the next stage of our journey, we carry all that we've learned with us. Failure to learn the lesson contained in any experience we've been through means that we have to go through it and learn it all over again. In that sense, ten can refer to a beginning, or a place in life where many events merge, or to a completion in which "oneness" is achieved as a result of the integration of all that has occurred along the path.

Astrology

The earliest tarot decks displayed their astrological correspondences. Many modern decks continue this tradition. You don't have to be an astrologer to interpret tarot cards, but knowing the meanings of these ancient planetary and star-linked symbols provides another medium through which to probe the depths of the tarot.

For instance, The Emperor is related to Aries, which rules the first house on the zodiac wheel. Each arm of his throne is decorated with a ram, Aries' symbol. Any associations you have with Aries may offer insight into what this card suggests about a given situation.

Table 5 (see page 37) shows the astrological correlations devised by the Order of the Golden Dawn in the early 1900s. Arthur Edward Waite, member of that order, who created the ubiquitous Waite Tarot deck, illustrated by Pamela Colman Smith, popularized those correspondences.

If you already have your own astrological associations for the cards and they make good sense to you, go right ahead and continue using them. For instance, if you use Aleister Crowley's correspondences (see *The Book of Thoth,* which is about his tarot deck), you would interpret Judgement using his title of The Aeon and relate it to the element fire, instead of using Waite's zodiacal correlation, which is Pluto and fire. It's best to use whichever starry scheme fits your own personal understanding.

Archetypes

Each major arcana card is linked to an archetype, a symbolic representation of a quality that is universal in human experience. Carl Jung described an archetype as a primordial image reflecting basic

Table 5. The Major Arcana and Astrology.

Card	Correspondence	Astrological Glyph
The Fool	Uranus/Air	♅/△
The Magician	Mercury	☿
The High Priestess	Moon	☾
The Empress	Venus	♀
The Emperor	Aries	♈
The Hierophant	Taurus	♉
The Lovers	Gemini	♊
The Chariot	Cancer	♋
Strength	Leo	♌
The Hermit	Virgo	♍
Wheel of Fortune	Jupiter	♃
Justice	Libra	♎
The Hanged Man	Neptune/Water	♆/▽
Death	Scorpio	♏
Temperance	Sagittarius	♐
The Devil	Capricorn	♑
The Tower	Mars	♂
The Star	Aquarius	♒
The Moon	Pisces	♓
The Sun	Sun	☉
Judgement	Pluto/Fire	♇/△
The World	Saturn	♄

patterns or universal themes common to all peoples, and that are played out on the stage of life in all times and all cultures. An example of an archetype is the wise old man. When studying the tarot, you can identify The Hermit who carries the staff of wisdom as the old man archetype. Every ancient culture honors those who hold a lamp of wisdom that illuminates the path of life. The Hermit finds his counterpart in the ancient Egyptian god Thoth, procurer of wisdom, and in the Greek god Hermes, thought to be the father of alchemy, as well as in the Greek philosopher Diogenes, who is said to be the historical figure on whom the old man carrying the lamp is based. Myths often depict archetypes because their stories embody dominant themes or dramas played out repeatedly throughout history, illustrating the struggles of humanity and beliefs about the origin of life, sacred and mundane.

Each of the major arcana cards depicts a different archetype that can be discussed in regard to its significance today as well as in reference to numerous myths and cultures. Table 6 gives a partial list of correspondences between the major arcana and archetypes.

If you recognize an archetypal theme different from those listed in Table 6, continue to use it as long as it contributes to your readings.

Table 6. The Major Arcana and Their Archetypes.

Card Number	Card Name	Archetype
I	The Magician	Trickster
II	The High Priestess	Divine Maiden
III	The Empress	Mother
IV	The Emperor	Father
V	The Hierophant	Teacher
VI	The Lovers	Marriage
VII	The Chariot	Journey
VIII	Strength	Hero/Heroine
IX	The Hermit	Wise Person
X	Wheel of Fortune	Destiny
XI	Justice	Judge
XII	The Hanged Man	Sacrifice
XIII	Death	Rebirth
XIV	Temperance	Virtue
XV	The Devil	Evil
XVI	The Tower	Passage
XVII	The Star	Guide
XVIII	The Moon	Intuitive
XIX	The Sun	Source
XX	Judgement	Transition
XXI	The World	Home
0	The Fool	Child

Color

Color is a one of the primary indicators of the emotional content depicted in each card. Throughout our lives, we learn cultural associations with color. All we need to hear is: "I'm seeing red," "I'm feeling blue," or "She's green with envy," and we have all the information we need to know the emotional state of the person described. How we interpret color gives us one clue to understanding a card's message.

To interpret the cards in relation to color, begin by analyzing your own associations with the various colors. They may be different from mine. For instance, instead of associating green with envy, you may associate it with nature, aliveness, or peace of mind. It's not important for you to learn my associations with colors, but you need to understand your own. When you recognize your feelings about the colors, you'll have a valid system for interpreting the significance of card colors. If you're doing a reading for another person who mentions his or her own feelings about a color, you should respect and use them. Table 7 gives a summary of color associations.

Table 7. Color Associations.

Color	Association
Violet	Spirituality, royalty, idealism, inspiration, release
Blue	Emotional concerns, reflection, depth, enlightenment
Red	Power, love, sex, intensity, vitality, heat, anger, blood
Yellow	Intellect, conscious awareness, sunny energy
Orange	Success, courage, vigor, regeneration, warmth
Green	Prosperity, harvest, growth, healing, jealousy
White	Positive energy, protection, purity, peace
Black	Negative energy, the shadow side, pain, death

Gender

Each card has both masculine and feminine attributes. If you're reading for a woman and she chooses a card representing her personal self or her outlook, address the qualities of the card in a feminine context, even if the illustration on the card depicts a man.

If you're reading for a man and the card representing his self is one that illustrates feminine attributes, such as The High Priestess, be prepared to speak about feminine qualities in relation to the masculine. This doesn't mean that the man is homosexual (although occasionally this may be the case). Often, when a feminine card is pulled to indicate a man's conscious awareness, it's a signal to talk about his qualities in a softer, gentler manner, including attributes usually assigned to women such as sensitivity, intuitiveness, and nurturing.

Carl Jung described archetypal masculine qualities as the *animus* and the archetypal feminine qualities as the *anima*. When either anima or animus qualities exist but are discouraged, hidden, or repressed, they end up as part of the person's "shadow," a term Jung used to describe the sides of the personality that are not consciously displayed in public, and of which the person may even be unaware. The Devil major arcana is associated with this shadow, which includes specific tendencies that are hidden because the owner hasn't accepted them or has fears associated with them. Shadow qualities aren't necessarily bad. They may be attributes that most of us view as positive, but that the person has disowned, ignored, or neglected.

The anima and animus qualities take on a somewhat different character with each card. The Hierophant or Hierophant's animus qualities, for instance, include telling how things are and being an authority figure. When animus is tempered with anima, he becomes a wise, knowledgeable, sensitive guide whose counsel is well suited to the person who consults him (or her, if the reading is for a woman). When animus is exaggerated and extreme, the Hierophant becomes rigid, dogmatic, and authoritarian, more interested in the trappings of his (or her) position and presumed superiority over those who consult him (or her) than in being truly helpful to them.

Similarly, the anima qualities of The Empress include being a mother figure, with everything that implies about nurturing and protecting. When tempered with animus, The Empress will recognize that true nurturing includes encouraging others' autonomy and independence, and will encourage their steps in that direction and provide support when they need it. When anima is exaggerated and extreme, The Empress becomes overprotective and smothering and doesn't let others step out to find their own way in the world.

Both animus and anima qualities are part of being a whole human being. Both include sensitivities and abilities that every person needs. Since many (but not all) cultures encourage men to express animus qualities and hide anima qualities (and vice versa

for women), it's easy for both men and women to end up as cari-
catures and stereotypes. As a result, men in such cultures tend to
screw up their relationships because they don't hear what their
women need, and the women end up dependent and needy
because they don't learn to do for themselves. As we learn to let
go of these stereotypical limitations, men may see remarkable
improvement in their relationships with people of both genders,
and women may find that they're capable beings who can depend
on themselves to do what they need to in the world.

Reversal

When you shuffle your cards and lay out a spread, some cards are
right-side up and some are upside down, or "reversed." When you
turn over a card, lay it down just as it is. Don't turn all the cards
upright. When a card appears in a reversed position, you give it
almost the same interpretation you'd give an upright card, since it's
the same card with the same symbols. But the reversed position
suggests that the attributes are in some way upside down and need
some kind of adjustment to be put in correct order. The general
rule of thumb is that reversed cards illuminate the need for some
sort of work to be done to realize the qualities that the card represents. For example, The Empress indicates the fertility of love.
When reversed, instead of representing love, it points to the importance of the need to take care of the love in some way, to trust love,
or heal the heart. The interpretive focus is on love, but there is
work to be done to get it right. Instead of the road to love being
happy and smooth, there are bumps to jolt the emotions.

Let your intuitive perceptions help you interpret a card's reversed
significance. When working with reversed cards, assess immediate
concerns and evaluate whether the symbols refer either to a quality
that's present and too powerful, or one that's apparently weak or
underdeveloped and needs to be developed or strengthened.

You may also have a sense, either from the way the person
speaks and moves or from some intuitive source you can't quite
identify, that one or more of the reversed card meanings are rele-
vant, even when the card comes out right-side up. If so, bring them
into your reading, for there's a good chance that you'll be right. If
the person says something like, "No, I don't see how that fits," then
drop it and move on. A good reader, like a good counselor or psy-
chotherapist, will follow clues that lead somewhere and forget
those that don't.

CHAPTER 4

GUIDELINES FOR READINGS

It is exciting, sometimes upsetting, but deeply encouraging to feel yourself in action and apparently knowing where you are going even though you don't always consciously know where that is.
—CARL ROGERS, *FREEDOM TO LEARN FOR THE 80S*

As you react to the images on the cards, your feelings, intuitive impressions, and inner associations will mix with the tarot symbols, coming together in a dialogue with the unspoken, universal language of the subconscious. By looking at the patterns that emerge in many different spreads, you become familiar with their imagery, which speaks both through your analytical intellect and through the mysterious, misty realm of your subconscious mind.

Readers who combine the richness of the cards' symbolic discourse with their knowledge of human nature can become remarkably accurate in divining unspoken realities. Your mind needs to be open, and your self-centered concerns have to move out of the way. Intuitive insight at its best is nonjudgmental and free of prejudice, but this doesn't happen by itself. It requires that we step out of our personal biases long enough to hear and feel another's inner world.

Some of us are naturally more sensitive than others, but many such differences in sensitivity are due to early learning. Early in life, in the family, in school, and elsewhere, we receive recurrent messages that either encourage or discourage our trust in our perceptions of people or situations. Even people who have been conditioned to mistrust their intuitive perceptions, however, can learn how to listen once again to messages that are apparent to those who are open to them.

The art of tarot reading combines sensing your own and the

other person's feelings in the moment, understanding how to interpret the symbols on the cards meaningfully, and using your intuition to probe the unknown. Believing in yourself is the key to success. You won't get very far in any intuitive practice if you expect it to be overly difficult, or think it's something only other people can do.

When you first try to read the messages in the cards, keep things simple and let your mind play with ideas. Notice both your thoughts and feelings about the pictures and symbols, and be open to whatever they seem to tell you. If you aren't asking the cards a question, but are just looking for such messages as the tarot may offer, you can seek whatever wisdom the cards present in the moment. First impressions usually hold a crucial clue, so don't disregard them. Notice any symbols that jump out at you. Be open to symbolic meanings on as many levels as you feel are appropriate and trust what you're noticing and feeling. Look through your third eye of wisdom to use important insights in giving interpretive meanings for the cards. Wisdom is more than knowledge—it includes paying attention to how and what you say and do. This can be nourishing and helpful for you and, if you're reading for someone else, for the other person.

If you plan to give card interpretations, you'll need to know how to discuss symbols in relation to love and emotions. Since other people are sure to ask about their love life, be prepared to discuss the cards in relation to friendship, romance, and even sexual concerns. (Career and money tend to be the second most frequent concern.) Thinking about the symbols on a heartfelt level will help you relate to the diverse emotional situations you'll encounter in your readings.

Reading for Yourself

Looking to the cards for answers to your personal questions can be a wonderful way to enhance understanding and inner growth. Look at your own real-life questions in relation to card symbols, and become familiar with your own interpretive values. With a little contemplation and practice, the cards will offer fresh insights. Your ideas and feeling-intuitive associations with the card symbols will weave a story that relates to your question or situation.

Some readers claim that it's difficult to divine their own fortune since they are invested in what happens, but others open their intuitive minds to symbolic information about their own life. Until you experiment repeatedly with giving yourself readings, you won't know whether you can do so successfully or not.

Nonetheless, for contrast and comparison, it's also good to have someone else do your reading, someone who is not partial to your own sense of reality and doesn't already know your hopes and fears. In addition, by watching another person do a reading, you can study how others give meaning to the symbols. When you sample others' readings, you'll find qualities in them that you like and others that you don't. Once you experience a bad reading, you'll have firsthand experience of what never to do when giving your own readings.

Reading for Others

When you're reading for others, speak from your heart and mind, from both the right hemisphere (intuitive side) of your brain and the left hemisphere (logical side). In each moment, look for a balance of reasoned, linear thinking and intuitive, nonlinear thinking. If you do a reading only from your intellectual understanding of the cards, you'll have mostly a mechanical connection with your art. If you read solely from the intuitive side of your mind, you may forget to make concrete, practical connections with the other person's experience. Even though each reader learns to interpret the cards in his or her individual way, most clients need commonsense interpretations that relate explicitly to their interests and questions. Unless you are in a trance state, your psychic voice will include both intuitive impressions and logical assessment. First impressions often provide the strongest intuitive insights, so don't ignore them.

We are all psychic to a greater or lesser degree. Each of us has a sixth sense to help guide us through life. Some of us listen to our intuitive feelings; others ignore them. Trusting your hunches or feelings about tarot symbols will help you discern their meaning in relation to the person for whom you're reading. With time and practice, you'll develop more confidence in your sensing and intuiting self. In the same way that you strengthen any muscle when you use it repeatedly, your intuitive mind becomes stronger as you consistently call on it to work for you. At the same time, remember that most of us never get to the point where we're always right, so don't browbeat yourself when you're not and don't insist that your client accept your insights when they don't feel right.

Information given to a reader in advance can bias interpretation of symbols during someone's reading, or change the discussion of a card's significance. Because people often mask their motives for getting a reading, and some don't really want you to know what's on their mind, your logical mind can be deceived about what a person's problem really is. I've had clients who told me about their situation before their reading began, only to later find that they disguised their true question due to guilt or fear of self-disclosure.

Often the cards are most effective when you act as a guide who assists others in making their own discoveries. When clients realize something for themselves, it's usually more powerful than anything you can tell them. So be careful of falling into the trap of trying to be "the all-knowing one." Remember the postmodern insight that everyone has a different story to tell about any event, that another reader would see it somewhat differently than you do, and that the client knows more about his or her personal experience than you can possibly know. You can never fully know another's inner world, any more than he or she can experience yours.

The card's meanings should relate to the actions and qualities of the person asking the questions. Sharpening your awareness and trusting your intuition allows you to grasp something of the essential nature of whoever is sitting before you. Your eyes and ears will be assessing a person before you read them. Even before people sit down, notice how they hold themselves and how they move. Are the messages in their posture and their gestures hard or gentle, demanding or supplicating, tired or energetic, friendly or reserved? If they reach out to you, they probably reach out to others. If they hold their arms close to their body, they probably have a hard time making contact. You can sense much of this before the person utters a single word.

Voices also carry messages. Does someone sing or whine? Are the words fast and breathless, centered and focused, or faint and hard in coming? In *Gestalt Therapy Verbatim,* Fritz Perls, the founder of Gestalt therapy, suggests imagining that some kind of music is playing in the background as the person speaks. Do you hear chamber music or Beethoven crescendos? Hard rock or relaxed reggae? Scary music from a suspense movie or a love song? For a moment, let your intuitive self listen to the sound of the voice while paying no attention to the content. Then, if you must, don't feel embarrassed to say, "Will you please say that again? I was distracted for a moment." (Most people would much rather be asked to repeat something than go unheard.)

Just as you want to see what each card, in either the upright or reversed position, has to say to this particular person in his or her present, specific life circumstances, you'll want to look for connections between the card and the sensory information you're receiving. If someone has a bandaged, black eye, this obvious information may play a role in your reading. A robust, pregnant woman will certainly get a different interpretation of the same card that is being read for a woman who is weeping about someone dying. Obvious logical clues about a person's life will mix with your intuitive reading of symbols, just as intuitive clues about them will mix with your logical reading of symbols. The world of the tarot is a different world, a house of multicolored, oddly shaped carnival mirrors where perspectives that we're accustomed to in daily life sometimes make sense and sometimes are turned upside down.

The Golden Rules

Neutrality is a key part of the attitude required to do a good job as a reader. At its root, it means keeping your mind clear of judgments. Try to look at, listen to, or sense what's occurring with the person you're reading without reference to any judgment about the person or his or her lifestyle or behavior based on preconceptions you may hold. If you read cards with a hidden agenda or prejudgment of the person or the question, your analytical mind rather than your intuitive self will be doing the thinking and the speaking. Your rendering of the card's message will be slanted to fit your prejudgment and quite likely will not be helpful. Many people have perspectives that are different from yours, and attitudes that don't fit perfectly with your view of the world. Nurture positive perspectives on another's situation, but don't use your position as a reader to try to tell them your way is better.

Taking a few moments to transport yourself into a centered, calm mental state before you begin a reading can help you be objective. Before starting a reading, set your own words, mental pictures, and feelings off to one side, and, for a moment, just sense your breathing. Let your intuitive or feeling nature be receptive to what the other person thinks and feels. Once you begin the reading, you can practice a psychological technique called "bracketing," if necessary. When you notice your own feelings and thoughts about what the person is saying come up in you, mentally place brackets around those responses and set them off to the side. (You'll have plenty of time to think about them later if you like.) One of your objectives in the first stage of a reading is to place yourself as completely as you can into the other person's interior world. Avoid the phrase, "I know exactly what you mean," however. No one ever truly does.

When you first begin giving readings, you may want to start your session by saying: "I'm imagining that you think . . . Is that right?" Ask questions that can help you check out which of your guesses or intuitions are correct. Unless you have strong reason to disbelieve a client's statement, accept what they tell you rather than try to persuade them that your intuition is correct. Part of your reading will be a reflection of how clients construct their own reality. Sometimes people are in denial of their own truth, and sometimes they lie about things they're trying to hide. Most of the time, however, those who seek your guidance are sincere.

As you get farther into the reading, it's all right to respond with brief statements of your own feelings, as long as they don't invalidate your client's. You may even tell very brief stories, but keep the spotlight on the person you're reading. This is their moment, not yours.

Another golden rule in a reading is not to give negative readings or paint bleak pictures that leave clients feeling worse after talking with you than before they came for the reading. Whatever your clients' situation, emphasize options for their growth and improvement. Don't highlight the negative. Instead, find ways to help people rely on themselves, take more responsibility for their actions, and create positive directions in their lives. Avoid creating self-fulfilling prophecies, in which someone who thinks that a negative event will happen unconsciously acts in ways that bring about the event. Be very careful about the kinds of expectations you help create!

Even if you perceive your client's world as falling apart, you can be truthful without engendering pessimism. For centuries, people have used these mystical cards for guidance away from difficulties and as a means to enhance reality. When you use them for these purposes, you're working with the angelic spirit of inspiration, and can influence your clients to aspire to their highest good. If I see a strong negative message in the cards, I use my discretion as to whether I talk about it or not. If a problem is going to occur anyway, the person may need a source of hope, rather than fear, to get through it. Look for ways in which the information you discuss can help clients cope with their lives. Consult the cards for guidance about some kind of positive action that may be possible.

Many times people say, "I'm afraid to have my cards read because I might see something horrible." One of my own teachers offered a principle for dealing with such fears. She said, "If you can tell the person how to fix it or prevent it, talk about your premonition, but if you're only going to frighten them, keep your suspicions to yourself." Her message emphasizes the importance of not letting your words create a dark mental state for your client. Because your mental energy is shared when giving readings, use a harmonious approach as you discuss your concerns. For instance, if you intuit that a person has cancer, instead of telling them your suspicions, you might suggest a medical checkup. Say that you feel an energy imbalance in a certain part of the body. Never diagnose or prescribe any drugs or home healthcare remedies. Unless you're a doctor who is legally able to give medical advice, doing so could land you in jail. People who are trained as medical intuitives do use their sixth sense to work with people's health problems, but you need medical credentials if you're discussing a prognosis or prescription for any illness.

Your words have a power to heal or to harm, and your client may think about them for a long time. Sometimes people remember what a reader or psychic has told them for the rest of their lives. You may hear a client repeat, word for word, what they heard during a reading 10 years ago as if it were yesterday. Don't suggest impending accidents or health problems, or tell people when they're going to die. Such comments only promote fear and anxiety.

Also, don't try to convince a person of things they're not ready to hear. If something seems perfectly plain to you, but off-the-wall to the person for whom you're reading, trust that their resistance to hearing it is serving some kind of a valuable protective function for them. The reason we all have psychological defenses is that there are realizations or realities that we're not ready to handle. Respect your clients' limits. If you suggest something in three different ways and they brush aside the suggestion every time, they're telling you that, even if you're right, and even if what they're doing is self-destructive, they're not ready to hear it now. They're locked into some self-image, attitude, or behavioral pattern that they're unwilling to abandon at this time. Your task is to discover what they are open to hearing that can be of use to them. Then focus on that.

Be a mirror for your clients and reflect beneficial information to help clarify their path. Encourage self-esteem and personal worth. They're trusting you to be their oracle, so give them the best energy you can. And if you're being paid for your readings, you'll get better references if people walk away feeling good.

When a client seems less than happy about something I've told him or her, sometimes I say, "The cards that come up are what they are. My interpretation of what they mean for you may be right or it may be off the mark."

You may feel uncomfortable in the role of prognosticator, and may worry about being "psychic" and foretelling events correctly. Don't. Although you can use the cards as springboards for predictions, they're most beneficial as tools to nourish personal growth. Their magic lies in their ability to enhance understanding of the meaning, purpose, and direction of the evolving Wheel of Life. Don't try to do something you can't do. Don't feel even a little bit embarrassed to say something like, "I don't foretell the future. I simply use the cards to help you clarify your own thoughts and feelings, so you can make the best decisions that you can." For many readers, that's reality.

When the major arcana card Death appears in a spread, people become alarmed. You need to be able to discuss this card with your clients in relation to other meanings besides physical death. It does not necessarily mean that your client or someone they know is going to die. Even if you're intuiting that someone will die, keep it to yourself to avoid a possible mistake in your judgment. Death makes most of us nervous, and if you focus on physical death in your reading, you may trigger serious anxieties and perhaps even depression. Physical termination of life is only one of many possible meanings associated with Death. A person may be dying in a symbolic sense. He or she may be undergoing a major change in life, dying to what has been in the past and being reborn by gaining awareness of a new reality. You can interpret Death as a radical change in a person's belief system and an energizing time for moving in new directions. Intensity of emotion, sexuality, transformation, rebirth, and the occult are some other common meanings of the Death card.

On the other hand, if a person has a terminal illness and doctors have determined that the person will die soon, then you may have to talk about their physical death and their concerns associated with it. At these times, it is not only appropriate, but necessary. In some cases, you may be able to help them overcome their fears and come to perceive death as simply a part of the great river of life that, even as they and others come and go, flows on through the world and time.

When people who are in good health seem unduly preoccupied with death, it may be a clue that, in some way, they're not living as they wish. In general, the fuller and richer a person's life is, the less likely they are to be preoccupied with death.

Another golden rule is: Don't discuss your client's problems with others. Respect for their privacy will give people faith in your practice. A tarot reader should maintain confidentiality just as fully as a psychologist or attorney would. People cannot open their hearts and tell you their deepest concerns if they think you're going to make their story into neighborhood gossip.

CHAPTER 5

THE READING PROCESS STEP-BY-STEP

Synchronicity means the simultaneous occurrence of a certain psychic state with one or more external events which appear as meaningful parallels. . . . I found 'coincidences' which were connected so meaningfully that their 'chance' occurrence would represent an astronomical degree of improbability.
—CARL JUNG, *SYNCHRONICITY: AN ACAUSAL CONNECTING PRINCIPLE*

I prefer, when possible, to do readings in a quiet, serene environment. Then the client and I are both more focused and our rapport is likely to be better. Candles, incense, crystals, magic stones, or bubbling fountains are often found sitting near readers who use mystical objects to enchant their personal space. Sometimes I'll put a small sword, a cup, a wooden staff, and a stone disc or an old Chinese coin with a square hole in the center on my table, to represent the four suits and The Magician's tools.

Of course, if you're a therapist who uses the tarot in your counseling office, a soft chair and a box of Kleenex may be just as appropriate. Wherever you do your readings, the more effort that goes into creating your sacred space, the more comfortable you'll feel in deciphering how a card unlocks the secrets of the person for whom you're reading.

Beginning a Reading

After you've created a comfortable and inviting physical space to work in, and have mentally centered your energy, you're ready to begin. It's time to shuffle the cards.

If you're reading for someone else, you can shuffle the cards or let your client do so. If people say they don't know how to shuffle, tell them to mix the cards together however they wish. When handing them the cards, explain that, while they shuffle, they should think of something important going on in their life. Why do they want a reading? Perhaps they have a question, or they may be worried about something. If they don't have any questions, I ask them to pay attention to the most significant events going on in their life, or I give them the option of simply seeing what story the cards tell. Usually, I interpret their cards in relation to something in their immediate or distant past, their present and immediate concerns, or the future. In a brief reading, such as a three-card spread, if clients ask specific questions about the future, then I may forget the past and present and look at what all three cards say about the future.

Most beginning readers ask their clients what questions they want answered during the reading, and use knowledge of their expressed concerns to guide card interpretation. Once you become comfortable and experienced in tarot readings, you may start to ask your client to think their question silently and not tell you what it is. You and your client may both be amazed when you witness the power of the tarot to answer unarticulated questions. Don't expect this to happen the first time you do a reading. With regular practice, however, you can learn the skill of answering questions by reading symbols in the cards, even when the client hasn't told you their question.

Cutting the Cards

While my client is silently thinking about a situation or question, he or she will be shuffling the cards. When the client has finished shuffling, it's time to cut the deck. Because the left hand corresponds with the right hemisphere of the brain, which is associated with creative, intuitive thinking, I suggest that clients hold and cut the cards with their left hand.

Methods for cutting cards while doing a reading vary. Some readers will cut or have their client cut the cards into two stacks, and others cut into three or four stacks. You may want to experiment with different card-cutting procedures. Your personal experiences will guide you to the card-cutting system that works best. The stacks don't have to be the same size. There may be ten cards in one stack, and forty in another.

When I'm giving readings at a gathering where I'm walking around rather than sitting at a table, it's difficult to ask people who are standing to shuffle and cut the cards. Instead, I fan them in my hand, and ask people to use their sixth sense to pick their cards. It's easy to see how this works. Ask yourself a question, then fan or spread the cards on your table. Close your eyes, move your hands over them, and let your intuition choose a card. Let this card's symbols answer your question.

Laying Down the Cards

In most readings, you'll place the cards in a spread where predetermined card positions represent certain attributes or aspects of life. If a card is in the position representing the past, the symbols are read in relation to past events. If a card sits in the position of the subconscious mind, the images are described as qualities that live in the depth of the psyche.

There are numerous, widely used spreads, but since our focus here is on love and relationships, we present those which are valuable in finding answers to emotional and compatibility questions. These spreads will help answer such questions as: Will I find love? Does he/she love me? What are the limitations or complications of that love? What can I do to enrich our relationship?

Don't be alarmed if you've studied qualities for a card's position other than those given in our spreads. Use what you've previously learned to enhance your understanding of a card's position when you create your layouts. Your intuition, present awareness, and depth and breadth of vision are the most valuable keys to determining the implications of the cards.

In addition to interpreting individual cards in relation to their places in a spread, you should coordinate each card's message with the significance of the card(s) next to it. For example, if The Empress sits in the position relating to present time, discuss her qualities not only in connection with present concerns, but also in reference to the cards surrounding her. If The Empress, who is associated with the power of love, is sitting next to the Three of Cups, a card linked with the expansion of emotions, her dominion will be discussed differently than if she is placed next to the Eight of Cups, which indicates secrets or anxieties about love.

When you're comfortable interpreting cards in relation to each other, you'll be ready to create in-depth spreads and give compatibility readings. If you're just learning how to read cards, work with one card at a time and focus on simple spreads.

"Yes" or "No" Spreads

When you're doing readings for others, undoubtedly you'll be asked questions such as: "Can the cards tell if my boy (or girl) friend loves me?" and "Is my love faithful to me?" Be prepared. Most people want to hear that they're loved and their partner is loyal. However, if your client is willing to risk looking for an unpredictable answer, you can use a one-card or three-card spread. These uncomplicated spreads offer immediate answers to questions requiring a swift yes or no reply.

A one-card reading is easy. Shuffle and cut the deck. The first card you turn upright will give the answer to your question. For example, if I want to know if a person who attracts me might become interested in dating me, I shuffle the cards and think about this person and my question. Then I cut the cards into three stacks, pull the top card from the middle stack, and look at the symbolic message it communicates. With a positive card such as The Sun, I assume a yes answer. With the Five of Swords, however, which implies some type of communication struggle, I interpret the card's answer to be no. Negatives represent no. Positives are associated with yes.

The trouble with this approach, of course, is that the card's answer can be abstract, or my interpretation of it may be wrong. If your psychic powers are working well, they'll help you with the answer. If they're not, hedge your reply instead of giving a straight yes or no, and suggest that the person stay alert for further information.

Another approach, which I prefer to use when possible, is to interpret the card not as providing a simple answer, but as indicating what the person can do to improve the chances that events will turn out as they wish. In the example above, The Sun might indicate that drawing more fully on the warm, outgoing side of my character will increase the chances of the other person's interest. The Five of Swords might mean that I need to do a better job of listening and sharing.

The Basic Three Card Spread

The three-card spread can be used by itself, or it can be added to another spread when you need more clarification. To create this spread, first think about your question, then shuffle the cards. Hold the deck face down in your left hand and cut it into three stacks. Take the top three cards from the center stack, lay them in a horizontal row, and look for your message. The left card represents the past, the middle one the present, and the right card the future, or resolution, of the situation. (See figure 1, page 54)

Past, present, and future are thematic components that occur in most readings. Understanding where a person is coming from, how they're dealing with the present, and where they're going offers a solid foundation upon which you can build a meaningful reading.

Also, when reading with three cards, you must determine what their relationships imply about the answer to the question being asked.

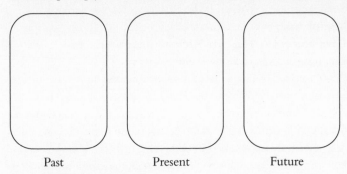

Past   Present   Future

Fig. 1. Sample three-card spread

In some cases, rather than viewing three cards as past, present, and future, it is useful to view them as what's inside a person, the present situation, and other people or outside forces. If the cards don't quite seem to answer your question, it sometimes helps to pull another one or even two.

The Many Uses for the Three-card Spread

When you add a three-card spread to an already existing one, such as the seven-card chakra spread or the Celtic Cross spread, it can help clarify ambiguities. For example, if the last card in a seven-card spread is the major arcana card Judgement, which signifies transitions, and you want the cards to say more about the implied transition, pull three more cards and place them directly on top of the Judgement card. That gives me the tarot's verdict on the direction in which judgment will be made.

Sometimes at the end of a reading, your client may decide to ask just one more question. You can either reply to this "one last" question by looking at the spread that has already been discussed, or let the person draw three more cards to answer their additional question. It doesn't matter whether you're working with ten, twelve, or even more, cards in a spread. You can always include an additional three-card spread.

The Celtic Cross Spread

The widely used Celtic Cross spread is a ten-card layout in which particular cards represent specific influences that may affect life's journey. (See figure 2, page 55) The card positions are as follows:

First card: Present concerns.
Second card: What's presently crossing the client's path.
Third card: Ego, how the client appears to the outside world.

Fourth card:	The client's inner nature.
Fifth card:	The past.
Sixth card:	The immediate future.
Seventh card:	The future environment.
Eighth card:	The client's future position.
Ninth card:	The client's hopes or fears.
Tenth card:	Future resolution, or outcome.

Cards numbered one through four discuss present concerns, card five signifies the past, and cards six through ten correspond to the future. By breaking the ten cards into groups representing past, present, and future, you create a coherent sequence in which you can discuss the direction a person's life is taking. Using this format, you can give interpretations similar to those you gave with a three-card spread, but with more cards, symbols, and interpretive possibilities.

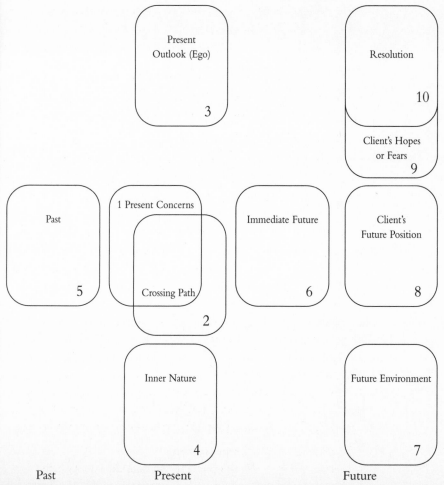

Fig. 2. The Celtic Cross spread

The Chakra Spread

The seven-card chakra spread (see figure 4, page 57) can reveal the mental character and emotional personality of the person you're reading. Using this spread requires knowing a little about the tantric depiction of consciousness represented by seven energy centers. Each of these centers, said to be located at different points along the spine, from the tailbone to the crown of the head, is connected with different human needs and physical functions (see figure 3 below). Each card corresponds to the qualities that relate to a specific chakra, and thereby says something about how a person deals with life, love, and sexuality. Table 8 on page 57 gives a summary of the energy centers and their correspondences.

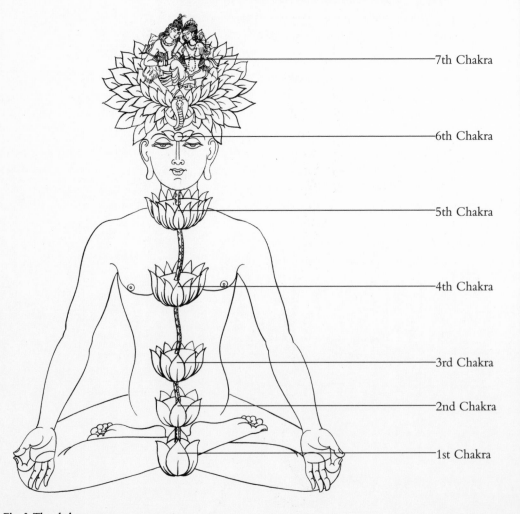

7th Chakra

6th Chakra

5th Chakra

4th Chakra

3rd Chakra

2nd Chakra

1st Chakra

Fig. 3. The chakras

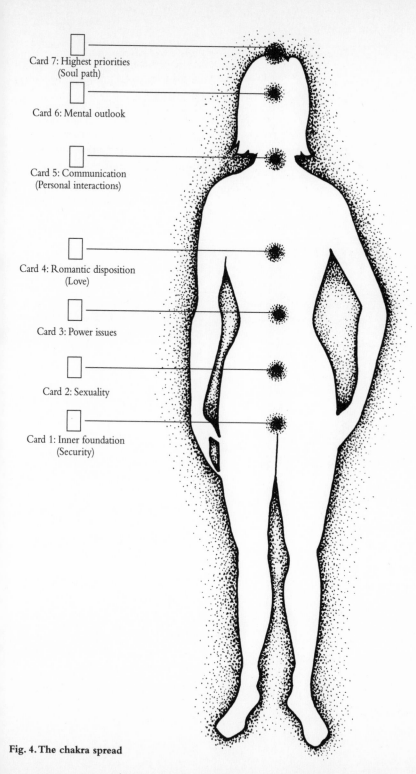

Card 7: Highest priorities
(Soul path)

Card 6: Mental outlook

Card 5: Communication
(Personal interactions)

Card 4: Romantic disposition
(Love)

Card 3: Power issues

Card 2: Sexuality

Card 1: Inner foundation
(Security)

Fig. 4. The chakra spread

Table 8. Chakras and Their Correspondences.

Chakra Number	Chakra Name	Keyword	Location	Primary Associations
1st	Muladhara chakra	Security	Root of the spine	Survival needs, food, shelter, and clothing; physical and psychological security; self-esteem; body awareness; energy flow; grounding, and matters concerning the material, earth plane. It is home to the kundalini spirit, which represents the inner potential for awaking to higher consciousness.
2nd	Svadhisthana chakra	Sexuality	Reproductive organs	Sexual activity, physical passion; a woman's lunar cycle; birthing instincts, fertility; emotions; family concerns; excitement; sensuality; jealousy, fear; the element water.
3rd	Manipura chakra	Power	Near solar plexus and the navel	Digestion; processing of psychic energy; desire for power; assertiveness; anger; ego demands, willpower; physical vitality; the element fire.
4th	Anahata chakra	Emotion	The heart center	Love, compassion, happiness, sadness, faith, expansiveness, and air; the breath of life that gets you in touch with your feelings.
5th	Vishuddha chakra	Communication	The throat	Sound; the ability to communicate; hearing, singing, talking, creative self-expression or repression; sensitivity, reliability, clairaudience, understanding, and awareness. This chakra gives words to the feelings of the other chakras.
6th	Ajna chakra	Intuition and intellect	The point between and slightly above the eyebrows	This is the abode of the third eye, the mystical doorway of intuition and clairvoyance; consciousness, where the left brain intellect meets the right brain; intuition and spirituality.
7th	Sahasrara chakra	Spirituality	Crown of the head	When this center is open, it is compared with the full moon or a lotus with one thousand petals. Here is where your inner nature is liberated from tethers of ignorance, and you can experience direct perception of truth, wisdom beyond logic, and love beyond measure. It has to do with detachment from personal ego-attachments, selfless concern with the welfare of others, and transcendent states of consciousness—the ultimate called "cosmic consciousness."

To create this spread, select one card to depict each of the seven chakras. Arrange the cards in a vertical line and describe each position in reference to the chakra it represents. (Begin with the bottom card and put each succeeding one above it, as you turn over the cards.) Discuss the card in the first position in relation to qualities linked with the first chakra, the second card in relation to the second chakra, the third card with the third chakra, and so on. Since each chakra represents a different kind of personal quality, this spread lets you symbolically view the energy and emotional characteristics of the person you're reading. You'll need to assess whether the card refers to the client in general, the situation, or to another person in relation to your client. The card positions for the chakra spread are as follows:

Card One: The foundation card. This represents the basic, underlying structure of the situation (or person) in question, the root of the matter, the bottom line. It refers to security issues, whether physical, financial, or emotional.

Card Two: Sexual magnetism. It may also refer to passions, sexual issues, hormonal mood swings, jealousy, or desire for a family.

Card Three: Power issues, dominance versus submissiveness, obsession with control versus willingness to share power, competitiveness, or gut-level instincts in reaction to people or situations.

Card Four: Love, romantic nature, open- or closed-heartedness, willingness (or unwillingness) to love and be loved, unconditional love, honesty, and compassion.

Card Five: Communication; willingness to truly listen to what the other person has to say rather than hearing the other only in terms of one's own interests and biases, articulate speech and other creative self-expression; disclosure of or secrecy about thoughts and feelings.

Card Six: Nonverbal communication; penetrating observation and awareness; the ability to intuit feelings; intellectual understanding; humanitarian desires.

Card Seven: Highest priorities; soul commitments; transcendence of egocentric reactions; broad concern for, and action directed toward, the welfare of others; great joy in moment-by-moment events; fulfillment; spiritual awareness.

The Double-Chakra Compatibility Spread

One of the most frequent tarot questions that lovers ask is: "Are we compatible?" As people share lives together, the chemistry between them constantly evolves. Ultimately, time is the true oracle of how well their energies mesh. Even so, the cards offer useful insight into how people connect, and how they don't.

The fifteen-card chakra compatibility spread illustrates the strength or weakness of the connection between two people. It shows how people's energies align in essential ways: finances, sex, power issues, love, communication, psychic/spiritual energy, and soul purpose.

Once you're comfortable doing the seven-card spread described above, you'll be equipped to move on to this compatibility spread, which is a composite of two-chakra spreads. Start by laying two even-card chakra spreads side by side (see figure 5, page 61). One line of seven cards represents the person asking the question, and the other line represents the other person involved in the relationship. Lay the cards in pairs, choosing the first-chakra cards for each person, then the second-chakra cards, and so on. Lay cards for one person next to the corresponding cards for the second person.

After you have seven pairs of cards arranged in two vertical rows, select a fifteenth card. Place it in the middle of the spread between the cards in the fourth row to illuminate the nature of the bond between the heart centers. If the fifteenth card is positive, compatibility is likely. If negative, it depicts some kind of challenge to harmony and points to emotional work that needs to be done.

To understand the overall potential for compatibility, in addition to looking at the three cards sitting in the fourth row, you must compare the cards sitting above this row with the cards sitting beneath it. This comparison between higher and lower centers allows you to determine the potential for balance, harmony, and overall compatibility. Adaptability and getting along together is analyzed by comparing cards vertically as well as horizontally.

You'll be seeking clues from this spread about how the two people exchange energy via their chakra points. This spread provides interesting clues to the interactive qualities of emotional and behavioral patterns. It provides information about how two people's energies and emotions connect. If you're doing a couple's reading and both people are present, each can choose his or her own seven cards.

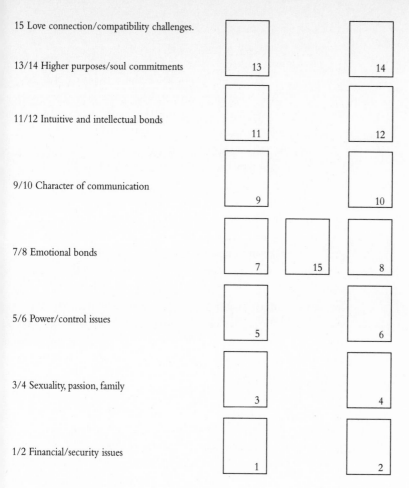

15 Love connection/compatibility challenges.

13/14 Higher purposes/soul commitments

11/12 Intuitive and intellectual bonds

9/10 Character of communication

7/8 Emotional bonds

5/6 Power/control issues

3/4 Sexuality, passion, family

1/2 Financial/security issues

Fig. 5. The double-chakra compatibility spread

For insight into a couple's compatibility, compare the symbolism and imagery in each pair of cards. For example, see what the bottom pair suggests about first-chakra energy for both people involved in a reading. Are the symbols on the cards friendly, complementary, antagonistic, or disconnected? What parallels or differences do they seem to suggest about what the partners need in order to feel psychologically, physically, financially, or intellectually secure?

Cards 3 and 4 in the second horizontal row signify the couple's passionate or sexual energy, interest, or inhibitions. Cards 5 and 6 form the third row, and indicate power and control issues. How is decision-making shared or not shared? What are the explicit or tacit rules about how each partner is allowed to be strong and directive, or required to be weak and compliant?

Cards 7 and 8 (and the 15th card that has been placed between them) comprise the heart-chakra row, which indicates the heart connection. These three cards speak of the potential for true love. The nature of the heart connection between two people can inspire or deepen, weaken, or destroy a relationship.

Because the three cards in the fourth row sit between the top six and the bottom six cards, they are positioned in the center of the spread. The three rows above the fourth row represent higher awareness; the three rows beneath it indicate lower awareness. The central row is the balancing point between them.

Cards 9 and 10 can show the way partners communicate verbally or don't communicate with one another. Cards 11 and 12 create the sixth row, and represent the couple's ability to share ideas and philosophies and to communicate nonverbally. Whether a couple shares a similar world outlook, or whether their viewpoints clash in some way, is depicted by these cards. A difference in outlook can be the spice of life, the ruination of a relationship, or of little consequence. The cards will give you clues as to what's probably important to discuss.

The last card pair, cards 13 and 14, form the top horizontal row. They reflect the joint purpose, or soul connection, of the couple. This row indicates if a couple's higher purpose and goals are harmonious, and if they are spiritually compatible. Couples that connect well on this level are sometimes called "soul mates," but total connection on this level is a rare gift, and many deeply rewarding relationships occur without it.

The double-chakra spread can also be done as a couple's reading, with both partners present. It may be framed as a compatibility reading, or as a reading about how to improve the relationship or how to handle a particular situation. Whatever is lost in terms of willingness to disclose sensitive thoughts and feelings is usually more than made up for by the immediate feedback from the other person about the concerns that each articulates. Such readings can be rich. They can also be demanding.

Other spreads can also be used in couples readings. When partners sit down for a reading, and I ask whether they want individual readings or a couples reading, sometimes what emerges regardless of their choice has some individual implications and some relational ones. The cliché "go with the flow" often applies perfectly here.

PART II

THE CARDS
AND THEIR
STORIES

CHAPTER 6

THE MAJOR ARCANA: CARDS OF WISDOM

I saw a Man and a Woman naked and beautiful. . . . Their
Love was . . . a prayer and a sacrifice; through It they . . .
received the highest revelations; in Its light the deepest truths
came to them; the magic world opened its gate.
—P. D. OUSPENSKY, *THE SYMBOLISM OF THE TAROT*

Reflecting on the 22 cards of the major arcana and their archetypal themes can open your mind to the deeper levels of their
messages and help you integrate these insights into your daily life.
Walking through the world in the company of The Fool, The
Magician, The High Priestess, The Empress, The Emperor, The
Star, and their companions can bring out seldom expressed sides
of yourself, and help you use already developed abilities more
effectively.

Although our text uses the Waite Tarot deck for illustrations, it
is not dependent on images within a specific deck, so it can be
used with traditional or modern cards. Since our focus here is on
unveiling the cards' symbolic power to mirror the emotions and
give insight into the world of romance, don't expect discussions of
other concerns, such as health, career, or money matters.

Keywords help you get a quick glimpse of each card's meaning.
Our keywords are in no way the only ones you can use to describe
the cards, but they are a good starting point for learning their significance.

When you read our interpretations for Major Arcana cards you
will find a correspondence called Most Compatible Card Partners.
Astrological sun signs and trines are used for determining which
Major Arcana cards are friendly or favorably linked with other

major cards, which can help you determine couple compatibility. When compatible cards appear together in a person's spread, it increases the probability that the situation being questioned contains positive elements or a relationship has the potential to move in a harmonious direction.

The sexual play section can help you make your sex life more delicious. In regard to sex itself, we realize that there's no one "right" way to do it. For every person and every couple, satisfying sexuality reflects our inclinations, dispositions, and personal history. There are no exact answers or perfect formulas. What delights one person or couple may not please another.

The reversed card sections are appropriate for cards that come out upside down in the reading. This position can be either literal or metaphorical. That is, a card may appear right side up, but during your reading, your sense of your client's struggles may suggest to you that the energies depicted by that card are being utilized in an "upside-down" manner—perhaps in some self-defeating way. You may find it appropriate to refer to that in your interpretation. Remember, however, that people want to leave their readings feeling good rather than bad, so phrase your reversed interpretations in ways that may help them get a better handle on counterproductive patterns.

0. THE FOOL

THE FOOL.

§ ROMANTIC INTERPRETATION:

With springtime in the heart dawns the infinite trust in love that only a fool is strong enough to give. The Fool is divine love and bliss in the moment. It is realizing intuitively that our past and future truly meet only in the present; that whatever we do, we do now, not letting our expectations and anticipations blind us to the possibilities that this moment offers.

Free of duality and innocent of pretense, The Fool dances with Rama—the god of romance—and walks the path of the openhearted. Listening to the music of the salsa of love, The Fool trusts spontaneity and the intuition, and relies on his or her heart for guidance. There is great wisdom in The Fool's ability to embrace the now, drink the nectar of consciousness, and move in no direction, yet be moving in all directions at the same time. Just as a flower opens its petals to the sun, so does the spirit of this card embrace the light, joy, and playfulness of love. It is a reminder to listen to your playful inner child.

§ EMOTIONAL INTERPRETATION:

Love springs forward as The Fool is willing to move with the frisky spirit of the Jester, who in days of old was often the King's confidante, privileged to hear the secrets of the most powerful figure in the land. This archetypal joker who is really the wise person in disguise, has the confidence to walk near the precipice of vulnerability without falling prey to worries about "what if?" Connected with the inner meaning of the words "free-spirit," The Fool's emotions are liberated from apprehension, oppression, and repression.

Imagine yourself the bright fool, and trust your inner knowing. With a particular person, you may have an intuitive sense that you can reveal a part of yourself that you usually keep hidden, and thereby open the way for them to reveal themselves more fully to you in return. Out of that sharing can come opportunities for rewarding moments that the more careful, closed-off part of you would avoid. Even if you don't know the direction of your emotional path, you can find your way by trusting your inner knowing in the moment.

§ SEXUAL INTERPRETATION:

Without attachment, The Fool is open to life and everything it offers. He reminds us to stay in touch with our youthful

Key Meanings: Divine folly, freedom, innocence, a free spirit; leaving insecurities and ego concerns behind

Loving Qualities: Carefree, trustable, accepting, loving

Loveless Qualities: Refuses commitments; gullible, lacks foresight

Astrological Connection: The planet Uranus—a masculine sky deity in Greek mythology—linked with the unpredictable and untamable and the element air, breath of life

Most Compatible Card Partners: The Lovers, The Chariot, and Judgement

- 67 -

0. THE FOOL

innocence and adventurous vitality as we reach to possess the bliss of the moment. If you have expectations, it's better to let them fall from your mind, for it's the physiological chemistry of your present connections that creates the immediate reality. Following the fancy of the heart, anything may happen. Let your mind open to feel the flow of fiery excitement tingling deep within. The heated lava of passion erupts as orgasmic desire dances in rhythm to nature's urging. Normal is whatever you and the other person decree, as conventional limits may be put aside. An androgynous figure, The Fool is free of any sexual identity crisis. Heterosexuality, homosexuality, bisexuality, or whatever—all is fair for The Fool in love, if you and your partner think it is.

❀ SEXUAL PLAY:

The Fool lives in the moment, concerned about neither the past nor the future, but fully present in the here and now. He has no preconceptions about how things are "supposed to be done" that get in the way of lovemaking. Lacking such preconceptions, The Fool pays great attention to what a partner does or doesn't like. If his partner wants to take the dominant role, he'll surrender and willingly defer to her request, or if The Fool is a woman, she won't be so foolish as to pretend she is satisfied sexually when she isn't. Lacking any pretense or expectations, The Fool is willing to say, "I need more of that," or "I don't care for that," and also to ask what the partner loves, likes, or dislikes. Many of us are reluctant to say or ask such things, out of fear that the partner will think that we love him or her insufficiently because we can't mind-read all his or her desires. The Fool has no such fear and speaks freely, so this card is auspicious for improving sexual communication. Tell your partner what you like (or don't), and ask what your partner likes (or doesn't).

❀ REVERSED CARD INTERPRETATION:

The reversed Fool often indicates the error of being spontaneous and open without listening to your own wisdom about what suits you and what doesn't, what's dangerous and what isn't. Don't do something on impulse because others urge you to, but make sure your own wise inner voice says yes before you act. Since your fantasies about what you want can get in the way of being aware of danger signals from others or the environment, be aware of nonverbal messages and "all is not well" signs instead of wandering off in dreamland. The most dependable clues tend to be in your body: If you feel a tight stomach or shoulders, clenched fists or jaws, or some other similar signal, it's probably a sign saying, "No, that's not right for me," "This is foolish!" or at least, "I need to do this more slowly and thoughtfully."

0. THE FOOL

THE MAGICIAN.

Key Meanings: New beginnings, responsibilities, or desires of love; finding or using your own magic

Loving Qualities: Keen insights, charisma, boldness

Loveless Qualities: Egotism, preoccupation with responsibilities

Astrological Connections: The planet Mercury—mythically personified as a wing-footed messenger for the gods—and qualities such as good communication, mental clarity, and inspirational intelligence

Most Compatible Card Partners: The Lovers, The Hermit

1. THE MAGICIAN

1. THE MAGICIAN

❧ ROMANTIC INTERPRETATION:

In the realm of love, The Magician represents taking a first step or beginning a new direction. Wishing for intimacy must be replaced with a bold willingness to move toward finding it, or toward hearing and touching the feelings and sensitivities of your partner.

What's real can get lost in the mists of expectations if you don't ground your ideas in overt communications. Expressing yourself clearly helps bonds of trust develop and can create an environment where understanding heals fears. When apparent agreements feel vague or hazy, ask for clarification.

The Magician's energy is turned on. Playful, spontaneous, charming, and interested in ideas, this person often is intellectually stimulating and adventurous. Be ready to travel to romantic places. If you're not in a relationship, be willing to initiate communication with people who attract your interest.

❧ EMOTIONAL INTERPRETATION:

Sitting home alone, analyzing your relationship or your lack of one will get you nowhere. Thinking, an attribute of The Magician, needs to be turned into action.

On the other hand, The Magician can also signify a deepening of self-empowerment, self-love, and understanding. You can use your mental energy to create magic in your love life, by using your time alone to develop interests, abilities, and self-confidence that will make you more attractive to others. This is a good time to start laying an inner foundation that will enable you to manifest your dreams of love in reality.

As you sort through emotions, listen to the inner truth of your heart, distinguish your own desires and needs from what others tell you "should want," and direct your efforts toward winning in life and love. Today your journey begins anew.

❧ SEXUAL INTERPRETATION:

The magic of the moment inspires saying yes to sexual intimacy. Just as Mercury, the planet associated with this card, moves rapidly around the Sun, you might find yourself moving quickly toward the object of your affections. If you're already committed to someone, pleasures will abound, or if you're out with someone casually and looking for some fun, you might go farther than you initially intended. Don't be fooled by the alluring qualities of a Mercurial lover, who is complex, curious, exploring, and open to testing the limits. Many magicians think they're good in bed and like to prove it.

❧ SEXUAL PLAY:

Gently, through the power of touch, The Magician may invoke passion by giving the partner a massage (after, of course, asking if the partner would enjoy it.) First the back and legs are massaged, then the partner turns over and the front is massaged gently. Then The Magician begins long, light strokes from each distant point on the partner's body to the area of greatest sensitivity, the genitalia. Let your fingers exert just enough pressure to electrify sparks of pleasure with your touch. Start by making a single long stroke from one shoulder to the center of the love body, then make a similar stroke from midway between shoulder and neck, then from the middle of the forehead, and so on like rays of the sun coming inward rather than outward, each stroke enticing sensual pleasure and the longing for more.

When you feel drawn to lie together, consciously match your breath by inhaling, together, pausing together, and exhaling together, hearing and feeling each other's bodies as you do. (One may need to breathe more slowly or the other more rapidly.) This can help the partner whose sexual rhythms are faster slow down to the other's pace.

❧ REVERSED CARD INTERPRETATION:

When reversed, The Magician can indicate shallowness rather than substance, or someone who may be stuck on an ego trip—"Look how great I am!"—which leads to a disregard of the other person's needs and feelings. This sometimes has its place on the world's stage, but is strictly a short-term high in intimate relationships where the magic has to involve both people. If it doesn't, it will eventually be poisoned by the pretensions of The Magician and the resentments of the one whose magic is disregarded.

The reversed Magician can also represent someone who is living in illusion, trying to make you (and perhaps himself or herself) believe he or she is something different than he or she really is. Beware of deception.

On a personal level, it can indicate that you think yourself inadequate and are trying to be something other than you are. This can lead to confusion, self-deception, and the fear that you'll be found out. Look out for the loss of energy that goes into keeping up a front and detracts from the spontaneity and realness of a relationship.

THE HIGH PRIESTESS

Key Meanings: A vibrant, intuitive woman who sees clearly into the hearts and minds of those she loves; strengthening the intuitive sense

Loving Qualities: Understanding, caring, and kind

Loveless Qualities: Can be cold, distant, and veil emotions

Astrological Connections: The Moon, linked with Diana, Roman goddess of the hunt, who is mystically skilled with a bow and arrow that can penetrate the psyche's depths

Most Compatible Card Partner: The Chariot

2. THE HIGH PRIESTESS

❧ ROMANTIC INTERPRETATION:

The High Priestess represents a powerful woman who prefers an equally strong partner. Because of her meditative nature, her inner light reflects calmness just as the Moon reflects the Sun's light. Deeply sensitive, and desiring to give her love only in a relationship that proves to be true, she strives for the closeness and intimacy that compatible partners can find. Although sometimes shy in expressing emotions, this energetic woman is capable of listening with her heart and has great insight into others' feelings. As a friend or as a lover, harmony is her law of communicating, and she strives to create balance in her everyday life. Don't expect her to lower her standards where values are concerned, for compromise is not her path.

❧ EMOTIONAL INTERPRETATION:

Strength of spirit moves The High Priestess forward on the game board of love, removing insecurities or self-doubts. If you are the person (male or female) represented by this card, the harmonious balance of finding your truth comes through meditative reflection. Using your intuition and attuning to the soul of the matter at hand helps you fathom the nature of the situation around you, even if shifting moods and emotional ambivalence make you change your mind about what choices to make.

Your dreams may play a part in helping you see into the depth of your own psyche. The Moon, which is linked with this card, corresponds to feminine energy, emotions, intuition, and the subconscious mind. The High Priestess relies more on her intuition and nonverbal sensitivities than on rational analysis to guide her in thought and action. As a result, looking within and being in touch with your deepest feelings is this card's key to finding answers to important questions.

❧ SEXUAL INTERPRETATION:

The High Priestess represents a woman with magnetic sex appeal, but one mentally strong who takes her time before saying yes to a sexual rendezvous. Even though she may know a secret formula for turning you on like you've never felt before, she'll want to make sure that you're receptive to her sensitive nature before she makes a move. For her, a genuine closeness in partnership is necessary before sharing on a sexual level. Courtship precedes physical involvement. Usually domestic by nature, she will want to bring you home for dinner and find out all about you before she knows if you're the right person for the gift of her passion. If this intimacy is lacking, she'll choose celibacy.

❧ Sexual Play:

In some traditions, The High Priestess represents a virgin goddess, like Artemis of the ancient Greeks, so if you are her lover, approach her with great care and tenderness, as if she has never been made love to before, and you are the one who has been chosen to initiate her into this mystery.

Awake in the ecstasy of the moment, The High Priestess may use feathers or fur to tickle playfully her partner's love spots. With gentle cat bites, she nibbles on sensitive places to arouse her partner's passions, and then sits astride her magician in a kneeling position where she can freely move her thighs up and down on his magic wand. (A pillow beneath the lover's buttocks may be advisable to bring both pelvises to the same level). The Priestess then takes charge of carrying out the sacred ceremony, remembering to alternate between passion-arousing movements and slower, cooling ones—perhaps touching and caressing sensitive parts of the body—to prolong their mutual pleasure.

❧ Reversed Card Interpretation:

This card may signal a reluctance to enter close relationships. Perhaps because of painful past experiences of abandonment or loss of loved ones, The High Priestess may shy away or sabotage the relationship when someone gets too close. It can also mean that the person represented by this card (which might be you) insists on others fitting the confines of his or her expectations and projections, or tries to change others to fit them. If so, the person may need to work on developing mutual give-and-take so he or she can accept others as they really are, rather than whom he or she wants them to be. One partner may put the other on a pedestal of expectations that the other can't possibly fulfill, and then lose interest when the other turns out to be an ordinary mortal rather than an embodiment of those expectations.

Negativity can inspire doubts about romance. With a positive attitude and attentiveness to what is occurring in your psyche and your surroundings, you'll find the path to living a successful life, in and out of the sexual arena.

THE EMPRESS.

Key Meanings: A big-hearted, nurturing woman who laughs with her heart, loves with her smile, and lives with passion for life; gifts of the heart, fertility

Loving Qualities: Optimistic, friendly, compassionate, and affectionate

Loveless Qualities: Shows favoritism, overindulgent

Astrological Connections: The planet Venus, equated with the goddess who bears the same name of this "morning star," a universal symbol for love, passion, creativity, music, drama, and poetry

Most Compatible Card Partners: The Hierophant, Justice

3. THE EMPRESS

3. THE EMPRESS

❧ ROMANTIC INTERPRETATION:

A very favorable card for romance, The Empress indicates the sharing of positive emotions and the rewards of love. A symbol for Venus, this card can represent a beautiful, loving woman, Aphrodite incarnate, who is lighthearted and loves to play. Her charming nature can lift spirits by finding the humor in life—even in serious situations. This card also suggests that you can expect to find happy moments and exciting prospects for increasing the pleasures of your heart. Wherever your passion is directed, you'll feel energy and inspiration. If you're in a relationship, you'll find it easier than usual to let go of old patterns that are no longer helpful, and will find your heart open to resolving problems in which you may previously have felt stuck. By becoming aware in the moment of what's going on in both you and the other person, you can move toward a mature love in which romantic notions are placed in a perspective that is healing to the heart.

❧ EMOTIONAL INTERPRETATION:

The Empress represents a wise woman, a wife, or even a Mother—someone emotionally mature who uses her love and wisdom to improve life. She may channel energy to help get creative projects underway or fertilize their completion. Whatever the direction you're turning, something of value will accelerate your progress. Feelings blossom with the warmth of optimism and find expression in some uninhibited way. Moods in the moment swing toward happiness. You may find yourself infatuated with a new love, indulging in obsessive thoughts about your heart's desires, or looking for sure ways to navigate through negative emotions. It's time to overcome difficulties in love, even if it means seeking relationship counseling. Understanding, hope, and faith in your future are key words for this card.

❧ SEXUAL INTERPRETATION:

This card, linked with the goddess of love, denotes times that are favorable for enjoying sensual intimacy and physical pleasures. When you walk in the footprints of Venus, kindness and affection are freely given. The heart opens to communications that inspire trust, fuel the passions, and make you feel good about yourself. You may be attracted to someone charming who has allure and sex appeal, or has an attraction for you and lets you know it. Encounters can be fun and have a positive long-range effect on you, but if sex for recreation rather than procreation is on your menu, make sure you practice birth control so you won't get any unexpected surprises, since this lady also represents the fertile seeds of life.

☙ Sexual Play:

The Empress loves to be pampered, and delights in providing pleasure for her companions. Lovemaking might begin with a bath or shower for two, with partners covering each other's bodies with suds, sensuously washing each area of the body, gradually moving toward the most erotic points. She and her lover might use their soaped, foamy bodies to wash and massage one another. In the bedroom, The Empress enjoys wearing alluring and regal nightgowns. Foreplay is slow and savory. Desiring to turn on as well as be turned on, The Empress may feed her lover chocolate through the labial doors of her sacred sanctuary.

☙ Reversed Card Interpretation:

When reversed, The Empress points to the negative attributes of love and sexuality. Too much Venus can point to an obsession with love or sex in a way that loses sight of everything but desire. You or the person represented by this card may be too fickle and flirtatious. This person may be driven to fulfill his or her desires, regardless of others' needs and feelings, such as a woman who goes after another woman's husband, or a man who makes a play for another man's wife.

Alternatively, it can indicate a strong attraction to one who is attached to another, coupled with the wisdom and ego strength to realize that the most you can be is dear friends, because it's wiser to avoid the complications that an affair or sexual encounter would bring. Still, you or the other or both may feel the regret of something that might have been, but is not meant to be.

Also, when reversed, this card can be linked with a person who doesn't want to give love. She (or he) may not be ready to make a commitment to nurture or assume a mothering role, either because she's not at that stage of her personal development or because her heart has closed up in response to a painful past, and she's having a hard time opening it again.

THE EMPEROR.

Key Meaning: A strong person with will power, high energy, courage, self-motivation, and financial acumen; leadership

Loving Qualities: Vibrant, passionate, sexy, high-spirited

Loveless Qualities: Aggressiveness; competitive nature

Astrological Connections: Aries, sign of the ram with spirited will and determination, who dares to climb the loftiest crag

Most Compatible Card Partners: Death, The Tower, Strength, Temperance

4. THE EMPEROR

❧ ROMANTIC INTERPRETATION:

A powerful or influential man who is near you in your life could become your lover or have a strong physical attraction for you or you toward him. Whatever the state of your love life, you will feel his presence. The Emperor points to the potential for a strong relationship to develop, or for you to own your power in a relationship. For example, even though you may consider a Herculean man to be your perfect mate, you have to be careful not to surrender your power to his masculine influence, or give him authority over your own decision making. Women sometimes see him as a father figure, or unconsciously, a combination father-lover. Since The Emperor sits on the throne of domination, it is natural for him to assume the role of leadership. He wishes to rule well and wisely, for the benefit of his people and community.

❧ EMOTIONAL INTERPRETATION:

This card can indicate that you or the person represented by this card may be trying to control emotions with logic. Most Emperor-type personalities like to believe that feelings can be dealt with directly, but they may have difficulty discussing them. It's usually easier to focus on business or administrative concerns. After all, how can an empire be ruled if finances are not in order?

The more psychologically developed Emperor has lived through failure, difficulty, perseverance, success, and victory, and may be sympathetic to the sufferings and problems of others. He may have sacrificed love on the road to power and felt the hunger of the heart acquired from that sacrifice. Such an Emperor has to learn how to balance worldly interests with inner emotional desires, and may still need reminders that love is as important as power.

❧ SEXUAL INTERPRETATION:

Often a mature person, The Emperor is an attractive "turn-on," someone who has experience in dealing with the world, including, but not always, the realm of sexual intimacy. Because this card is associated with the Sun sign Aries, which is ruled by Mars, the planet of physical stamina and sexual potency, it indicates heated currents of intensity. Rams, by nature, have strong, persevering energy that can keep them going and going, even when others are ready to slow down or stop. Characteristically, The Emperor is a strong-willed person who doesn't easily take no for an answer, so don't encourage him unless you're ready to go the full distance. If your connection with The Emperor is physical, you can probably look forward to his passionate endurance, sensual stimulation, and penetrating depth.

SEXUAL PLAY:

Surrendering to the allure of his lover, The Emperor buries himself in his mate's tenderness with beckoning kisses that electrifyingly say "I want more!" He has learned to use his strength appropriately and with restraint, tempered by sensitivity and compassion. (He did not become Emperor by ignoring what occurs in others' hearts, but by being acutely sensitive to it).

Widely educated in worldly ways, he favors the ancient Chinese rhythm of nine light, shallow thrusts followed by one deep one. The light thrusts may barely touch the doors of the sacred entrance or slightly enter the hidden sanctuary, while the deep thrust may be vigorous or very slow and languorous. The pace may vary, slowing, even stopping, when climactic excitement threatens to overwhelm him. This delicious rhythm, which may be used with any sexual position, helps prolong lovemaking.

REVERSED CARD INTERPRETATION:

When reversed, The Emperor may refer to impatience, impotence, problems with power, or power struggles in sexual, emotional, or worldly realms. It can refer to a fear of success and consequent self-sabotage, or being out of touch with one's purpose.

It may also denote frozen emotions, frustrating sexual experiences, an unwillingness to give of oneself or make commitments in a relationship, or difficulty expressing feelings. And it can signal an attachment to relating from a position of power instead of one of openheartedness. There may be an inability to be in the present or a feeling that nothing is going fast enough, with a narrow field of view that excludes the larger effects of one's actions. This rigidity in defining success can be present even when the success that is sought is idealistic.

4. THE EMPEROR

- 77 -

THE HIEROPHANT

Key Meanings: A spiritual, metaphysical, or philosophical person with ethical courage and high values; connecting with your higher purpose

Loving Qualities: Strong-minded, vibrant, and creative

Loveless Qualities: Stubborn, inflexible, possessive

Astrological Connection: Taurus, the bull, a sign of strength of spirit, passion, perseverance, and strong emotions

Most Compatible Card Partners: The Empress, The Hermit, The Devil

5. THE HIEROPHANT

☙ ROMANTIC INTERPRETATION:

It can take time for this person, who has a tendency to stay somewhat distant, to open his or her heart to you, but once it happens, he or she becomes deeply committed. Inner beauty tends to act as a magnet to attract The Hierophant partner, for in most cases, outer appearances are less important to him or her. Although they may be practical and down to earth, Hierophants hold on to their ideas and desires with all their being. There is nothing lightweight about the personality of the Hierophant, who views love as sacred. He or she won't get seriously entangled without feeling a soul connection (but may get involved on a casual level without making a commitment.) Emotions root in ardent desire.

☙ EMOTIONAL INTERPRETATION:

This card signifies receiving a helping hand and an opportunity for some kind of beneficial change because of it. A trusted friend, teacher, or spiritual person may offer you guidance to help you find answers to your emotional questions. Open communication brings greater depth of understanding and new perspectives on your future. Your pendulum of desire (or the other person's) may swing among material, emotional, and intellectual concerns, awakening inner awareness that helps you see through veils of illusion or confusion. The card points to grounding your hopes and emotions in reality, and although glamorous, romantic dreams may stir your imagination, your overall well-being should be nourished with pristine clarity.

☙ SEXUAL INTERPRETATION:

The Hierophant usually desires a relationship that offers more than sex, and once involved, is intensely loving and passionate. Because this card is connected with Taurus, which is ruled by Venus, a symbol of love, beauty, seduction, and pleasure, it indicates that the chances of finding happiness in the bedroom are greater than average. When a love affair unfolds, you may experience tantric sex—the alchemical union of two souls—if both you and the other person exert sexual energy with spiritual awareness. Childish love games of testing the limits and pretending detachment or indifference can be overcome with sensitive, honest communication that solidifies trust and opens a willingness to give unselfishly on sexual levels.

✧ SEXUAL PLAY:

The Hierophant arranges a setting for the sacred ceremony of joining two bodies and souls. Designing an altar to acknowledge the four elements of creation initiates the rite. To honor the element earth, flowers are offered to his love, while for the element air, sweet smelling incense burns near his bed. To pay homage to fire, the element linked with passion, candles light the room, and for the element water, a cup or shell is filled with wine or juice.

With caring silence, the Hierophant's lover presents the temple of her body as an offering of joy. The Hierophant kneels to worship the goddess of love standing before him. Running his hands lightly over her torso, he undoes her clothing to reveal her naked beauty. He banks the passionate fire burning in his loins with the coolness of his breath to slow and center himself, then tastes the magical ambrosia of sweet seduction that flows from the pulsating portal between her legs. Surrendering to the wishes of she who offers herself, the Hierophant invites her to choose the manner in which the offering of sacred love occurs.

✧ REVERSED CARD INTERPRETATION:

When reversed, The Hierophant can indicate someone who is committed to an inflexible view of a religious, political, or economic doctrine or other ideology. In the interpersonal sphere, this tendency may mean dogmatic commitment to an idea of how a relationship should be, and a lack of flexibility in viewing himself or herself, the partner, or their relationship. This can interfere with the mutual give-and-take that contributes to making a relationship healthy. It can be rooted in personal insecurity that causes the person to feel inadequate unless expectations established earlier in life are met. Impervious to hearing, seeing, or sensing how the partner really is, the reversed Hierophant may make the other feel diminished, invalidated, or invisible. A compulsion to control the nature of the relationship may not leave enough room for the partner's true self.

Head-on confrontation with these inflexible views is likely to lead only to escalating conflicts, because self-esteem and security are tied to being "right." Arguments with such people often get stuck on general principles that have little to do with the actual situation at hand. But if you can offer loving support for the other person at the same time that you quietly follow your own inner guide in the relationship, you may be able to gently redefine your basis of relating, and The Hierophant may even let go of the need to always "be right."

THE LOVERS.

Key Meanings: People with inquiring minds and energetic spirits share a vision of love; passionate intimacy, making the right decisions

Loving Qualities: Versatile, openhearted, communicative

Loveless Qualities: Unyielding, criticizing, insecure, demanding

Astrological Connection: Gemini, sign of the twins, mentally agile and ever mindful of the dualities in life and love

Most Compatible Card Partners: The Magician, Justice, The Star

6. THE LOVERS

6. THE LOVERS

❧ ROMANTIC INTERPRETATION:

Eros shoots his arrow of love. Marriage, commitment, or some kind of a bonding of emotional ties may be on the horizon, or may already have been made. You may find a fertile oasis of mutual sharing and caring in the desert of loneliness, or experience harmony after a time of discord. Your mind searches for and finds a path leading to improvement of intimate communications. Love's mysteries are revealed, and you may find yourself making decisions about important matters concerning your romantic destiny. Your confidence and self-esteem are likely to grow as a golden opportunity to enrich your emotional life comes your way. Ordinary reality becomes infused with the sublime.

❧ EMOTIONAL INTERPRETATION:

Just as the twins of Gemini can see down two different and opposite paths at the same time, so does this card indicate seeing the nature of duality. You will have to make decisions about the directions in which you let your heart move, and about the actions you take as a result of those movements. You may find yourself juggling emotional choices as Eros smiles wryly, watching you try to go in two directions at the same time. Mercurial quickness of thought can keep things interesting and moving quickly. Your dreams and realities may fit seamlessly and beautifully, or you may have to reshape your dreams to fit the forms of life and love that offer themselves to you. Trying to manipulate realities so that they fit your preconceptions creates struggle. Remembering that your life story unfolds day by day—and that the very nature of human existence prevents you from knowing the outcome in advance—can help you flow toward your emotional future without fear. You might even get something better than what you're hoping for.

❧ SEXUAL INTERPRETATION:

Lovers meet and share physical pleasures, creating a bond of intimacy. Since Mercury, the planet of communication, rules Gemini, The Lovers' astrological correspondence, speaking your mind is included with sexual play. Communications, mostly fun and deeply sensual, are mixed with calling genitals by playful names like "Mr. Big" or "Tushie McGee." Sounds of nature such as bird calls or whale songs make The Lovers' erotic utterances echo with vibrations of lust, longing, and urgency. The Lovers seek flexibility, spontaneity, and living in the moment. Seeking ways to be mutually loving, respectful, and caring, as well as passionate in a relationship, turns on the spirit of romance.

8 SEXUAL PLAY:

Responding to music that has a rhythm and quality that fits both of their moods, The Lovers shed their clothes and begin to dance. First apart, then closer, they touch momentarily, let their bodies brush against each other spontaneously and sensually to provoke sublime intimacy, then move apart to fan desire's fires. At last, bodies entwine and intermingle, and express what they feel. Caresses of the dance give way to caresses on the bed or a futon on the floor. Mercurial logic struggles to provide balance, but when passions glow warmly and burst into flame, the magic of orgasmic ecstasy draws love's consummation near. Two souls together, through breath, mind, and body, link to feast on the banquet of erotic love.

Once they have entered oceanic caverns of sexual pleasure, both partners lie very close together and hold each other tightly in a loving embrace for a momentary eternity. Then as they begin to move, each pays attention to the other's level of arousal. If their movements threaten to cast one or the other over the orgasmic abyss too soon, they stop moving or use light hand pressure to signal the partner to stop moving long enough to draw back from the climactic brink in order to prolong the excitement. As their bodies sway in sexual union, they are overcome by the storm that sweeps through undulating waves of delight.

8 REVERSED CARD INTERPRETATION:

While the opportunities of love bring sunshine into your heart, difficulties may lurk in the shadows. One of these is betrayal or an imbalance of love, as expressed in the cliché "Love is blind!" One may be in love while the other says or implies that they're in love without really being sure about their level of commitment. Usually the more committed person senses this imbalance at some level, which can lead to insecurity, jealousy, and attempts at overcontrol, which may have effects just the opposite of those that were intended. If I demand more than you want to give, it may frighten you away. So if my love is stronger than yours, I'm in a troubling bind: I want to draw you closer, but I have to hold you loosely instead of tightly to avoid driving you away.

6. THE LOVERS

Another reversed meaning involves the problem of projection, in which you see the other person as having all the qualities you wanted in another and blind yourself to the ways he or she differs from your expectations—for now. This opens the door for future trouble, as your illusions fall away. Or, out of your insecurity and need to be loved, you may give up your own needs and inclinations in order to fit your beloved's expectations. These are opposite sides of the same coin, both involving a lack of a clear sense of boundaries of where I leave off and where you begin.

Another danger is that "I love you" may really mean "I want you to meet my needs and desires, but don't expect me to meet yours." True love involves *mutual* respect and caring. Without that two-way flow, it's only a facsimile. Without intimate communication (that is, each partner truly listening to and hearing what the other needs), love is endangered. And if The Lovers are concealing important desires, feelings, and intentions, then truly intimate communication, which inevitably involves a dimension of trust and transparency, is impossible and the love is tragically flawed.

7. THE CHARIOT

THE CHARIOT.

🙚 ROMANTIC INTERPRETATION:

Like the two sphinxes (or horses, depending on the deck) trying to pull The Chariot in different directions, contrasting forces such as past fears and future dreams may tug at you. If you are not in a committed relationship, you may be examining the single life. Perhaps you're unsure about making commitments, while you reach out to enjoy the fruits of love and yearn for the security of a good relationship. Or you may have had enough relationships that were not so hot that your own company seems better than what you've found available out there. If you're in a partnership, you may be weighing the pros and cons of your situation or of some new way in which you might like your relationship to grow.

As the charioteer, you have the strength to guide the opposing forces within you, and the responsibility for doing so. With the chances for pleasure and rewards come the risks of uncertainty and pain. You'll have to decide which path is best for your heart, body, mind, and soul to follow at this moment in your life. Thinking analytically, listening to the voice of your intuition, and finding the center from which your action springs will help you overcome ambivalence and discern what directions are best for you. What do you most want for yourself now?

🙚 EMOTIONAL INTERPRETATION:

Self-inquiry stirs emotions, and memories rise to the surface. Willingness to look within yourself helps uncover the road to recovery from painful experiences and can free your spirit to move boldly. This may be your time to sing a hopeful song of romance. Balancing logic and intuition helps feelings flow toward an expression of harmony. Rushing toward the future disturbs the present. Be willing to allow your "now" to unfold at its own pace and witness it with total awareness.

The ebb and flow of moods may accompany changing life circumstances that bring new opportunities. Since some of these changes endure, while others are doors that open briefly and then close, it is important to be flexibly responsive to each moment's demands without too much focus on future expectations. Don't obsess about issues needing clarification. At the right time, you'll hear your answers whispered from within your psyche, or from the voices of the other or others who are involved.

Key Meanings: Force of will (often unconscious) drives one forward; balancing the forces of duality; advancing toward goals

Loving Qualities: Generous, understanding, compassionate

Loveless Qualities: Moody, possessive, overprotective, and sometimes crabby

Astrological Connection: Cancer, sign of the crab, emotionally serious, yet playful while moving through high and low tides of love

Most Compatible Card Partners: The Moon, Death

❧ SEXUAL INTERPRETATION:

Because The Chariot is linked with the zodiac sign Cancer—which is ruled by the Moon, a symbol for the feminine, emotions, imagination, the subconscious, and esoterica—this card embraces a spectrum of sexual possibilities. Sex magic, bondage, and delicious forms of erotica such as whipping the pony or joining the mile high club can be invoked when the mind is free to create sexual reality in a playful manner. But if inner values are not respected, if you and the other(s) involved do not listen to one another's needs and sensitivities, then playfulness can be transformed into hurtfulness. The wheels of The Chariot can be brought to a halt by the sensitivity deeply embedded in our emotional nature, so fire can suddenly turn to ice if you don't treat your partner with respect. Unselfish giving that shows consideration for the other's wishes and individuality—not penis or breast size—keeps a lover happy and coming back for more.

❧ SEXUAL PLAY:

The Chariot symbolizes instinctual, passionate energy swiftly turning the wheels of sexual love. Giving yourselves over to the moment with wild abandon (while taking care to respect the other's feelings, needs, and limits) turns up the heat. Passions are evoked as your fingernails playfully race down the course of your lover's back, letting dominatrix rule with the wild whip of willful teasing. Whispering the word no and alternating soft breaths and tongue-licking kisses in the ears inflames desire. Continue kissing your lover's head, neck, and shoulders again and again, moving downward. Slowly, with awareness, trace the bones of your lover's pelvis with your tongue until the temptation to invite the charioteer's steed through the hidden chamber's doors can be withstood no longer. Thrusting movements accelerate at a stallion's gait. Spanking or stroking the buttocks playfully, the charioteer urges or quiets the steed into a dance that perfectly fits the moment until the enchanted destination is reached.

❧ REVERSED CARD INTERPRETATION:

The charioteer's tendency to move strongly and rapidly can lead to a narrowed awareness with which you overlook unintended consequences of an action, or unseen possibilities in the act not chosen. Just as indecisive or timid action can be confusing, inadequate understanding of the other can sabotage the best intentions. Insensitivity to effects of one's words or actions on another can produce a lasting feeling of injury, resentment, or even a desire for revenge that may erupt at some unknown future time.

If love or commitment is in question, but physical intimacy is in play, questions may not be answered concerning the direction of your encounter. Underlying influences or hidden agendas may keep surfacing. The result may be either fond memories of a delightful episode, or regret and a wish that you had done things differently.

If you are truly indecisive, as symbolized by the sphinxes pulling in different directions, or if you know that you're not ready for a commitment, it may be important to communicate that, so that you don't lead the other person to believe that your chariot is going in their direction. Clarity is crucial, as it's so easy for people to believe what they want, sometimes even in spite of what another person is saying or not saying.

STRENGTH.

Key Meanings: Strength of spirit and positive energy enables one to overcome obstacles; fortitude; potency of purpose

Loving Qualities: Radiant energy, courage, and creativity

Loveless Qualities: Arrogance and the need to control

Astrological Connection: Leo, the celestial lion, a playful romantic who is true to heartfelt emotions

Most Compatible Card Partners: The Sun, The Emperor, Temperance

8. STRENGTH

8. STRENGTH

❧ ROMANTIC INTERPRETATION:

A positive attitude promotes emotional prosperity and helps you find the inner strength to succeed in love. Use your intuition, look into your inner crystal ball, and see how love and happiness are within your grasp. Strength includes telling yourself that you have the ability to succeed, visualizing positive results, and taking concrete steps to create success in love or worldly matters. Such steps may be large and bold, or small and careful, in accord with what you feel capable of doing successfully at this moment. The important thing is to be willing to make your move.

If you're in a relationship, dominance versus submission may be an issue. Improve chances for love by avoiding power struggles. Be attentive to noticing when you're caught in a power struggle—especially when the issue you're both being stubborn about is not a major one in and of itself—and when possible, simply let go and step out of the struggle. Courage is needed to do this—courage to try a new and more flexible way of being with yourself and your partner. Being kind and generous, even with your partner's need for space, acts in your favor. Mutual encouragement of each other's strengths and interests provides a foundation for an enduring relationship. When each person helps the other grow and develop, both or all can prosper in love, wisdom, wealth, accomplishment—or all of these.

❧ EMOTIONAL INTERPRETATION:

Creative self-expression blossoms when the heart is optimistic about today's opportunities and tomorrow's fortunes. The lion personality, powerful and persevering, is passionate and fiery, likes receiving attention, enjoys getting his or her own way, and has the power to see deeply into others. If your inner lion feels small, realize that your confidence will grow and blossom as you engage in repeated actions that express your life force at the level at which you can be successful now. Even the greatest of lions starts out as a cub. When you open your heart, sometimes you may be anxious, but to the lion, that's just part of life. Like the lion, you can patiently wait for an opening, and then move swiftly to ensure your well-being. Saying "Yes!" to your hopes and dreams opens up opportunities for happiness.

❧ Sexual Interpretation:

Since Strength is associated with Leo the lion, the only zodiac sign linked with the Sun, this card signifies the potential for sizzling, hot love. Warm and inspirational, the Sun's positive energy can help you gain love's victory. Tingling sensations intensify and passion dominates, for the playful, affectionate nature of the cat is hard to suppress. When moving the fires of sexual desire into the bedroom, plan carefully, and consider the possible consequences if love's juices flow freely. Strength, being linked with Leo, the horoscope's home for children, indicates the potential for fertile seeds being planted.

❧ Sexual Play:

Taking a shower or bath together is a relaxing and playful prelude that leaves you both feeling sparklingly refreshed. Mirroring every movement your naked partner makes, accent your passionate acts with punctuation marks of playful sounds. Growling loudly is not only fun, but a clear signal that the love instincts are inflamed. Courage and strength, allies for initiating untried recipes for making love, are called upon to liberate animated foreplay. After the yoni fills with love's juices, the woman, kneeling on all fours on the edge of the bed, invites her partner to enter her secret temple of pleasure from behind like a lion mounting his mate. As he stands behind her, he moves to embrace her body with his own, caressing her breasts, her sides, her back, and the secret portal that beckons his approach. With his hands stroking her tenderly, he enters with long, easy strokes.

❧ Reversed Card Interpretation:

Strength sometimes takes the form of a tendency to dominate. The dominator is too locked into his or her own need for control to allow others to assert their own strength. This often leads to verbal, emotional, or physical abuse by the dominator. (Often the acceptance of such abuse by the dominated is tolerated because that's how love was packaged in childhood by a dominating parent or other adult, and that's the only way the dominated person knows how to accept it.) While a relationship based on controlling the other person may work in the short run, in the long run it almost always turns poisonous and interferes with the growth of everyone involved. Often it involves the psychological mechanism called "displacement": A weaker partner, being unable to return aggression toward the stronger, becomes aggressive toward the children or toward others who are even weaker, thus perpetuating a cycle that is passed from one person or generation to another.

The irony is that in most cases, the dominator learned his or her role by being rendered powerless at the hands of a dominating role model, leading both to the desire for revenge—which is later displaced onto others—and to a mastery of the large and small cruelties involved in acts of domination. In this sense, domination is not strength but weakness. The truly strong help others find their own strength, rather than victimizing them.

The reversed Strength card can also point to fear, insecurity, giving away your power, and acting out the role of victim. Or it can indicate that you tend to let your body lead your head in following your passions, and later feel remorse for doing so.

9. THE HERMIT

THE HERMIT.

§ ROMANTIC INTERPRETATION:

The Hermit represents drawing on your inner resources to transform or enrich what you bring to a relationship. Emotions are communicated, and through this communication, you may come to a resolution of a conflict or undergo a transition in your awareness of the truth of words spoken. If single, you may find your strength to stand alone and come to terms with being a "free spirit." Aloneness doesn't mean loneliness to The Hermit, but strength of mind and independence.

Sometimes, the very act of taking time to give to yourself without feeling like you have to please others, even if in little ways, can be healing in and of itself. You can use logic and constructive introspection to find answers concerning the next step of your romantic journey, reducing insecurities and stirring inner healing.

§ EMOTIONAL INTERPRETATION:

The figure on The Hermit card (in those decks where the figure is male) is said to be the ancient Greek philosopher Diogenes, the best-known teacher of the Cynic school, which emphasized naturalness. In different iterations of his legend, the light of the lantern he holds was meant to find truth, or to find an honest person. Diogenes advised searching for your own inner voice and ignoring the standards, allures, and goods of conventional society. Feelings are empowered as your mind seeks the direction of your emotional path that will lead to your evolutionary growth. The Hermit looks within to gain self-knowledge and come to conclusions about future directions. Exploring personal issues helps you understand your ways of being in a relationship as well as your needs to be separate and independent. The Hermit does not, however, remain apart from society: After withdrawing into yourself to listen to your inner messages, you're ready to reach out with greater awareness and inner composure to another, or to others, to create or deepen relationships.

§ SEXUAL INTERPRETATION:

Virgo, the virgin, corresponds with this card, so be willing to make love with the mind as much as the body. Mercury, which rules Virgo, is the symbol for analysis, quickness of thought, and intelligence, and its influence demands mindfulness and heedful

Key Meanings: Developing your inner resources; contemplation without attachment; letting go; the search for truth

Loving Qualities: Sensitivity, open-mindedness; perceptive

Loveless Qualities: Overly analytical reasoning; hard to approach

Astrological Connections: Virgo, the zodiacal virgin whose heart gazes at love's sensory garden first with mercurial intellect followed by impassioned emotion

Most Compatible Card Partners: The Magician, The Hierophant, The Devil

awareness. Focus is on creating the ultimate loving experience, but remember, for The Hermit, passion needs to be mentally stimulating and provocative to set the mood for love. Spiritual connectedness breaks down barriers of isolation or feelings of separateness. Revealing too much of your body or soul too soon can lead to nervousness or embarrassment that slows down sensual contact, but taking a candlelit, romantic bath with a partner can remove the threshold of physical or psychic distance.

℘ Sexual Play:

Rub your hands together to create friction and ignite fiery Shakti energy in your palms. Allow yourself the gift of giving your own body a massage, whether kneading sore muscles deeply, rubbing lightly and sensuously, or both. When the rest of your body is content, take a spoon of your favorite love oil, pour it into your hands, and rub them together to heat the oil. Once it's warm, sensually stroke the most intimate parts of your own body until you feel aroused. Play with bringing your sexual energy up your spine to your heart center. Hold your breath still, and then exhale breathing the sexual energy out from your heart center. Let any tightness or tension in your body fall away as you exhale. Then let your fingertips explore your personal zone of sensory delight. Imagine the energy of your physical pleasure lighting the candle of self-love in your heart as stimulating contractions arouse the current of your own sacred essence.

If you're with a partner, as you lie together, each of you can watch the other's ritual of personal pleasure.

℘ Reversed Card Interpretation:

This card can indicate a lack of reaching out to others, or a compulsion to have everything thought out and programmed in advance. Living in the past constricts the future, while living solely for the future steals the life and vitality from the present. Old habits can be a prison, giving you hang-ups, and interfering with life's zest and flavor. Excessive nervousness, the dour face, and the tight sphincter can interfere with the relaxation and playfulness that we all sometimes need. It may be important to work on letting go so you can relax and enjoy the good fellowship and fun around you.

The reversed Hermit who endures hardships stoically can also reflect excessive reclusiveness and the feeling that you have to "do it all yourself," with no help from others. You may benefit from looking for help and comfort in talking through your problems with a trusted friend. You may need to learn to work on problems collaboratively, instead of feeling like you have to do everything yourself.

WHEEL of FORTUNE.

Key Meanings: The wheel of life turns, bringing change—often good fortune, progress, and success; preparing for new possibilities

Loving Qualities: Light-hearted, adventurous, altruistic

Loveless Qualities: Insensitive, narcissistic

Astrological Connection: The attributes of the planet Jupiter, linked with ancient deities known for wisdom and foresight

Most Compatible Card Partners: Temperance, The Moon

10. WHEEL of FORTUNE

℘ ROMANTIC INTERPRETATION:

Your love life may swing higher or lower than usual, depending on the turning of the wheel of fate, but whatever direction emotions flow, you can expect learning to be part of your journey. Mostly, this card represents exuberant energy, success, and good fortune. If you're undertaking something that involves more risk than usual, however, be sure you take extra time to look at possible future consequences of your acts before you boldly jump forward. For people enjoying the fruits of romance, this card can indicate gaining insight into your emotional direction and increasing your clarity about the commitments you do or don't want to make. If you're single, this card signifies the hand of fate expanding your world of relationships and romance. An upswing in flirting and dating may occur.

℘ EMOTIONAL INTERPRETATION:

Since Jupiter, the planet linked with this card, is connected to ambition, progress, expansion, philosophy, and spirituality, it is usually considered auspicious when it appears in your tarot spread. Self-knowledge and a deeper understanding of your inner emotional nature come with Jovian activities. Be alert to rotating the wheel of life in your favor. Look for ways you can turn emotional problems or conflicts into opportunities for growth and success. As you think of solutions to problems, both internal and external conflicts will diminish. Events may hold up a mirror for you to see yourself reflected with an improved sense of self-esteem, greater appreciation of your inner spirit, or a glimpse of a new side of yourself that can take advantage of your personal power. Letting go of the past or unreal expectations can help you to be emotionally open to potential trysts, or to respond emotionally in new ways to old situations.

℘ SEXUAL INTERPRETATION:

As the wheel of fortune turns, luck turns in your favor, and intimate encounters may become more likely. If you're already involved sexually, they may become more delicious than ever. Happiness prevails when your lover's eyes say "Yes!" to playful affection. Physical energy, including sexual energy, may heighten, and you may find yourself easing comfortably into erogenous zones. Your experiences bring you a more conscious awareness of your body and health strategies for your sexual well-being.

Opportunities to be involved with multiple partners or partners of the same sex may be presented to you. Bedroom values may be challenged by new circumstances. Your body and your life are your own, so pay attention to what you truly want to do and what makes sense to you. Avoid being driven by others' "shoulds" or expectations, either toward conventionality or unconventionality.

§ SEXUAL PLAY:

The gypsy of the soul dances passionately toward the touch of love's pampering. As hands massage the welcoming body, sensual warmth opens the gateway of love. With consent, fingertips moist with love oil gently titillate the erogenous zones before temptation's tango changes into a waltz of sexual embrace. After fingers have lightly and sensitively opened her inner gate, the tongue moves onto that sensitive spot known in ancient Chinese texts as the "pearl on the jewel terrace." Then with a long breath, slowly exhale on your partner's pleasure spot to engage her deepest desire. If she has not already, she may moan out for your mighty jade stalk to enter. Venture in slowly, avoiding climax, and enjoy pleasure's depth. Then withdraw and resume titillation with the tongue once again until you bring her almost to climax before you stop, and then enter again. All this may be repeated numerous times, to allow you to prolong your enjoyment of an ecstatic feast of the senses.

§ REVERSED CARD INTERPRETATION:

When reversed, this card sometimes points to the end of a relationship, to a time to move on and come to terms with letting go, so you can spin the wheel again. Or, it can indicate that a particular pattern or phase in a relationship is ending or should end—perhaps one that's no longer healthy or helpful, so that you might find more happiness by relating in different ways or moving in new directions.

The upside-down Wheel of Fortune can also signify inertia, lack of progress, or a feeling of being psychologically stuck or stifled. It can mean that you respond to a potentially constructive change, or possibility of change, by staying stuck in counterproductive, old habits and patterns instead of flowing with a new opportunity.

Alternatively, it may mean railing against an unwanted turn of fate instead of making the best of it and moving on. You may be spending too much time and energy being consumed with frustrations or worries about the inevitable.

JUSTICE .

Key Meanings: Becoming centered, finding inner balance, and weighing the positive versus the negative helps measure the truth of the heart

Loving Qualities: Friendly, easygoing, affectionate

Loveless Qualities: Indecisive, vulnerable

Astrological Connection: Libra, sign of the scales that balance mind and emotions, trust and doubt, passion and fear

Most Compatible Card Partners: The Empress, The Lovers, The Star

11. JUSTICE

❧ ROMANTIC INTERPRETATION:

You may find yourself drawn almost equally toward and away from a romantic involvement, but the desire for love or companionship can act like a magnet pulling you toward romance. Someone who is your complete opposite may attract you. Rather than throwing yourself into a questionable situation, pay attention to whether your initial self-disclosure and trust are reciprocated to an equal degree. Balance the weight of strong feelings with logic and common sense as you gauge the direction, nature, and power of your attractions. If a romantic opportunity is present, it's up to you to discern whether it's right for you, or whether some aspect of it makes it wrong.

Questions involving compatibility, commitments, or marriage may need to be answered. The scales of justice indicate that it's important to balance your emotions with your common sense and make decisions from a centered place within yourself. If you're in a partnership, both of you need to give and receive to an equal degree. If you don't, you may be better off standing on your own for the time being because sooner or later one of you will probably start resenting the inequality.

❧ EMOTIONAL INTERPRETATION:

Justice signifies using your power in the service of compassion, mediation, and the reestablishment of harmony. Trust plays a role in fertilizing a bond of love. Be willing to trust, so long as the other also displays trustworthiness in word and deed. If your trust is welcomed, validated, and reciprocated, you will be able to make decisions concerning the extent of your emotional involvement.

If you're already in a relationship, you and your partner may move into sharing feelings on deeper levels. You may analyze the pros and cons of your emotional direction, as the scales weigh your heart's leanings and your intuition's messages. Keep your mind clear of insecurity (or at least notice when and how your old insecurities crop up so you can avoid running aground on them) so that your love can act as a strong foundation for creating harmonious relationships. Make space in the flow of your daily events for your happier, loving, inner spirit to express itself. It's time to create magic in your life.

৪ Sexual Interpretation:

Justice is associated with sign of the scales, Libra, which is ruled by Venus. Because this planet is associated with the goddess of love, Aphrodite, and all things beautiful, pleasurable, and loving (even houses of Ladies of the Night), this card is an indication of the enjoyment of fathomless depths of passion. Affection and sexual magnetism intensify. Compatible partners join in deep and sensual bonds of intimacy. But such depths in their fullest are not given lightly. If you're single, this card is auspicious as it can indicate attracting a playmate. Be willing to be the enchanter or sorceress. The more you believe in your personal power and are confident of your sexuality, the easier time you'll have attracting a partner. The focus is on passion, pleasure, and fun—as you balance them with heartfelt emotion.

৪ Sexual Play:

Get naked with your lover except for your underwear. Without using your hands, use your teeth to take off your partner's undergarments. When your mouth contacts sensitive parts, your tongue licks playfully. Move into the position commonly referred to as "sixty-nine" in which you're facing each other and each of you has your has your head in the direction of the other's feet and your lips where you can kiss each other's tantalizing tidbits. If your partner is female, use your tongue to explore all possible forms of pleasurable contact and penetration, from pausing at the pearl on the jewel terrace to sucking it into your mouth, and penetrating as deeply as your tongue can go. If your partner is male, tickle the underside of the tip of his majestic member with your tongue. Then let your mouth cover the tip and gently pull it with your lips. Hold your breath with awareness of the sexual energy flowing within. When you exhale, imagine yourself blowing this essence from your sexual center to your lover. This position balances natural forces of giving and receiving, masculine and feminine energy.

৪ Reversed Card Interpretation:

Upside down, Justice points to lack of sensitivity, loss of harmony, and being out of balance or off center. This may mean a one-sided relationship (or relationships) in which you or the other person put out more energy than is reciprocated, either by grasping at connections unsuitable to you or by feeling mistrustful even when another's affections are sincere.

Aphrodite holds the scales of Justice. When they're out of

balance, her energy can turn into indiscriminate eroticism. This can be fun while it lasts, but be careful to steer clear of unwanted long-run consequences. Unbalanced Aphrodite energy can also flow into jealousy or possessiveness in which you lose your mental and emotional balance. Perhaps the other person becomes resentful of your attempts at control and your restriction of his or her autonomy. This could destroy a relationship you hoped to cultivate. Commitments may be broken.

11. JUSTICE

12. THE HANGED MAN

THE HANGED MAN.

✕ Romantic Interpretation:

The Hanged Man often indicates a person hung up on love, who is trying to live passionately and fully. This may be in the context of a current or past relationship, or of hoping or looking for a new one. While keeping your priorities in mind, your ideals need to be down to earth in order to find fulfillment.

If your romantic present isn't satisfying, instead of being frustrated, look for new directions to find potentials for positive change. If you're seeking romance, stop being shy or living in your dreams, start to communicate with people who are interesting to you, and ask someone for a date.

Your willingness to express yourself from a place of inner strength will help you find a friendship, form a partnership, or strengthen ties within a relationship. With new acquaintances, "first lines" don't have to be great, but just sufficient to open the door to conversation within which both you and the other person can assess or express your interest in further involvement. If you're in a relationship, don't expect your partner to guess what you want. Be explicit about your desires and needs, and tactfully share your feelings about matters that are important to you.

✕ Emotional Interpretation:

Something interesting is bound to happen if you get up the courage to show your vulnerable or playful sides. Adventure and knowledge come from sacrificing comfort and extending your feelings beyond familiar limits. Try letting go of fears and speaking your true thoughts and feelings. If communications aren't right, trust your intuition to lead your emotions to help you act, speak, and listen at whatever depth seems to fit your personal situation and another's willingness to respond to you. Notice your ways of holding in and holding back, and remember that you can breathe deeply, smile, and reach out with your eyes and arms.

Because Neptune—the planet associated with sensitivities, dreams, visions, and psychic realities—is connected with this card, it is an indication that you need to validate your feelings with reality checks so that you don't get lost in nebulous clouds of hopes and desires. This card represents illumination through evolution, so expect to learn to recognize the deeper reality that you're living.

Key Meanings: A person may be hung up in ideas or feelings, may see things from a new angle, hear them in a unconventional way, or have a different sense of a situation

Loving Qualities: Sensitive, dreamy, romantic

Loveless Qualities: Over-sensitive, unrealistic

Astrological Connection: Planet Neptune, linked with king of the sea, who plays with the trident of power while living in an ocean of romantic dreams. Also, the element water and the flow of emotions

Most Compatible Card Partners: The Moon

8 SEXUAL INTERPRETATION:

Patience is a good remedy for inhibitions if you're feeling hung up or fearful of intimacy. If you're unsure of yourself, move slowly in exploring sexual possibilities with your partner. Even though sex is a physical act, it can also be a spiritual experience.

On the other hand, hot pursuit of alluring, sensual pleasures can break through inhibitions. Imagination comes into play as sexual arousal intensifies and fantasy mixes with intimacy. Immediate fulfillment, however, may be at a cross purposes with long-term values, causing indecision.

Playfulness is a key to enjoyment. Passion flows from within your being when you reach out to share it with another. Physical expressions of love will teach you a lot about yourself, so be willing to grow with the kisses you give. Remember, however, that emotional attachments are often formed with the consummation of love, even when you don't intend them to be.

8 SEXUAL PLAY:

Close your eyes and smell your partner's body perfumes. Explore the dimensions of passion's possibilities by using all your senses. Licking, tickling, or very gently biting each others' nipples, lovemaking begins and lighthearted fun is the focus. Tickling sensitive spots and blowing in the ear playfully excites the mood, as nibbles and kisses are exchanged. She lies on her back and he on his side next to her, draping his upper leg between hers where their fingertips can easily meander across each others' pleasure gardens and when the time comes he can easily move into her. This dance of passion is languorous and relaxed, with partners thoroughly hung up in each moment until the arrival of the next.

If you like, you can use The Hanged Man card as permission for sexual fantasy. Who's that movie star you always wanted to make love to? Or that passionately alluring person whom you know is off-limits? This card lets you enter the theater of your mind where you can close your eyes and transform your partner into anyone you please, and your partner can do the same. (If you wish, you can even play at it together: "Who would you like me to be tonight?" each of you asks the other.)

8 REVERSED CARD INTERPRETATION:

Reversed, The Hanged Man usually indicates focusing on some trouble in your relationship, or your approach to relationships.

You may find yourself hanging on to something that's not helpful to you, and needing to let go.

At its extreme, this card may refer to emotional desperation, to grabbing at anyone who comes along regardless of suitability, or to clinging to a dead relationship after it's time to let go. This can lead to one-night stands when you hoped for more than that, or to such an emotional dependence on the other, or on the other's fulfillment of your own expectations (and/or vice versa) that neither of you allows the other room for individuality and growth. As a result, such partnerships are usually codependent, often stormy, and sometimes physically or emotionally abusive. Learning to feel more secure within yourself can help you improve your ability to create a good relationship. Outside resources such as a couples counselor may help you and your companion move harmoniously together. Family therapy can be useful (and sometimes essential) if kids are involved.

DEATH.

Key Meanings: Endings, transformation, new beginnings, rebirth of intimate involvement, sexual forces

Loving Qualities: Passion, sensitivity; deeply emotional

Loveless Qualities: Possessiveness and jealousy

Astrological Connection: Scorpio, sign of the scorpion, warrior of the heart and champion of romantic, sensual love

Most Compatible Card Partners: The Tower, The Chariot, The Moon

13. DEATH

13. DEATH

❧ ROMANTIC INTERPRETATION:

A strong, magnetic attraction or intense emotion may alter the next step of your life's journey. Hold on to your heartstrings and don't let your sensitivity or composure be shaken by the thought of change. Responding flexibly to the demands and opportunities of the moment is necessary for emotions to evolve.

An internal change may move you toward finding new ways to perceive love and reach out to others, or to appreciate sides of people in your life you hadn't recognized as important. You might find a new degree of clarity in deciding which potentials of your own you want to develop, and give new life to sides of yourself that have been dormant or stagnant.

If you're in a relationship, a change in your circumstances or your outlook could open a different door, and you might begin doing things together that you've seldom (or never) done before. Or the changing direction indicated by this card might involve one or both of you individually creating new emotional realities. Even if you don't want change, trust that, in some way, what is coming is for your highest good.

Every time you gain something new, you administer death to other possibilities, so appreciate and enjoy what's valuable in your present romantic situation, whatever it may be. Time will help you find the best solutions to love's riddles.

❧ EMOTIONAL INTERPRETATION:

Tomorrow can create exciting possibilities for change, but if you're worried about the unknown and don't welcome the new, these changes could put you on an emotional roller coaster. If you're worried about the future, do something active to release your stress. (Physical activity, for example, helps strengthen your body while calming your nerves.)

Just because you're capable of diving into the depths of your emotions doesn't mean that you have to spend all day in them. But don't try to push your true feelings out of your awareness, either. To gain perspective on your situation and your options, share your feelings and thoughts with trusted friends, or go on a spiritual sojourn that quenches your soul's thirst for inner wisdom. Working to develop new personal directions and greater emotional balance might be to your benefit.

Although the future is always unknown, you have the stamina to run long distances. Keeping a clear focus on your goals brings you face to face with what you need to do to find success. Events unfold when it's time for them to do so.

☙ SEXUAL INTERPRETATION:

A tender embrace opens a portal to sensual awareness and physical pleasure. Be open to new possibilities and experiences. Look for ways to create something turned-on and wonderful between you and your partner. Symbolizing rebirth, this card may mean that it's time to drop an old lover who thinks you exist only to satisfy his or her sexual needs and shows no sensitivity to yours, or it may be time to vigorously—and perhaps tantalizingly—reeducate him or her in how you like to be loved. If you're single, the temptation of sexual pleasures will entice you, and make you think more deeply about how to find a lover.

Because this card is associated with the Sun sign Scorpio, which rules the genitals and reproductive organs, it has a powerful link with sexual activities and procreation. Extensive love making, multiple orgasms, heightened pleasure, and invigorating sex are all potentials indicated by its presence.

☙ SEXUAL PLAY:

Death symbolizes rebirth, transformation, and change. Are you willing to dance with the unknown and merge with your partner in an untried way? This card is a reminder to go beyond old preferences and try something different to awaken heightened sexual awareness. A new position, a different way of talking about sexual needs or preferences, or a willingness to experiment with your fantasies or unspoken physical desires brings you in contact with fresh possibilities.

Is there anything in your sexual encounters that you do out of sheer habit, even though it has come to seem stale and routine? Is there anything in your lovemaking that your partner doesn't especially like? (You might ask him or her.) When you get this card, it's a good time to bring your awareness into the moment and renew your contact with your partner so that the two of you can find ways of lovemaking that step out of your usual patterns and fit the moment's fancy.

If your partner's "dead tired," but you're feeling amorous, ask permission with your hands to initiate lovemaking. A woman receptive to a man's desire can passively allow him to enter. In *The Mythology of Sex,* Sarah Dening says that according to the seventh-century Chinese sex manual by T'ung Hsuan Tzu, a skillful lover might at one point "push in as slowly as a snake entering a hole to hibernate," and at another "rise and then plunge low like a huge sailing boat braving the gale."

§ REVERSED CARD INTERPRETATION:

Upside down, the Death card refers to events or changes that are unwanted and perhaps unpleasant, or even wrenching. These might create great anxiety about your future. If the changes are not severe, they may seem more frightening than they have to be if you're trying to hold on to what has been, but can no longer be held on to.

The reversed Death card can also point to an emotional connection that has died, or is slipping away, making the situation painful and difficult, as in a relationship where the love is gone but the partners are still involved because they're afraid to let go, or want to stay together for financial security or for the sake of their children. In some instances, it can point to a dysfunctional pattern of sexual encounters or even an actual physical death.

By looking at what cards surround the Death card in your spread, you can see whether it's pointing to something negative or positive, something to break away from or something to pursue. Also, neighboring cards may suggest some way to lighten the situation, or provide more insight into the dilemma.

14. TEMPERANCE

TEMPERANCE.

❈ ROMANTIC INTERPRETATION:

Temperance involves the inner discipline of choosing between what's healthy and helpful for you, and forgoing what's not. This is a time to develop your moment-by-moment awareness of how the people and environment around you cause you to feel and act. Encourage passions and surround yourself with influences that are connected to your soul and discourage those that are not. Finding ways to bring your romantic inclinations into balance with the whole of yourself opens the door to deeper intimacy.

The card points to the importance of communicating with your higher self and bringing the light of your spirit into your relationships. Being centered in inner awareness allows you to live in the truth of your heart. You have the power to move beyond fears that have held you back, or perhaps even to let go of them entirely. This will help you become inwardly stronger and more effective and authentic in relationships.

One of the Seven Virtues, temperance suggests that you can find more harmonious ways to handle discordant issues, in which you and the other person can feel both supportive of one another's needs and supported in your own. Say no to emotional debris that you don't need to rehash yet again, and to invitations or demands that lead in directions that aren't what you want.

❈ EMOTIONAL INTERPRETATION:

By listening to the voice of your feelings when you first become aware of them, you move toward living with your emotions in an appreciative and effective way rather than being overwhelmed by them. Reaction gives way to foresight, mastery, and personal integration. The ideal combination of yin-yang, positive-negative, and solar-lunar energy cures anxieties about love, and boosts the desire to communicate about inner realities. Philosophizing about your current state of affairs needs to be balanced by looking at how your ideas and ideals work in reality, keeping your perspective down to earth. Listen to your real feelings in the present moment, and refrain from counter-productive criticism.

Few relationships are perfect in every way. Looking at what's good and beautiful about your commitments can sweep away

Key Meanings: Harmonizing inner and outer realities, spiritualizing your life; moderation; learning to say "No!"

Loving Qualities: Generosity; a positive, adventurous spirit

Loveless Qualities: Insensitivity, superficiality, intolerance

Astrological Connection: Sagittarius, sign of the archer, part human, part centaur, who demands heart-to-heart, intimate relations

Most Compatible Card Partners: Wheel of Fortune, The Emperor, Strength

pessimism. More often than not, your emotions are your friend and guide. Together with your eyes, ears, and your awareness of the tension or relaxation of your muscles, they're an important part of your intuition about what you need and what you don't. Keys to peace of mind are at hand. Your task is to find and use them. You might even try calling on your guardian angel to help you with your love issues.

☿ Sexual Interpretation:

Linked with Sagittarius, Temperance embodies the symbolism and idealism of its ruling planet, Jupiter. It embraces philosophical understanding, education, expansion of consciousness, and higher aspirations—qualities that make this card a beneficial influence for you, even in the bedroom. The centaur, mythical beast symbolizing this fiery sign, is well hung and reputed to be easily aroused. When you consider combining all the above traits, they point to the possibility of sex that's exciting, passionate, yet sensitive and thoughtful or thought provoking. If you're considering jumping into a sexually turned-on opportunity, consider whether it feels like it will nourish your spirit or just fan the flames of heated physical desire.

Give yourself credit where credit is due. You might just be irresistible to your partner, making affairs of the heart move swiftly under bed covers. Take the time to enjoy the magic of the moment you're capable of creating. Stay attuned to your own sense of what's right for you, relying on your own reason and intuition rather than other people's "shoulds," preferences, or pressures. Your decisions today affect your emotions tomorrow.

☿ Sexual Play:

This is a card of chaste or innocent lovemaking. It strengthens our ability to respect limits that may be necessary due to social circumstances, a physical condition, age, or other reasons. Partners may make love in any way they wish except for mouth kissing mouth, hands or mouth touching genitals, or genitals touching each other.

Focus not on what's excluded but on the possibilities of what's available: touching, looking, smelling, stroking, embracing—any way you wish except those that are off-limits. Make love as deliciously and imaginatively as you can through special actions and contact. Massage, dance, and words of love are permitted. Rediscover the wonder of such simple acts as running your fingers through your partner's hair, holding your partner's hands, or tracing the delicate bones on cheek or shoulder. Your body is an altar for letting the divine awaken within you. Embrace the space of sacred energy that the two of you are creating. If you like, breathe the sound of "Aum" in unison with your partner. In some cases, young people may want to make this card a central object of contemplation and a source of guidance until the age and sense of personal maturity arrives at which they are ready for full sexual engagement.

❧ Reversed Card Interpretation:

Upside down, Temperance can point to thoughtless indulgence and excess, making decisions that take you away from peace and harmony, and not following your better judgment or your informed intuition. It can also mean wild indulgence even when that's dangerous or inappropriate, or a lack of balance of other kinds. To reverse this, work on sharpening your moment-by-moment awareness of what you're feeling. Notice when you do something that takes away your inner peace or emotional balance (that is, practice awareness without self-condemnation). Say "No!" to such an act or pattern when you feel yourself beginning to do it or fall into it, and choose to act differently instead. Disciplining your passions rather than giving yourself over completely to them may be an important task for you.

14. TEMPERANCE

- 105 -

THE DEVIL .

Key Meanings: Lust, negative thinking, bad connections, emotional manipulation, attachments that breed sorrow, danger

Loving Qualities: Energetic, dutiful, and determined

Loveless Qualities: Melancholic, distant, heartless

Astrological Connection: Capricorn, combined sign of mountain goat and dolphin, who is willing to climb high peaks of love in search for a compatible mate

Most Compatible Card Partners: The World, The Hierophant, The Devil

15. THE DEVIL

❡ ROMANTIC INTERPRETATION:

The Devil card is associated with the challenges that come with romance. When it appears in your spread, it is often a warning to protect yourself from danger or harmful activities. Lust entices passions. You may be tempted with desire for someone you know is wrong for you or not available to you, or find yourself in a power struggle, or feel intimidated by an aggressive person or authority figure.

Hunger for a relationship might influence you to participate in a situation that is not healthy for your emotions. Perhaps your partner is influencing you to do something that is in conflict with your ethics. When you go along with demands that don't agree with your own, you're apt to end up being, or at least feeling, trapped in situations that are not good for you, engaging in behaviors harmful to you or others, or in patterns of negative thinking. In such a case, you can be true to yourself by summoning up the courage and discipline to assert your will. Taking care of yourself by speaking your truth or taking space when you need it helps you from getting angry or burned out.

❡ EMOTIONAL INTERPRETATION:

Saturn, a symbol for the teacher, restrictions, and heavy responsibilities, is associated with Capricorn, the astrological correspondence to The Devil. This astrological connection points to facing the karma of your deeds, and to important lessons for the soul that can be found in your present situation. Ask yourself, "What am I supposed to be learning from this experience?" Look for the value of the challenges you face, which may include moving toward better internal communication with yourself, for The Devil often refers to personal disintegration in which one side of you turns a blind eye to what another side is doing.

With The Devil also comes the possibility of taking things too seriously or getting lost in melancholy, so remind yourself to lighten up, and make your life more fun-loving and carefree. Or it can mean the opposite—to stop making light of everything, and be serious about what needs to be taken seriously. In either case, it refers to the importance of change in your existing patterns. The surrounding cards in the layout will help you discern which way to go.

Developing positive attitudes about your love life will help strengthen your self-image, make you more secure within yourself, and give you the strength to ask for what you need to be happy. Instead of focusing on outer relationship dynamics that may be outside your control, work on perfecting your inner relations with important sides of yourself.

❧ SEXUAL INTERPRETATION:

You've picked the card that can mean great sex, but sometimes in exchange for lost peace of mind. When you give yourself over to the pleasures of passion, make absolutely sure that you'll be practicing safe sex before indulging. You don't want to wake up one day to a nasty surprise such as a sexually transmitted disease (STD) or an unwanted pregnancy.

Lust may tempt you to taste the succulent fruit of a relationship that's too hot to handle. If so, despite the pull of passion, be sure you get a clear picture of the entire situation, and the possible consequences for you and your partner, before you decide to go ahead. Be alert: catting around can get you in trouble!

If you're married or in a similar commitment, you may be focusing on frustrations in love or sexual relations, causing you to question the purpose or depth of your commitment. Focusing too heavily on your problems can hamper fun in the bedroom and leave you feeling frustrated or angry. Save some mental energy for the flames of passion.

❧ SEXUAL PLAY:

Who knows what outrageous forces will come out to play on the stage of your sexual dreams when The Devil card is pulled? This card is sometimes interpreted to mean being lost in lust or your mind, instead of staying in touch with your true feelings and those around you. Such fetishes as whips and chains and leather boots come from being caught up in cravings for power, excitement, or bondage games.

The use of such items is okay, as long as both "master" and "slave" enjoy playing and the dominance-submission game remains a game and doesn't slide into being serious or threatening. A way to ensure that is to take turns of equal time in each role, and to agree in advance that if the other does something you don't like, you'll use an explicitly agreed-upon phrase like "please don't do that," and the other will instantly comply. (Without such limits, if the game ceases to be a game for either partner, it can lead to permanent and irrevocable loss of trust in

15. THE DEVIL

- 107 -

the other as well as lasting psychological damage.) You can also use the card as a reminder to do something devilishly good that you know your partner loves but that you don't do very often.

If either partner regards sexuality as something dirty or sinful (as this card may seem to some readers to imply), The Devil may indicate an opportunity to discuss those feelings, and the experiences that gave rise to them, with a highly trusted partner or friend. If there's something devilishly difficult in your sexual relationship that one or both of you just don't know how to handle, consider a consultation with a professional couples counselor or sex therapist.

❦ REVERSED CARD INTERPRETATION:

Reversed, The Devil can involve a misuse of power, either the manipulation of another person for your own selfish ends, (sometimes with the aid of alcohol or drugs), or the other person doing that to you. This may be manipulation with malicious intent, using power to harm others and inflate one's own ego. It can also refer to being chained to a situation in which something has been lost, or you aren't happy, but you don't know how to change or fix the problem.

The Devil can frighten the strongest of lovers so that impotence or frigidity rules. On the other hand, The Devil reversed can be a positive sign, in the sense of "Been down so long, the only way to go is up." It may signal that the time is right to go through and out of something that has been troubling you. It could mean that the turbulence in your life is giving you the kick in the ass that you need to make you look at your fears or problems and get through them.

15. THE DEVIL

16. THE TOWER

THE TOWER.

✤ ROMANTIC INTERPRETATION:

The Tower, associated with the intense energy of Mars, crumbles from being hit by a bolt of lightening, and when you get this card, you're being cautioned: Look for inner balance because you're going to need it to keep your life flowing in harmony. Just as a concrete tower may fall, plans or commitments may crash or be shaken. The ego is strong, but even the powerful can fall. Assess where you can fortify your romantic interests.

This may be a time when you need to protect what you hold sacred. Yet this protection may involve taking constructive steps in relation to needs that another person has articulated. Your loving ties may be tested by fate. Uncertainties may bounce your emotions like a ball on the waves of a stormy sea. Affairs or undertakings may be be jolted, tested, or ended by an unpleasant occurrence.

If you're not in a committed relationship right now, don't re-enact the same old patterns of relating that have been shaken by life, perhaps time and time again. Open your interests and try different possibilities in the kinds of people you choose to relate to and the kinds of things you choose to do. Your old habits are like boundaries that you've stayed inside. Try taking steps outside them in a way that's adventurous yet true to yourself.

✤ EMOTIONAL INTERPRETATION:

The intense energy shown in the falling tower may reflect the overwhelming power of outside circumstances. It may also represent an unexpected eruption of your own emotions that have been locked up by defense mechanisms you have built around them, as shown by the stone from which the tower is built. Jealousy or insecurity at a level you didn't realize was part of you may create inner tension or outer difficulties. Things may not be working out the way you think they should, or you may need to deal with complex issues that require great emotional energy.

Results of your past efforts may not be what you were expecting and you may have to adjust your attitude and actions to keep your spirits high. If you're in a relationship, you may feel the need to sever the bond or strengthen the commitment, depending on your situation. Some aspect of your awareness is due for a change or an uplift.

Key Meanings: Intense forces bring unexpected events into your life, and plans are altered, or you make a change in your life patterns that creates a crisis, a changing flash of awareness

Loving Qualities: Spontaneity, strength, passion, and sex appeal

Loveless Qualities: Too intense or too much ego; easily angered

Astrological Connection: Fiery attributes linked with the planet Mars and the Roman god of War who shares the same name

Most Compatible Card Partner: The Emperor

When The Tower shakes, superficial ideas and half-truths fall away. The advice others have been giving you may not be appropriate. If it feels wrong, you probably need to rely more fully on your own inner sensing and knowing, and perhaps talk about your situation with others who can bring fresh and unbiased perspectives. You may come face-to-face with some aspect of your self-image that's not a true reflection of who you are. If so, it's a very important insight. Since many others can see the true you even when you don't, becoming aware of how you really are is a key part of a good relationship. As the tower indicates, all self-deception eventually must be swept away, or else anything you've built on top of it one day will crumble.

Whatever direction you're going in love, be willing to trust that ultimately you'll find your rewards for facing fully the challenges of this moment.

🜨 SEXUAL INTERPRETATION:
The Tower sometimes indicates an exaggeration of sex into debauchery, such as wild parties that turn into orgies, partner swapping, or exhibitionistic sex to impress others or make money. Sexual realities may topple, leaving one angry or unhappy.

One way or another, the phallic-looking tower is falling, and symbolically this can indicate sexual problems. It can point to impotence, sexual dysfunction, or kinky sex that may have nothing to do with love. The dysfunction might be an excessive timidity that keeps you or your partner from getting fully and freely into the flow of lovemaking, perhaps because of messages or prohibitions from many years ago that still trigger inhibitions or other feelings in your present life. If this is the case, getting out of your thoughts, going fully with your passions, and getting completely into your sensory experience in the moment might be the answer. Just as the visual presence of a lightening bolt is threatening, so are one's comfort zones and preconceptions about reality tested by the unpredictable, and sex can definitely play a role in this.

🜨 SEXUAL PLAY:
As The Tower falls, people may drop from respect or lose their emotional balance. False promises or lies intended to provoke favors of intimacy may become apparent. Someone can romantically talk the language of tantra to impress another, but have no wisdom or understanding behind his or her words. In this case, there is no sexual liberation, but only the toil of lessons to be learned so one can become more aware of how to distin-

guish light from darkness, reality from falsehood. The crashing of circumstance associated with this card can ultimately bring spiritual illumination and awakening of heartfelt truth—or, depending on your attitude, continued blundering about in darkness.

If The Tower points to coping with some kind of difficult or painful transition, making love can play a healing role. As talk turns to touch and excitement rises, lovers prepare for worship in the temple of delight. When she lies on her back and signals that she's ready, he kneels before her temple. She presses her feet up against his chest so that she can move her feet upward or downward on his chest to adjust her body to find the most delicious angle of penetration. If he tries to come in too deeply for her comfort, her feet can push against his chest to signal him to move more lightly. Also in this posture, his moistened fingertips may play with her magic button to increase her excitement while they are entwined.

❦ Reversed Card Interpretation:

The situation around you may be changing radically, more than you're comfortable with, making you want to cling to the old and familiar. Perhaps you've been surprised by startlingly turbulent and unexpected feelings deep inside you, so you resist making changes that are called for by the present state of affairs. Trying to hold on to the past under such circumstances brings only difficulty or useless self-pity. The not-so-easy answer is that you may have to adapt to your new circumstances, whether these are dangers, losses, limitations, opportunities, blessings, or some combination thereof. Try not to worry, because in our dualistic world, emotional storms are often followed by sunny days and balmy seas.

A challenging path may beckon. It may be an outer path or an inner one, but in either case, you'll have to find ways to walk along it. Several alternative paths may require you to make choices. Begin your moves with your actions, thoughts, or feelings—whichever is most feasible—and other sides of you will follow. If your choice is not to change anything, chances are that you'll stay stuck in the rubble of that which has fallen!

16. THE TOWER

- 111 -

THE STAR .

Key Meanings: Clarity, optimism, a willingness to act to realize your hopes and dreams, improvements, nearing fulfillment

Loving Qualities: Friendly and understanding

Loveless Qualities: Rebellious, spiteful

Astrological Connection: Aquarius, sign of the water bearer, who pours heartfelt emotions into the cauldron of love, earning, through valor, a way into your heart

Most Compatible Card Partners: The Fool, The World, The Lovers, Justice

17. THE STAR

17. THE STAR

❧ ROMANTIC INTERPRETATION:

Looking deeply into the pools of subconscious memory and awareness helps you find answers to love's riddles. Your inner perceptions of emotions and your insights into the character of others are probably clearer than usual at this time. You are less likely to be deceived by other's pretenses and appearances that try to disguise or hide underlying realities.

If you're in a relationship, you might experience a deeper level of communication, intuitive connection, or feeling of fellowship. If single, your ability to love may expand while you're learning to enjoy your freedom and independence. Your feelings of confidence and self-esteem grow stronger as your awareness of your inner spirit increases. Harmonious feelings expand as you do things you like to do as well as things you have to do. Paying explicit attention to your dreams, daydreams, sensations, and feelings in the moment can help you learn to focus on the present, open your heart, and improve romantic potentials.

❧ EMOTIONAL INTERPRETATION:

Stargazing or wishful thinking can inspire sentiments, but emotions need to be down-to-earth to create a balanced outlook on love. Don't waste time trying to count every star in the sky or analyze every aspect of your emotions. This is a good time to explicitly appreciate your strengths and your ability to intuit your path to happiness. Give yourself the gift of increased self-confidence. Whether or not your heart is bonded to another, give up focusing your thoughts on your fears and instead focus them on endeavors that are meaningful to you.

Your zest for life, expressed in ways that respect others' needs and individuality, can bring new friendships and emotional experiences. Just as a boat captain can use the stars to navigate the seas, use your inner powers to improve your situation and find your path to happiness. Keep your faith in yourself and your dreams.

❧ SEXUAL INTERPRETATION:

The Star is connected to the Sun sign Aquarius, which is ruled by both Saturn, symbol for the teacher, karma, self-discipline, and responsibilities; and Uranus, whose influence brings unexpected changes, revolution, and the desire for freedom.

In the bedroom, this combination can be challenging. Saturn's energy says yes to conformity and tradition, and Uranus rebels against them. While one voice inside you may say, "Go for it," another may say, "Wait!" Your truth must rest on a foundation of love for both yourself and others if your connection is to be nourishing, for loveless sexual encounters often turn harsh or poisonous.

Sometimes a sexual identity crisis can occur, but you will find illumination if you're patient and listen quietly to your inner voice. To reduce confusion, gain inner clarity, and have greater access to ecstasy, follow the light of the star, or the healing power of love within yourself.

✣ Sexual Play:

Touching sensitive spots and exchanging kisses generously—at unexpected as well as expected places on the body—inspires partners to move deep into love's trance. When partners have caressed each other to a point of great excitement, the man sits up in a cross-legged position with his manly power exposed. Facing him, the woman sits in his lap, wraps her legs around his waist, and locks her feet together behind him. They sit motionless for a few moments, synchronizing their breathing, until both are inhaling and exhaling at an equal rhythm. Then she opens her gates of paradise and slips his penetrating staff inside her secret retreat. They sit motionless again, tightening and relaxing their instruments of joy. In this position that classically expresses the yoga of love, they then begin to move harmoniously together as if they were two stars merging in an infinite sky. They move back and forth or in a circle, softly, strongly, or sometimes pausing altogether when the passionate fires of liquid delight push them to the brink of orgasm. It is possible for a couple to remain joined in this position for a very long time before exploding into the flames of final ecstasy.

✣ Reversed Card Interpretation:

When the Star card is upside down, you may find yourself stumbling around in the dark, without starlight or optimism to guide you. Stuck in darkness or confusion, you may despair, failing to see the light of hope that can guide you.

Or the meaning can be just the opposite, that you may be overly optimistic, too hopeful, or naively trusting, so that you need to be careful that someone doesn't take advantage of you. Rely on your awareness, intuition, and wits to tell you when trust is appropriate and when caution is the order of the day. Follow your inner insights and tune in to what's going on around you. Whatever this reversed card may mean to you, the best antidote is, "Don't worry, be happy!"

18. THE MOON

THE MOON.

§ ROMANTIC INTERPRETATION:

The Moon points to forces and inclinations that dwell in the depths of your psyche, perhaps unrecognized by your everyday mind. Subconscious impulses may move within you, causing you to question your romantic path.

Even if you're unsure of your direction in love, trust your intuition to offer guidance concerning the best path for you now. Deep inward searching can bring your unconscious memories, thoughts, and yearnings to the surface. Be wary about what others want you to do, because no one else knows your inner world as you do. Wait until you're centered in inner calmness before discussing important decisions with your partner or lover.

Life is usually easier when you trust yourself in the moment, even when changes are occurring. By adapting to circumstances and flowing with the forceful movements of emotional currents, you may find your situation changing in ways that differ from your old ideas and expectations. Just as the Moon is constantly evolving through its four phases—new, first quarter, full, and third quarter Moon, you may find yourself moving through waves of changing awareness. These changes can deepen your self-knowledge, expand your self-perception, sharpen your sensitivity of what others are feeling, and enlarge your comprehension of your external situation. Home is a good place to become secure in your emotional well-being and centered on your path.

§ EMOTIONAL INTERPRETATION:

Be willing to look into old memories and feelings that hold the key to understanding present emotions. Releasing old fears is part of the process of restoring balance and inner harmony. This opens you to receiving positive, creative, healing energies that bring the warmth and light of the sun to illuminate the depths of the soul and ease anxieties about the future. Maternal instincts or motherly love and affection, past or present, may affect your moods and emotions.

In addition to old pains and fears, your subconscious also contains positive attributes and potential that you may not be consciously expressing in your life. Carl Jung maintained that drawing on your unknown self, which he called the "shadow,"

Key Meanings: Intuition, dreams; diving into the depths of the subconscious; strong emotions, feminine attributes

Loving Qualities: Compassion, sensitivity, and imagination

Loveless Qualities: Helplessness and melancholy

Astrological Connection: Pisces the fish, who perpetually swims in the river of love, moving intuitively through up-and-down currents of emotion

Most Compatible Card Partners: Wheel of Fortune, The Hanged Man, The Chariot, Death

- 115 -

to find and express your less developed aspects is the central key to growth. This is especially true of your emotional life. Ask yourself, "What emotional qualities and moods are usual for me?" Then, "What are their opposites, which I allow little expression in my life? Am I ignoring important and valuable qualities that could enhance my existence?" These sides of yourself might point the way to enjoying relationships with people who are different from most of your past partners, or to opening new emotional dimensions with your present partner.

☿ SEXUAL INTERPRETATION:

Lovers meet behind closed doors, replace words with touch, and explore mysteries of sexual love. The forbidden fruit of a clandestine affair may be sweet, but complicate passion's delight.

Dreaminess, sensitivity, and warmth, all powerful attributes of Pisces, which corresponds astrologically to The Moon card, indicate the potential for a deep and caring intimate experience. Moon energy's gravitational effect on the Earth and the tides influences your ability to swim through heavy currents in the ocean of emotional desire. If you're not afraid to submerge yourself, you can dive into whatever experience is stimulating your interest. Being sensitive to the preferences of your partner can keep experiences flowing in a turned-on direction. Something beneficial may be stirred up in the cauldron of love.

☿ SEXUAL PLAY:

Lunar energy, linked with the feminine nature, focuses on womanly delights, the bosom, the yoni or vulva, and smiling satisfaction. Depth of imagination enriches foreplay, and dreamlike, erotic visions expand boundaries into the realm of desire where all possible sexual positions and movements may be encountered. Honoring the feminine is the primary rite connected with The Moon card, and touching the soul of your living goddess is consummation's priority.

Lovemaking may begin subtly and quietly like the night and stillness of the Moon against which may be heard the hooting of an owl, or a coyote calling in the distance. Lovers begin by covering each other with kisses. Piece by piece, clothes fall away, all but the scanty garment that covers the secret chambers that remain veiled to venerate temptation's mystery.

Through and around the cloth, the breath and tongue play delicately yet mischievously to arouse the keepers of the inner gate and beseech them to open without undue delay. The crescendo of excitement like a wave ready to crash upon the

shore inspires lovers to unite. As she lies on her back, her partner kneels before her and lifts her legs straight up like two tow-
ers and supports them on his shoulders. Caressing her legs with
his arms and chest, he gladly takes the meandering path to reach
the summit where ecstasy awaits.

ℰ Reversed Card Interpretation:

When The Moon is reversed, it can indicate a time when emotions are out of balance or emotional craziness is experienced
to some degree. You may become frustrated by a lack of communication with yourself by not listening to your intuition,
your deeper emotional realities, or your power for converting
your dreams to reality.

It is also linked to emotional troubles in relationships, most
especially with women or with the feminine attributes of a
man, which result from not being sensitive to the emotional
currents of the other person's being. Misunderstandings or difficulties in your relations with your mother can become overwhelming.

This reversed card can also reflect getting lost in your imagination by dreaming about a new relationship, a good relationship, great sex, or some accomplishment, success, victory, as a
substitute for the effort required to make the real thing happen.

Your sleep may be disturbed by scary dreams, which are
often messages you're receiving from your subconscious that
something may be amiss, in your psyche, your actions, or the
world around you. Dream interpretation may prove insightful.

THE SUN .

Key Meanings: Creative thought illuminates conscious awareness with sunny vibrations and happiness, awakening success

Loving Qualities: Warmhearted, playful, and positive

Loveless Qualities: Self-centered, domineering

Astrological Connection: The Sun is associated with masculine energy and the power linked with the Greek god Apollo, solar sage of music, medicine, prophecy, and creativity

Most Compatible Card Partners: The Emperor, Strength, and Temperance

19. THE SUN

❧ ROMANTIC INTERPRETATION:

Your own sunny nature shines! Positive ideas inspire your hopes. Inner strength awakens, giving you the energy to move beyond your fears and create a strategy for finding or deepening love. Look inward and outward to see how your attitudes are affecting your life and relationships. Are there corners of your being where you can let in more sunny, positive energy? What specific steps can you take to brighten your day and let more warmth and light into your life? Others are attracted to sun energy, and if you cultivate it in yourself, they'll be attracted to you.

The Sun is favorable for romance and creative self-expression. It can illuminate opportunities, but it's up to you to notice and take advantage of them. If you already have a partner, your journey together may take a lighter and brighter turn, or you may decide to bring a child into the world or create some other tangible miracle together. Because this card symbolizes fiery radiance and strength of mind, its presence in your spread is a sign that you have the qualities to accomplish your goals.

❧ EMOTIONAL INTERPRETATION:

Since The Sun card is associated with positive, happy vibrations, it indicates that sunny, warmhearted energy will keep the moody blahs away. Airing emotions through direct communication helps you understand the ground rules for building the romantic foundation for your future. Being flexible in matters concerning power, will, and desire helps you listen to the needs of your friends, lovers, or partners without getting entangled in power struggles. When you can identify such struggles in a lighthearted way that playfully invites stepping out of them, it reduces the odds that you'll get caught in them.

Just as a cat has nine lives, you'll survive your pain from past loss and difficult emotional stages as your life unfolds in pleasant ways. It is said that no heart goes unscarred, but the sun will always shine again to illuminate prospects for tomorrow. Restless, fiery affairs of the heart need to be tempered by common sense and an appreciation of practical realities. As mature children leave home, a relationship between partners may undergo transformation.

❦ SEXUAL INTERPRETATION:

Expansive, healing Sun energy opens your being to fun, pleasure, and touch! Stop looking at roadblocks to love and create visions of finding satisfaction and happiness. Dust off your self-confidence, because you may have to initiate. More acceptance of your body's perfection (even if you don't possess a model's figure) allows you to be comfortable with your sexuality. Fashioning a sexier you inspires the willingness to go out on the prowl. Be willing to arouse your inner temptress (or tempter), for your steamy self can attract the love that you desire. If you enjoy playing the flirt, your playfulness will help you get a VIP's share of lustful attention.

Affairs of the heart may make the lion roar, and also include tender moments in which you cuddle up like a kitty-cat to receive affection and a warm embrace. Matters in the bedroom will work out for the best in due time. If you do not find the sizzling temptations and intimacy you desire right now, find something wonderful to enjoy until that special time arrives.

❦ SEXUAL PLAY:

The darling of your heart's delight touches your soul and awakens the life force within. One lover begins by giving the other a "full body massage," which means using his or her full body, no part excluded, as the massage instrument rather than just the hands. Forearms, chest, head, legs—use any part of yourself you wish to stroke your partner. This is especially sensuous when you can cover each other's bodies with massage oil as you lie on a covered mattress. The partner receiving the massage lies on it, and the partner giving the massage whose body is covered with oil, slip-slide massages his or her lover's entire body. When a full-body massage is done on a bed, sans a coating of massage oil, the contact should be very light and gentle.

To culminate the massage, the male kneels astride his lover's legs, his weight on his knees and arms, titillating the moistened love button with fingertips. Then slowly, with awareness of her body's readiness, he descends into her golden gateway. At first he barely enters her, the end of his magic wand touching just the outer portals. While still inside he may lower his pelvis to rub or stroke hers with an upward motion, softly stimulating her with his pelvic bone. Gradually he lowers himself deeper into her sacred cavern as she tightens herself around him like a contracting sea anemone. Excited passion, tempered with slow movements, extends pleasure's boundaries as long as lovemaking can be sustained.

§ REVERSED CARD INTERPRETATION:

When The Sun card is reversed, it can be compared to the sun's warmth hidden behind clouds. For the time being, there is no sunshine, and the sun's rays of life-giving energy are concealed. Everything can seem dark and gloomy, impeding happiness.

This reversed card can also point to the compulsion to be powerful at others' expense, such as the narcissistic desire for more power or wealth, or for being the center of attention, with little thought for those who get left out. The tricky part is that people tend to be blind to their own selfishness (whatever form it takes), thinking that they really do deserve more of everything than others (often because of some underlying insecurity). But narcissism must be addressed and subdued, or it will be an ongoing source of dissatisfaction, regardless of favorable external circumstances.

The reversed Sun card makes a statement: reclaim your emotional strength, stop pouting or fretting, keep your egotism in check, and look for joy in each moment in whatever form it may appear. Get busy, because you have some work to do in order to meet your desires.

19. THE SUN

20. JUDGEMENT

JUDGEMENT.

❧ ROMANTIC INTERPRETATION:

Judgement refers to reaping the harvest of your karma—experiencing the consequences of your actions and choices. Your answers will come as romantic potentials are tested by the verdict of passing time. You or the other person may challenge the nature of your commitment, feel indecisive about continuing a relationship, or undergo transitions in love. Be willing to brave the fires of passion and the poignant pangs of disappointment to find the truth of your heart or the other person's. It's usually better to be clear about the nature and prospects of a relationship than to hang on to the hope that it will become something that it's not. If you're single, beware of expectations or demands you place on yourself involving love. No one promised that romance would always be easy, except in fairy tales, and even there the outcomes are sometimes a surprise.

Changes may appear on the horizon, and the more you're willing to respond creatively to events and circumstances that unfold, the easier your path will be. If you map out a plan for creating more happiness in your life that's based truly on who you know yourself to be and open to new discoveries about yourself and others, you'll feel more grounded when you travel through unfamiliar territory. Dust off your enthusiasm for adventure, and don't let frustrations get in your way of exploring new or different approaches to the relating and dating game.

❧ EMOTIONAL INTERPRETATION:

Dry your tears and protect your vulnerable emotions. The winds of change are blowing and it's time to let go of your fears and find the will to create success. Positive influences surround you, ready to help guide you on your path if you watch and listen to their messages. Something out of the ordinary may occur, accelerating your personal growth. If you fertilize these special moments with nourishing thoughts, you'll grow stronger. If you focus on the negative, life will prove more difficult.

When a conflict occurs and someone runs to you with their story, beware of making a snap judgment. Listen to everyone involved before you form a conclusion.

When you meet inevitable and unavoidable circumstances that signal change, walk gently toward your future with faith in your ability to make something positive out of whatever pres-

Key Meanings: Outcomes, evolution, the phoenix rising from the ashes, rebirth, and giving or receiving judgment

Loving Qualities: Depth of perception; truth-seeking

Loveless Qualities: Overly serious, unrelenting, self-righteous

Astrological Connection: Pluto, the most distant planet from the Sun, symbolically aligned with Hades, guardian of the underworld and god of stolen love, and the element fire, linked to strong desires

Most Compatible Card Partner: Death

ents itself. It takes courage to make the best out of unexpected events that might contradict your expectations and change your plans for tomorrow.

§ SEXUAL INTERPRETATION:

Temptress or tease, hot or not, love can evolve to a greater awareness of the truth of intentions. Whatever your romantic situation, Judgement marks a time of excited passion, so chances are good that your sex life will be turned on. Because Pluto, the planet associated with this card, corresponds to death of the familiar, you may confront unexpected or unusual romantic notions. Passion runs the gamut when you decide love's for real (and sometimes even when you're just playing make-believe.) A deeper connection or fond closeness bonds lovers' hearts and yields to permissiveness in the bedroom. Even if sexual juices have long been flowing in an ongoing relationship, don't be surprised if you meet some unknown aspect of your sweetheart's libido. If you're wondering whether a new friendship will take an erotic turn, you'll soon find out.

§ SEXUAL PLAY:

Begin with "couples yoga." You may wish to have some kind of quiet music playing—an Indian raga, or a New Age piece. Move into identical hatha yoga postures (such as the Sun Salutation) or dance positions. If you use the latter, mentally let go, and slow down aerobic or other fast dance movements to a yogic pace, letting every instance of touching your partner be soft and loving. Or, simply feel your body from the inside, and allow yourselves to stretch in whatever ways your bodies want to move.

With your emotions moderately cool—anticipating but not yet aflame, take at least 15 minutes to do yoga postures together, coordinating your breathing and your movements. Improvise positions in which you touch or stroke each other. You might sit with both feet touching and both hands touching, sensitively pulling each other back and forth in yogic stretches. Or you might stand side by side as you do a posture, and reach out to touch palms or fingertips.

As your excitement rises, invent a new posture that allows you to make more erotic contact with your lover as you stretch and move. Let that process evolve, at a leisurely and measured pace, until you are drawn together irresistibly in tantric union. Sensitive and unhurried, the offerings of love begin as lovers absorbed in the ecstasy of the moment find their way along the path of paradise.

⚄ REVERSED CARD INTERPRETATION:

Judgement reversed may refer to unwanted changes or unpredictable losses (which may be directly or indirectly related to your past actions). It can indicate being frustrated or having trouble coping with life's events. You may feel emotionally abandoned, hold on to fears or to others' criticism, or may be too judgmental of yourself or others. Constantly judging or criticizing yourself can lead to chronic low self-esteem—"I'm never quite good enough." This involves the introjection—taking into yourself—of others' judgmental evaluations of you as if they were your own, and can cause a loss of your identity and sense of yourself.

Your critical judgments of others may prove less then helpful. Judgment is a major barrier to good communication, since someone you judge can't feel fully accepted or welcomed in your company, and is likely to be either overtly or covertly irritated, resentful, or angry. Being judgmental is a strong habit that you can only conquer by cultivating moment-by-moment awareness of what you're doing, and letting go of your judgments when you see that you're forming them.

The reversed Judgement card could also mean that you're caught by a desire to inflict some kind of punishment or retribution on others. Even if you succeed in gaining temporary satisfaction from some vengeful action, it may make it harder for you to find lasting happiness. Spiritual teachers assert that forgiveness is a powerful cure for healing the body, heart, and soul.

20. JUDGEMENT

- 123 -

THE WORLD.

Key Meanings: Fulfillment of desire or completion of a cycle; new possibilities open; discovering passion's secrets; worldliness

Loving Qualities: Forgiving, selfless, kindhearted

Loveless Qualities: Unforgiving, stubborn

Astrological Connections: The planet Saturn—associated with a Roman god who fertilized the fields—karma, lessons, and our values which connect us with the truth of our inner self

Most Compatible Card Partner: The Devil

21. THE WORLD

21. THE WORLD

§ ROMANTIC INTERPRETATION:

The World indicates your potential to broaden your ability to love and undergo personal transformation inspired by intimacy. It also signifies a time to face emotional difficulties with resolve, and overcome them. Focus on what you want now, and structure your priorities so you can start doing what you need to do to find fulfillment. Analyze your values to see if they can help you make better choices about the direction you want to go in your romantic life. Then question your values to see if there's any way you can transform or integrate them to help you move past old limits or self-concepts that no longer fit who you've become.

Don't be surprised if your personal directions and boundaries are tested by a society that seeks to impose its priorities on you. Being true to finding your own way strengthens your power to free your soul from stagnation. You don't have to make someone else think that what's right for you is right for them, too. It may not be. As you find your wings, you may confront old feelings of insecurity and dependency, so be willing to let go of fears or self-criticism. The world holds many opportunities that will help you learn how to meet the challenges of the moment with an open heart and zest for life.

§ EMOTIONAL INTERPRETATION:

Letting go of attachments to painful memories helps you attune to your own spiritual and/or creative nature. When your heart is open, you live more in touch with your passions (and that sometimes includes your antipathies), and you become more at home with a variety of people and situations, and more insistent on your freedom to be yourself, yet respectful of others' rights and needs. If a lover restricts your freedom or acts as an authority figure toward you, you'll feel the restraints and may have to confront soul-felt issues.

Greater personal awareness may evoke a desire to meet your mate or creative counterpart, if you haven't yet done so. If you're in a relationship and it's running into snags, you'll be actively seeking solutions. Summoning up the courage to communicate your deep thoughts and feelings gives you a chance to work through problems and emerge both stronger and wiser. Naked emotions allow your confidence to grow, and new possibilities for success to open. The truly worldly person has a keen sense of when to reach out, when to hold on, when to withdraw, and when to let go.

§ SEXUAL INTERPRETATION:

Indulge with awareness. Safe sex is necessary in today's crazy world. Saturn, the planet linked with The World, points to time, order, restrictions, karma, lessons and higher authority, indicating that you may need to take precautions in your lovemaking. Structure in the bedroom may not be what you prefer, but listening to the wisdom of health's conventions can help your experiences be rich and rewarding instead of leading to troubles you definitely don't want. How exciting your relationship becomes depends on the magic of your connection, not the brand of condoms you choose. Dancing with passion keeps sexual spontaneity alive even when you practice health-conscious awareness. Because this is the last major arcana card, it signifies your experiences coming to a climax or fulfillment of some kind, perhaps moving you toward a new dimension of the meaning of tantric love, or a deepening of closeness in sexual communion.

§ SEXUAL PLAY:

Begin by sitting face-to-face across from your partner for a candlelight libation, whether at a table or cross-legged on the floor or bed, and whether of wine, juice, or any other drink that pleases you. Look into each others' eyes and recognize yourselves as sparks of the divine. As you worship the flame of passion residing in your partner's temple, choose your form of sexual play from any other card or any other source that pleases you. In The World, all other cards meet and mingle. Or if you like, as you play together, use a finger to outline your partner's soft secret curves as if you were drawing on an embodied canvas. Slowly and playfully, lick the line you have drawn on your partner's body, arousing and prolonging your sojourn in passion's realm. Then, the woman might kneel, astride her partner, and then bend forward to cover his upper body with her own and bring pleasure to his chest and face with long, massage-like strokes of her breasts. Renewal of emotions, contemplation on love, and heated forces of nature come together in passion's entangled embrace. As you feel the rhythm of your partner's movements, surrender to passion's enticing vibration. Joy mixes with prayer to honor the Great Spirit of love as unfathomable depths of sacred sexuality are timelessly explored.

21. THE WORLD

- 125 -

❧ REVERSED CARD INTERPRETATION:

The World card reversed often refers to something unfinished that's hanging over your head, such as an incomplete project that you need either to finish or explicitly let go. It can also indicate desire without fulfillment. This may be due to a lack of focus, suggesting that you need to be more specific in conceiving what you want and how you need to go about getting it.

It can mean resistance to expansion beyond your current boundaries and endeavors. Possibilities for adventure beckon, but circumstances may keep you close to home. You may be closing your eyes to wonderful opportunities or possibilities, in either your relationship, possible relationships, or your search for love. The opportunity may be something you've overlooked that's right before your eyes, or it may mean taking an intelligent risk and venturing beyond your accustomed limits. Look and listen and you may discover new worlds beckoning.

21. THE WORLD

CHAPTER 7

THE MINOR ARCANA: FOUR REALMS OF BEING

Nothing is mundane and no act can be relegated to the purely material. In fact, there can be no division between sacred and secular, because everything is sacred. . . . Everything is permeated and saturated with the divine Spirit.
—VANMALI, *NITYA YOGA*

Fire, water, air, and earth dance through the reflecting, symbolic mirror of the minor arcana cards to enliven the swaying rhythm of life's romantic twists and turns. A spectrum of life's struggles, opportunities, and qualities is portrayed in the minor, or lesser trumps. The wands, cups, swords, and pentacles that comprise the minor arcana are props setting the stage to answer questions about romantic mysteries and emotional concerns.

As you decode the symbols in each card, you're learning to unveil secrets concealed in this ancient oracle. Their wisdom is revealed to those who seek it and their light can guide the loved or lovelorn toward emotional comprehension and clarity. These cards can be used to inspire self-discovery and improve chances to win the game of love.

Now we step, in turn, into the worlds of wands, cups, swords, and pentacles, to get acquainted with each card in each suit.

Wands: Walking on the Wild Side

*Fire is the element which carries the senses into sensuousness,
the mind into flights of imagination and vision, the emotions
into a passion for living life in all its many dimensions.*
—MARINA MEDICI, *LOVE MAGIC*

Varied expressions of the gift of fiery energy appear in the suit of
wands. Disruptions and blockages of this gift, and indications of
how it can go astray—twisting our relationships and interfering
with the fulfillment of our potential—are also depicted in this suit.
These remind us to be alert to the limits beyond which our self-
expression can transgress the needs, feelings, and interests of others. Now we look at how this gift of active energy, excitement, and
passion appears in each of the cards.

ACE OF WANDS

ℬ Romantic Interpretation:

This first card in the suit of wands represents the igniting power of the element fire and the potential to illuminate the depths of the mind and imagination. Seeds of affection sprout enriching emotional experiences and hopes for new avenues of success. Lighting-up your mind, your emotions, and your creative self-expression can lead to rewarding friendships appearing on the horizon. You will be offered something of value, either tangible or intangible, that strengthens your sense of direction or increases your ability to move toward getting what you want. With fiery forces coming into play, it's important to realize that you have somthing valuable to offer others. Focus your thoughts and emotions on success, especially if you're experiencing romantic uncertainty.

ℬ Emotional Interpretation:

The warmth of love brings happiness, playfulness, romantic celebration, or even an engagement. Meeting people or a special someone, making new friends, or strenthening ties with old friends increases the richness of your social life. A night out on the town can brighten your outlook. Even though friends bring happiness and stimulate creativity, don't let others distort your decision-making process. Optimism and faith contribute to your inner growth and your discovery of outer possibilities for personal enhancement. The path to fulfillment of your dreams is more easily found when you balance emotional concerns with creative activities.

ℬ Sexual Interpretation:

A friendly glance can cause you to feel sexy and kindle the fires of desire. Playful teasing tantalizes soul-tingling interest. Notches on the bedpost may seem gratifying, but when the spirit as well as the body hungers for consummation, it is the nourishment of love that fills you with satisfaction. Heated experiences in the dating game arena may stimulate a surge in your sexual appetite as a sensual body, a smiling face, and welcoming arms offer alluring temptation. Your sex life is likely to get more interesting when you fan the flames of passion with positive efforts.

ACE of WANDS.

Key Meanings: Passionate beginnings; seeds of renewal; meeting new friends; relationship issues evolve; creative insights; productive inquiry

Reversed Meanings: Emotional freak-out; inhibitions, stagnation; being turned-off instead of turned-on; unfulfilled expectation; anxiety, disappointment

ACE OF WANDS

- 129 -

❧ REVERSED CARD INTERPRETATION:

The Ace of Wands reversed can point to all kinds of events becoming more intense. Overreaction to circumstances, or overheated conversations may cause agitation or anger. Frustration, stagnation, lack of trust, or inhibitions may need to be overcome. Spending your time worrying about love's direction can be a self-fulfilling prophecy that interferes with your awareness of opportunities when they arise. Be present with your experience instead of worrying, and trust that a heart-expanding breakthrough will come when the time is right.

ACE OF WANDS

TWO OF WANDS

❦ ROMANTIC INTERPRETATION:

This two symbolizes the action/reaction of opposites in the elemental domain of fire. The other side of love is hate; death stands next to life; spirit is linked to matter. Finding the center between fear and faith and transcending the ambiguities of uncertain emotions allows you to live joyfully, even if you feel lost in indecision or the need to choose between two paths. Ignite the fire of your inner romantic and explore creative ways to unleash your emotional attractiveness. Being alive to the freshness of the moment allows you to live spontaneously. Spoken words, body language, and your intuition can all be channels of communication. Look for recreational pursuits or projects that can open opportunities for love and play.

❦ EMOTIONAL INTERPRETATION:

If you're involved with someone, time and experience leads to greater clarity about the lifestyle and emotional makeup of the person you are with. Don't allow confusion or indecisiveness to dominate your attention. Questions involving the direction of your love life may soon be answered. Concentrate on developing and appreciating your best qualities, for your confidence can help light the fire of love or rekindle passion. Become aware of moments when a despairing attitude limits you, for moving beyond such limits can open a brighter horizon. Ask someone out to dinner or over for brunch and get to know them better. Your strength of spirit can deepen a friendship or draw in a playmate.

❦ SEXUAL INTERPRETATION:

Passion joins forces with desire and intimate connections occur. New lovemaking methods excite sensual ecstasy, while sexual love invigorates the desire for deeper intimacy and emotional explorations. In the bedroom, quality is often better than quantity. Don't blame others for not meeting your needs; instead, speak your desires and your questions that you need to have answered. Take steps to be prepared for sexual love: Have a condom, take birth control pills, or even get an emergency contraception kit. With birth control or STD concerns taken care of, your passion can be fulfilled without worrying about unwanted consequence.

Key Meanings: Emotional exploration; early stages of dating; a quest for answers to love's riddles; excitement; seeking fulfillment of desires; ardent choices

Reversed Meanings: Feverish emotions, disrupted plans, surprise, decreased faith, distance from a loved one, ambivalence stirs confusion, faultfinding

TWO OF WANDS

- 131 -

❧ REVERSED CARD INTERPRETATION:

This card symbolizes not being able to make a choice, or not attaining a goal you had hoped to realize. This may mean that it's not the right time to make decisions about the direction in which your heart or your creative energy needs to go. Or, it can indicate criticism or fallout from an emotional alliance. If someone is critical of you, instead of succumbing to being hurt, you can turn the spotlight back onto the critic. Identify how that person is being judgmental, describe how that affects you, and ask for more considerate communication. Use the magic of the wands to find ways to turn apparent vulnerabilities into strengths.

TWO OF WANDS

THREE OF WANDS

❦ ROMANTIC INTERPRETATION:

A pioneering spirit combats stagnation. Testing personal limits and having the determination to go beyond the familiar uncovers new realities and sometimes even profound wisdom. Intense desire can bring home hot romance for the night. Pursuing love may lead to a greater openheartedness within yourself, and sometimes reciprocated love as well. Your quest for nurturing experiences can expand your awareness. Strength to talk about emotional needs lies within, while circumstances may suggest appropriate discretion. A commitment to changing self-defeating behavior leads you closer to experiencing the pleasure of your desires. An opportunity to travel may arise.

❦ EMOTIONAL INTERPRETATION:

Don't be a slave to the quest for emotional perfection. Free your mind from inhibitions, as well as from idealistic expectations that finding love or a soul mate should come easily. This card represents the strength to jump hurdles and the ability to enjoy the present. Share positive emotions, and take responsibility for making your current situation a rewarding one, for the choice of an adventurous or sour attitude usually lies in your own hands. There is much for you to appreciate now, if you realize it. Your willingness to express yourself, even if you're a little shy in doing so, can enhance your ability to make good connections. Increased confidence may grow out of cooperative work or play. Helping others can bring joy and kindle the development of talents or specialized skills.

❦ SEXUAL INTERPRETATION:

There's isn't any boredom in the bedroom when your mind is turned-on. Connect with your inner fire, sizzling passion, and delicious effervescence. If you've made up your mind to seduce someone, buoyantly make the effort. If you're too shy to talk about what's on your mind, movements will speak for themselves. If the person you desire is guarded, give time and friendship a chance to evolve. Not everyone is comfortable with sexual advances, so sharing time getting to know someone and participating in activities that the other person enjoys may be the magic that unlocks the bedroom door. Charming and sensual is hot, but forget kinky stuff unless your lover is willing to turn on to your fantasy.

Key Meanings: Passionate desires; searching for emotional answers; adventure, expansiveness, flirtatiousness, integrity, cooperation, social networking

Reversed Meanings: Undeveloped talents; dependence, passivity, imitation, folly, instability, unrealistic idealism; leaving home; the end of a troubling situation

- 133 -

❧ REVERSED CARD INTERPRETATION:

Too many unfulfilling involvements or the frustrations of a triangular love affair cause distress. Since wasted romantic efforts give self-esteem a kick where it hurts, be attentive to cues that suggest yes or no before you transform hopes into expectations. On the other hand, a reversed three can also point toward ending a situation that has been causing you trouble.

THREE OF WANDS

FOUR OF WANDS

IV

❧ ROMANTIC INTERPRETATION:

Instead of worrying about romance, this card suggests that you be more aware of your creative potential, work on self-improvement by developing your talents and, when the time is right, romance will come. In regard to finding a partner, in an existing relationship, or, for that matter, in other areas of life, strengthen your sense of security by adopting a more optimistic outlook in relation to difficulties. Take small, doable steps now, and an understanding of how to take larger ones will follow. This card may also point to having trouble making up your mind, or to changing your mind about an important matter, especially if new information appears. It can point to a person or relationship that moves in one direction, then in an opposite direction, with great intensity in each case. You may find it helpful to give the analytical side of your mind a rest by listening to your feelings.

❧ EMOTIONAL INTERPRETATION:

At its best, the Four of Wands refers to domestic tranquility and a solid, nurturing relationship in which each person respects the other. When idealizing about romantic utopia and your highest emotional aspirations, however, stay in touch with the present and don't get lost in imagining that people or events are different than they are. Rigid expectations about how others are "supposed" to be may block your ability to enjoy them as they are. Build your way from small steps in emotional communication to larger ones, so that you have a firm footing and a sense of trust. Deepening mutual understanding with friends or your partner strengthens emotional bonds. Venturing beyond your usual haunts and broadening your circle of friends and acquaintances can enrich your social life or expand opportunities for romance. Be willing to take the lead in initiating friendships or suggesting activities.

❧ SEXUAL INTERPRETATION:

Make room for fun and excitement in your sex life. Stepping outside of your comfort zone by doing something different, such as placing an ad in a singles publication with a privacy code, may get you a playmate. However, before you explore unknown romantic territory, screen current prospects to make sure you won't be taking the wrong direction. Adult toys or

Key Meanings: Productivity; laying a foundation for success; getting to know yourself or your partner on deeper levels; strengthening self-esteem

Reversed Meanings: A bad temper; trouble in paradise; promiscuity affects intimacy; suppressed emotions; fear of commitment; compulsive behavior.

FOUR OF WANDS

- 135 -

erotic clothing can be funny or fun. Trying different positions or techniques to satisfy your lover, with verbal or nonverbal communication about what he or she does and doesn't like, can increase erotic enjoyment. Look for opportunities to know your sexual self better, such as by opening yourself to learn from your lover, and put on hold any tendency toward overanalysis.

❧ Reversed Card Interpretation:

Suppressed or neglected emotions can create an imbalance or visible hostility. Promiscuity during a relationship may be discovered. Disappointment due to a breach of faith, or lack of verbal commitment, can be overcome by taking refuge in creative or recreational interests. The direction of love evolves apart from demands and expectations.

FIVE OF WANDS

§ ROMANTIC INTERPRETATION:

Emotional qualities are heated in a single person or a relationship. Romantic situations can degenerate if you're not sensitive to another's feelings. If stress or anger is driving your communications, it may be better to be quiet than to speak your mind, unless you feel it's absolutely necessary. Saying critical or angry words when the atmosphere is already tense, anxious, or hostile may get you in deep water, unless you're unusually skilled in being tactful and considerate. It may be better to breathe, relax tight muscles, mellow out for now, and wait for a better moment to bring up what's bothering you. You can also learn to frame your comments in a way that accentuates what's positive in your interaction rather than what's negative.

Nonetheless, unless it's something that you can truly let go, you'll need to find a good time to voice your complaint so that it doesn't become part of a buildup of unspoken resentments. If love is true, it can withstand the heat of disagreement or upset feelings, and emotional maturity grows from dealing with love's issues. Actions speak louder than words. Doing something as simple as completing domestic chores that make your partner feel angry when they're left undone can lead to happy feelings.

§ EMOTIONAL INTERPRETATION:

Surrendering to the demands of the moment allows you to be alive in the present rather than being the slave of constant worry about the past or the future. However, if career demands interfere with time for love or sorting out emotions, find occasions to get away and clear your mind. Hidden dragons may pop unexpectedly out of deep recesses of the mind, and their fire may ignite a person's feelings or the emotional climate of a relationship. Adopting an attitude of unconditional acceptance of the other person, regardless of their mood or yours, keeps feelings in balance. Cultivating your patience and centeredness can help you stay grounded and defuse disputes before they escalate. When you get upset, seek the perspectives of cooler heads. Don't sweat the small stuff.

§ SEXUAL INTERPRETATION:

Five wands equal fiery libido impulses accompanied by the question of how to keep the fire contained so that it doesn't burn out of control. Passionate fires may be turned-on, but also

Key Meanings:
Communications intensify; stress creates a need to take a breather; systematic teamwork furthers respect; affection and accomplishment

Reversed Meanings:
Competition for love; confronting negativity; frustrated desire; sexual blocks; drowning in wishful thinking; gossip; mood swings.

- 137 -

FIVE OF WANDS

may be agitated by doubt, frustration, or anxiety. Anger may arise over major or minor disagreements, triggering quarreling or defenses that block intimate communication. An emotional power struggle may interfere with sexual desire and cause a partner to turn from hot to cold. The opposite, however, can also be true: A lover's quarrel doesn't have to end on a sour note, since sex is sometimes especially passionate after an argument. For a tantalizing twist, the person who's always "on top" may take a turn being on the bottom, or the more controlling person can surrender and ask their lover to take control. This switch can be informative and useful for both partners in regard to other aspects of life as well. Respect for the other's needs and feelings can enrich sensual pleasures.

ℰ Reversed Card Interpretation:

A competitive attitude toward another may turn a friendship sour or even destroy it. Trying to have the last word can leave the other either resentful or angry. You may need to confront negativity or mood swings in another person or in yourself. Remember that in time, negative situations pass. If you look for opportunities to learn from conflict, you can be a winner. You may need to find some kind of centering activity that reduces your level of emotional stress.

FIVE OF WANDS

SIX OF WANDS

⚝ ROMANTIC INTERPRETATION:

At one extreme, love can be self-centered, based wholly on feelings of "I want" and "I need," and at the other extreme it can be a conscious love that is as attentive to the other person's needs and wants as to your own. This card points to evolution in the latter direction. Romance evolves with greater understanding and consideration. If you're ambivalent or impatient about some aspect of your love life, and pressure is on for you to make up your mind, don't be persuaded to hurry up your process. Instead of getting lost in an emotional whirlpool, use meditation to find your center and help balance complex realities. Wait until you know what you want before you voice your decision. An important message may arrive, one that helps you make up your mind. If another person's inclinations don't fit your own, compromising, or alternating between your preferred activities, may be a solution.

⚝ EMOTIONAL INTERPRETATION:

More kisses are on the horizon! If you're single, release or relax your concerns about love by appreciating what's good in the your life now, and focusing on goals you can attain on your own. Celebrate who you are, even if you don't know what you want, or whom you want to be dating. Pay attention to your own preferences, and not parents', friends', or coworkers' expectations or "shoulds" about your romantic partners. Set positive emotions into motion by planning a party or other social event, or asking a friend or coworker to go on a date. (A lunch date is sometimes an easier or more appropriate first move than a candlelight dinner.) At times an "excuse" is a good connecting point, such as having been given tickets to the theater. (I have an extra ticket. Would you like to come too?) Don't forget that dates can liven up a long-term relationship. Appreciate the moment, for only when you get out of your head and meet life spontaneously do you fully touch the richness that it holds.

⚝ SEXUAL INTERPRETATION:

Six wands represent the stimulation of fiery passions. However, someone may try to coerce you into doing something that you'd rather not. (After a few glasses of wine, you might not notice.) Assert your will and say, "No, thanks," before anger or regret destroys your friendship. If you can't make a decision

Key Meanings: Attraction of opposites; approaching love the right way; intentions become apparent; victory; becoming more caring or compassionate.

Reversed Meanings: Facing unresolved issues; excessive dependency; possessiveness, jealousy; sexual concerns or ambivalence; not thinking things through.

about what you want, then perhaps it's best to honor your indecisiveness. Give yourself a little more time to see how your situation evolves and the obvious choice will become apparent. Likewise, if you're ready and the other person isn't, don't push too hard. If there is no indecisiveness, however, the card may represent hot and fiery lovemaking, so enjoy! Be gentle and sensitive. Experiment with different ways of touching and holding your partner during love making.

§ REVERSED CARD INTERPRETATION:

You or your partner may be disloyal or dishonest, or one of you may be afraid that the other will be even if it's not true, and may be tempted to make false accusations. This card is connected with hot emotions, so keep cool, check out the facts, and avoid premature or possibly unfounded doubts or anger. Acting "for love's sake" without being reasonable makes you appear foolish (even if someone is making a play for your mate).

SIX OF WANDS

SEVEN OF WANDS

❧ ROMANTIC INTERPRETATION:

Emotions mix feverishly with imagination. Your creative mind will enable you to win the various trials of love and life that the hand of fate presents to you. Your willingness to stand strong during difficult times and to face the unknown, both within yourself and in your relationship(s), is your ticket to your goals. Take the initiative and become active in resolving conflicts or finding pleasing solutions to dilemmas, while remembering that an open mind is necessary to tame opposition or transcend limiting dogma. When you express your sunny energy, it inspires others to open their hearts as well. New friends are made and dates are arranged. Write a poem or give flowers to someone you care about.

❧ EMOTIONAL INTERPRETATION:

Your emotions may be put to a test. Obstacles or difficulties are a chance to learn and grow. Be patient with your lover, roommate, parents, or children while you cool the fires of intensity and allow hot energy to diminish. Take time to be gentle and nurturing with those you love, and to smooth ruffled feathers with the healing spirit of love. Strengthen your personal magic with self-reliance, and give yourself more time to sort out your heart's truth and find the answers you seek. Life unfolds at its own pace, and tomorrow will bring greater clarity to your situation. From your experiences and what your body tells you, your heart's decisions become obvious. Don't be surprised if you find yourself becoming more deeply involved in an emotional alliance. Going to the theater or a musical performance with your lover or a valued friend is a great stress buster. Good luck in love may come your way.

❧ SEXUAL INTERPRETATION:

Inner fires are intensified as temptation tantalizes you. You might be asked to take part in some unusual sexual tryst that may or may not suit your emotional nature. Let the tension or relaxation in your body give you clues to what's right for you. When your mind and body listen to each other, you can stay centered and clarify your thoughts and feelings. Then you'll be prepared to move forward, stand your ground, or back away with certainty. If you're dreaming of having a better sex life, you

Key Meanings: Evoking fiery emotions; endurance; sexual attraction, tingling effects of hot communications; opportunity to date; becoming emotionally involved

Reversed Meanings: Learning about love the hard way; emotional confrontation; embarrassing moments; preoccupation with sex

might pick up the *Kama Sutra* or some other equally erotic guide to enhance lovemaking and get busy reading.

☘ REVERSED CARD INTERPRETATION:

Romantic fantasies may be draining away energy you could use for finding love. Disrespect for personal boundaries may provoke anger. Feeling trapped or stuck in negative emotions indicates the importance of change. If you're learning about love the hard way, take a breather and focus on the value of the lesson. Deal with uncertainty by being certain of the strength inside of you.

SEVEN OF WANDS

EIGHT OF WANDS

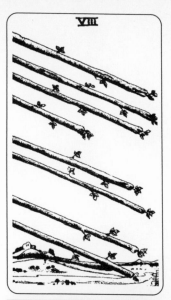

❧ ROMANTIC INTERPRETATION:

Eight wands represent the power of the element fire to inflame the mind and vitalize the will. When this force is awakened it ignites the strength, passion, and intensity that you must feel to be able to overcome obstacles, find success, and follow the path to joy, bliss, and love. Strong desire alters old concepts about limitations, making it possible to move beyond previous restrictions. It's time to use your best persuasive skills and promote your best interests. Assertive communication skills may come in handy if used with diplomacy. While rash or reckless action may lead to unwanted results, paying careful attention to all the elements of a situation opens opportunities for success. A wonderful man or woman may unexpectedly turn out to be a lover or best friend.

❧ EMOTIONAL INTERPRETATION:

Conflicting desires or inclinations can lead to frustration or anger. Wait for a favorable time to express your emotions and direct your energy with confidence. Whatever you put out toward others often either comes back to you in some way, has effects that go far beyond those you anticipated, or both. You may be facing an intense situation, a crossroad, or even a crisis. Such a crisis may be external, or existential—that is, one that involves a self-confrontation with some dimension of your way of being in the world. Balance intense emotions with practical logic that keeps perceptions in the here and now, for your worries may be worse than the reality you're facing. A short vacation or break from routine may provide the rest you need to energize your emotions. Nonconforming ideas may be rejected by family or loved ones, testing your commitment to live life your way. Creative outlets such as art or writing can energize your sense of well-being.

❧ SEXUAL INTERPRETATION:

Hot and spicy passions burn with intensity. Being bold in love-making can be favorable if you fan the flames of love in the right direction. Impatience won't help you get what you want, although flowers, incense, romantic music, and receptive communication might. The fire of sexual energy needs to be balanced with discrimination and sensitivity, or emotions may turn sour. Giving love is inspired by Cupid's arrow aimed at uniting

Key Meanings: Hot, flaming desire, heated passion; being close to success, but not knowing it; swift decisions, living in the fast lane; confrontation

Reversed Meanings: Lack of focus; being taken for granted; fear of breaking up; miscommunication; being scattered; sexual bias or harassment; difficulty

and entwining sexual forces and feeding the fires of enraptured, erotic communion. Consciously strengthening lovemaking muscles enhances orgasmic consummation. A romantic getaway shines the spotlight on *amour.*

§ REVERSED CARD INTERPRETATION:

Times are challenging or perhaps overwhelming. Being taken for granted breeds resentment. You may be getting anger or the cold shoulder from a friend or lover. If anger has been provoked, cool down, remember that hurt usually underlies anger, and look at what that hurt's about. Fears of separation or abandonment may be strong. You might break up with a lover, then get back together. You and your partner may have to look at how your relationship reflects other people's—or society's— expectations that interfere with your own needs and feelings, and change some of your ways of being with each other so that your relationship is truly your own.

EIGHT OF WANDS

NINE OF WANDS

❦ ROMANTIC INTERPRETATION:

Look at your heart's true desires and create a bonfire of passion with faith in your tomorrow. This card indicates waking up your passive self and asserting the fire of your will. Connecting with mentally stimulating people transforms life's perspectives. Education, travel to new places, or other events that enlarge your horizon bring new possibilities into focus. Spirited romantic notions generate a happy mood and enlighten the choices of good fortune. Smiling friends brighten feelings. The possibility of new love or an opportunity to have an affair may surface, but if you're already emotionally attached, beware of romantic whims and running aground on hidden reefs, for betrayal can provoke explosive reactions.

❦ EMOTIONAL INTERPRETATION:

Unwavering feelings light the torch of action. Heated passions burn wildly and restlessly. The direction of your emotions may be unclear, but uncertainties will be clarified with new insights that lie just around the corner. Own your power to be emotionally centered during fiery times. Just when difficulties in relationships or life projects seem insurmountable, you'll find that you have a hidden reserve of energy and determination that can carry you through to success. Traveling or getting out and about locally allows you freedom to live the life you dream of, while staying at home waiting for the phone to ring creates anxiety. It's probably a good idea to analyze your present course and assess whether you need to change direction, perhaps before you make a move. Be sensitive to another's feelings. If you end a relationship, whether it was fleeting or long-lasting, make your exit as gracious, considerate, and painless as you can. If you do, your former lover may become a valued lifelong friend.

❦ SEXUAL INTERPRETATION:

Emotions may evoke inhibiting fears due to unanticipated change, or tensions may build that make intimate love complex or difficult. Sometimes this card indicates anger or fighting in the bedroom.

On the other hand, enjoyment of bedroom playfulness may grow to a crescendo, intensifying longing for passion's culmination. It is advisable to slow the heat and pace of sexual foreplay with tantric rituals of love. You may move to a higher level of

Key Meanings: Emotional vitality; asserting your beliefs; resourcefulness; transformational decision-making; fulfillment of fiery desires; titillation; breakthrough

Reversed Meanings: Aggression; callous lovemaking; hard decisions; loss of faith; canceled plans; deception; guilt trips or emotional manipulation

excitement or a deeper connection through the power of un-hurried touch. Conception is a strong possibility if desires esca-late without a net of protection. Since this card represents the engaged potency of the element fire, considered by ancient scholars to be the life-giving force, it is linked with stimulation of the flow the semen that impregnates a fertile egg. Good communication about what your partner says yes and no to, whether verbally or nonverbally, is essential.

℞ REVERSED CARD INTERPRETATION:
Someone may lay a disturbing guilt trip on you, or you may act in a careless and uncaring way that causes the guilt to be deserved. Perceive your actions clearly, and be honest with yourself about them and their effects. Be prepared to feel emo-tions on deep levels, and go to the inner depths of your psyche, instead of papering over your deeper feelings. Obstacles (either yours or the other person's) may need to be overcome. Handle complex situations with sensitivity to other people's problems as well as your own.

NINE OF WANDS

TEN OF WANDS

☙ ROMANTIC INTERPRETATION:

This is a card of transition, either now or in the near future. Something is coming to an end or morphing into a new form, or something entirely new and different is emerging. The Ten of Wands also points to the power of the mind and will to activate potential, ignite success, and find resolution to problems. Harnessing the fire of the mind to develop concentration and mental discipline helps you use your creative energy to realize your goals, be they worldly or emotional. Instead of over-analyzing your emotions, find friends to share good times with, and give yourself permission to play. Letting go is important, especially of apprehension or anxiety. Follow your own guiding light. Unselfish giving of yourself to others brings satisfaction, but also be alert to times when it's necessary to give to yourself and recharge your energy.

☙ EMOTIONAL INTERPRETATION:

You may want to break away from a restrictive relationship or may be struggling to accept the limiting confines of a powerful bond. Perhaps it's time to take a stand and go in the direction your heart wants to follow, no matter what the opposition. Within an ongoing relationship, it may be time to speak more openly about what you need, or ask sincerely and listen more carefully to what your partner needs. This can lead to illumination for both of you, and to enlarging what you offer and allow each other. If you're single but don't have time for meeting people, a dating service could help you connect with like-minded partners. Be hopeful that any problem you face can be resolved. Out with the useless, and in with values and actions that further your integrity and peace of mind! Stability is gained by making a commitment to do what is important for you. A project may come to completion, opening the way for a new undertaking. You have the strength you need to fulfill your dreams.

☙ SEXUAL INTERPRETATION:

It is important to question what you want. Listening to your real preferences about your sexual identity lightens inner pressures. (This doesn't mean just your sexual orientation, but also how you express your sexual identity.) Get in touch with your playful fantasies, and look for a sensible means to reality-test them. Clarifying your ideas about what you want helps you get

Key Meanings: Questioning romantic fulfillment; having sexually gratifying experiences; improvements in family relations; progress toward goals; completion; perseverance

Reversed Meanings: Not trusting; feeling burdened; rigidity instead of flexibility; avoidance; blocked energies; repeating past mistakes; needing to put down a heavy load.

- 147 -

more of what you hope to receive. Desire, passion, mutual respect, and awareness are fruitful seeds to plant for sensual enjoyment. New lovemaking positions and sweet-smelling lotions can add spice to romance. It may prove beneficial to be open to others' sexual dreams, directions, and imagination, as well as expressing your own.

❧ REVERSED CARD INTERPRETATION:

You may send a lover packing, or feel burdened by unwanted responsibilities or demands. Grasping for love is a turn off. Someone may annoy you with his or her power trips or self-righteousness. Good communication is needed to prevent estrangement from sweethearts, if sexual relations prove to be uncongenial. If events have been intense lately, do something lighthearted.

TEN OF WANDS

PAGE OF WANDS

PAGE of WANDS.

§ ROMANTIC INTERPRETATION:

The Page of Wands opens his or her heart to all living beings, including plants and animals. This card indicates a youthful spirit, often someone who is naive, innocent, or ignorant of the ways of the world. Desire is the fire of the mind and this page, a romantic at heart, is learning how to focus his passions toward loving and winning. (Winning may refer to winning hearts and need not be competitive.) You may need only to look inward to realize that you know the direction you want to go and can find resolutions to problems; or you may need to listen to (or read) others whose knowledge about romantic affairs is greater than your own. Desires for interpersonal growth mingle with creative needs, inspiring you to advance in your profession or to find career opportunity in a place where you'll have interesting companions. Focus your energy on moving forward in settings where success and happiness can be found. The page's answers to romantic questions often come through actions or choices that spring spontaneously from the heart.

§ EMOTIONAL INTERPRETATION:

Steps may need to be taken to fulfill your passionate desires. Listening to the inner voice helps one to hear the soul's plight and enables one to organize time and priorities. You may feel uncertain and confused about what you want and how to get there, but you're learning to unravel tangled emotions—your own and those of others around you—and hear what each has to say. There may be lessons you'll need to master in order to fully enjoy what life has to offer. Understanding yourself better helps you to be sensitive to others' emotional needs, too, seeking your good fortune and theirs along the way.

§ SEXUAL INTERPRETATION:

Uncharted realms of love are waiting to be explored. Sexual energy and physical vitality are high, the imagination is powerful, and hope is soaring. Desire is like an electrical current and body heat burns like a forest fire. What you're going to do about these energies can become the main concern of your inner dialogue. Sometimes, because the page may be inexperienced in lovemaking, it becomes important to verbally say what you need in order to be satisfied. Experimenting with sexual possibilities, positions, and potent turn ons are all part of

Key Meanings: Being an apprentice in love, or ardent in pursuit of passion; earnest efforts; spirited interactions; openhearted contact; developing social skills for success

Reversed Meanings: A complacent person who is irresponsible or immature; lacking passion or motivation; stagnation; the need to refine lovemaking skills

uncertain explorations. An immature page may make bedroom promises or requests that will not be fulfilled easily (or, perhaps, at all).

❦ REVERSED CARD INTERPRETATION:
Piercing emotional energy burns without faith or direction. You may be caught in fears or in obsessing about a negative event or possible event. This page may be too immature to commit to a relationship or to focus on the future. Realizing that learning is a lifelong process, and that you don't already have to know how to do everything exactly right, may lighten up your attitude.

KNIGHT OF WANDS

KNIGHT of WANDS.

⅋ ROMANTIC INTERPRETATION:

This knight symbolizes a person with a warrior spirit who moves through life with boldness and energy. Determined and persevering, such a person usually achieves his or her goals. Some who are represented by this card have a penetrating ability to see through lies and insincerity, and are not easily fooled by superficiality or facades. Since relationship with such a person cannot be built on pretense, you'll need to be your true self or find someone else to play with.

Others represented by this knight are overcome by their own willfulness and their desire to win and control to a degree that makes them less sensitive to others' feelings. Since it's easiest for the Knight of Wands to relate to a partner who does not challenge him, developing a relationship based on equality and give-and-take with such a person is likely to require work. Usually attractive and engaging, the person represented by this card can be exciting and sexually alluring. When romantically turned-on, these knights are hard to turn off and are likely to battle relentlessly to win in romance.

Alternatively, this card can represent your own strength and determination to succeed in attaining what's important to you.

⅋ EMOTIONAL INTERPRETATION:

This knight engages life intensely—whether in work, play, or love—and with a strong, focused will. He corresponds to a magnetic person who can initiate many friendships, platonic or romantic. Flirtatious at heart, the Knight of Wands loves dating and courtship rituals, but when he or she finds a true mate, becomes possessed with strong emotion and is usually faithful to familial bonds. Often characterized as someone striving to climb the career ladder of success, progress and achievement are a big part of this person's emotional needs. Searching for the soul's truth and pursuing victory in life's endeavors, he or she actively pursues answers to love's questions.

This card can also symbolize entanglement of your own inner knight in a confusing battle of love and other emotions. You may have to fight your way through to gain clarity or find resolution.

⅋ SEXUAL INTERPRETATION:

Strong and easily excited, the Knight of Wands is energized by erotica and sexual desire. This knight who loves to adventure

Key Meanings: A socially outgoing person, individualistic and bold, striving for personal or romantic success; determination and using your will forcefully

Reversed Meanings: A confrontational or anxious person who doesn't yield or use their energy productively, or a lack of resolute action; love as conquest

- 151 -

beyond normal limits may be simply wild and eager, or reserved and self-contained on the outside, but wild and eager on the inside. When the doors of affection are opened, he or she uses the breath and tongue playfully to stimulate and provoke passion. Frequently insatiable, the word "more" is this warrior's battle cry. Open to pushing the limits, a swinger's group may be right for the knight if everyone consents to a condom agreement. Sometimes if too intoxicated, his sexual energy wanes, but even when drunk, this lover's an enormous tease and will test your will to say no to amorous demands.

✗ REVERSED CARD INTERPRETATION:
This card can symbolize a hotheaded person who worries too much about fame, fortune, and love's future. Or it may indicate that you need to confront a person or obstacle who hinders love or threatens your personal space. Also, it can indicate that love may be becoming stale or static, losing the luster and excitement of early romance, and that you need to take action to help improve your situation. You can respond to negative forces by adopting a positive attitude in your quest for love.

KNIGHT OF WANDS

QUEEN OF WANDS

§ ROMANTIC INTERPRETATION:

This queen symbolizes an industrious woman who directs her fiery will in skillful and constructive ways. An original thinker, strong minded, deliberate, and true to her beliefs, she expresses concern for family, friends, and community in the choices she makes. Loving by nature, she can become quite upset if someone she loves is affected by negative circumstance. Once you've gotten close to her heart, she'll be your advocate and strongest supporter. When you're involved with her, you gain something of intrinsic value. Also, this queen can point to your own personal power, including creative imagination and energy, to activate change or expand possibilities for improving your romantic situation.

§ EMOTIONAL INTERPRETATION:

The Queen of Wands depicts a powerful woman who is sensitive, strongly emotional, passionate, and physically active. She is determined, resourceful, and uses her creative ideas to achieve success. Typically she is outgoing, dates or goes out frequently, and enjoys diverse social events. If single, she is active and insightful about finding love. (She might even surf the Internet to send out signals to find romance.) If with a partner, she directs a great deal of attention toward her lover and building their relationship. She may be in your life as a lover or a courtly friend who is generous at giving support, encouragement, and counsel on matters of the heart. Also, this card can highlight the importance of relying on your fiery inner spirit and determination to fulfill ambitions and find happiness.

§ SEXUAL INTERPRETATION:

This queen is passionate and experienced, strong or gentle, as the occasion demands. She won't settle for an inept or bungling partner, although she is willing to initiate a less-experienced but willing partner into the deeper mysteries of sexuality that she has fathomed. Being turned-on is a green light for the pursuit of pleasure, as this card is linked with steamy, red-hot women who are comfortable in their bodies and enjoy their sexuality. Only a fool would take their favors for granted. If you're in an ongoing relationship and make a point of keeping your sexual relations alive and exciting, your mutual passions are not likely to wane with the passing of time. If you're single, be willing to

QUEEN OF WANDS.

Key Meanings: A willful woman who is receptive, daring, energetic, successful, and enterprising; your high aspirations, strength, and intuitive insight

Reversed Meanings: An irresponsible woman who is insensitive, insecure, or quarrelsome; or being lovesick, lacking understanding, love, or sexual power

QUEEN OF WANDS

- 153 -

look for amorous situations to heat up the expression of your romantic life.

§ REVERSED CARD INTERPRETATION:

Reversed, this queen indicates an insensitive or irresponsible woman who may pretend to be someone other than who she really is. She may not be confident or able to find love or happiness. Also, she can indicate powerlessness, frustration, or fault finding, an upset sense of well-being, or stirring the fire of anger or jealousy. Healing past sorrow may be necessary.

QUEEN OF WANDS

KING OF WANDS

KING of WANDS

🙲 ROMANTIC INTERPRETATION:

This king's dominion is will power, passion, creativity, and enterprise. He signifies the realized potential of focused action, the fulfillment of enthusiastically held desires, and unleashed energetic power. He can indicate a person whose wisdom idealizes the meaning of "the fire of the mind" represented by the wand, the very symbol of magical power. Usually clever and capable, he might offer you inspiration or clear insight into your personal situation. If you're receptive to his charming manner, you may be tempted to fall in love with him or look at him as your mentor. Drawing this card can signify your power to realize your romantic aspirations, and point to an awakening within you of courage and determination to win the battles of love and life. The results of wise past action drop like ripe fruit from a tree, increasing your ability to make clear, good decisions in affairs of the heart, even though the decisions are sometimes not so easy.

🙲 EMOTIONAL INTERPRETATION:

This king can represent a powerful man who crosses your path in a meaningful way. He is likely to be enterprising, passionate, and enthusiastic. He may or may not be sensitive to others' emotions. He is typically open-minded and outgoing, with a magnetic personality that others follow willlingly. Sincere, he enjoys entertaining, socializing, and the ecstasy of romance. He'll talk you out of stay-at-home habits that shut out meeting potential lovers. When he falls in love, look out, because he doesn't easily take no! for an answer. This wand can also represent the fire of your desire that burns with such intensity that you master whatever task is before you. Struggling against limiting ideas about what can happen leads to a breakthrough that opens doors of potential.

🙲 SEXUAL INTERPRETATION:

Forget casual communication. The book of sexual enhancement, the *Kama Sutra,* lies open on this king's table and he's been reading it. A strong will to enjoy life mixes with the fires of passion to light a path to the zenith of sexual pleasures. Burning desire creates climactic moments when lovers exchange lessons of the heart and loins and the masculine dominates. Seduction

Key Meanings: A man of action who can influence your life; self-assurance, strength of passion, capability; focusing your will power to maximize success

Reversed Meanings: A man who has lost in love or is not focused in life; blaming; not using your power, or using it badly; a bad temper; authoritarianism

and intercourse blend with creative imagination to open possibilities for wild and enriching sensual experiences. With your consent, he will take you beyond normal limits and inhibitions. Usually this king attracts willing potential lovers like honey attracts bees. Depending on his inclinations, he may be faithful to his partner, may respond to discreet invitations to liaisons, or may maintain an ongoing affair besides his primary relationship—or even a series of successive affairs.

§ REVERSED CARD INTERPRETATION:

Reversed, this card can represent a man who has gambled with love and lost, or suffered a decline in his will, sense of self-esteem, and personal power because of some misfortune. It can also point to you or another person being authoritarian and controlling, or blaming others instead of owning any responsibility for what has happened in a relationship. Power struggles may hinder love.

KING OF WANDS

Cups: Drinking from the Cup of Love

Your reason and your passion are the
rudder and the sails of your seafaring soul.
If either your sails or your rudder be broken,
You can but toss and drift, or else
be held at a standstill in mid-seas.
—KAHLIL GIBRAN, *THE PROPHET*

In the suit of cups, we plunge into the depths of feeling, and all the rest of the mysterious realm that lies beneath the surface of the personality in everyone. Love, lust, emotional fertility, pleasure, delight, receptivity, intuition, and imagination are all related to cups. So, too, are hidden intentions, insecurities and anxieties, confusion, jealousy, vanity, frustrated desire for intimacy, affairs and deception, and all endings and new beginnings in affairs of the heart. The deepening and enrichment of old relationships and the beginning of new ones are within the purview of this suit, in ways that will reveal themselves as we examine the cards one by one.

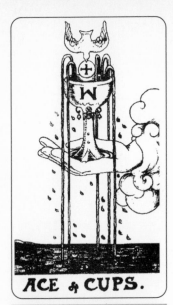

ACE of CUPS.

Key Meanings: First love; happiness; birth; starting a relationship; a new direction in an ongoing relationship; gifts of love; consuming passion

Reversed Meanings: Moodiness; fear of love; failing to initiate a desired relationship or a needed new direction; moving too fast toward love

ACE of CUPS

ACE of CUPS

⚹ ROMANTIC INTERPRETATION:

The hand of fate offers an adventure to swim in the depths of emotion. Experiences may awaken your dreams of romance, or deepen and enrich a present relationship. Optimism and faith mix with desires to help you cultivate love in the garden of your heart. As your hope turns the wheel of tomorrow's good fortune, stay in touch with your common sense to balance your emotions with realistic expectations of the future's potential. Let your feelings guide your search to find your heart's truth. Reaching out to others for greater support or nurturing opens up a new dimension in your experience. Tactful and considerate ways of expressing your needs can open doors to receptivity and more satisfying relations.

⚹ EMOTIONAL INTERPRETATION:

The deepness in the ocean of your psyche gives birth to treasures for your heart's delight. By drinking in the truth of what you feel, you can evolve in a way that gives you greater awareness and strength for your ventures in this uncertain world. Practicing patience will quiet your emotions and allow you to look into the mirror of self-reflection, to see more clearly into your inner being. The clearer, more perceptive self that emerges will be more engaging to others and better able to attract love or deal with issues in an existing relationship. This cup holds important keys to peace of mind, for drinking its contents will quench your thirst for emotional enrichment, happiness, and well-being.

⚹ SEXUAL INTERPRETATION:

Teasing sensuality kindles love's passion. Desires may intensify, inspiring a budding relationship to evolve toward intimacy and sexual union. The ebb and flow of attraction is strengthened by strong currents of lust. Arousing events may lead lovers to forget about safe sex in the heat of pleasure. Fertility bursts forth in new possibilities as promises of romance or commitment are spoken. A child may be conceived. Get ready for consequences that may blossom tomorrow once the seeds of love you have planted start growing. But beware: For better or worse, love's intoxication may be addictive.

⚝ REVERSED CARD INTERPRETATION:

When reversed, this card symbolizes mistrust or fear of emotional or sexual encounters. Stagnation can result from creating excuses that block new possibilities, or from refusing to let go of emotions that existed in a relationship that's no longer alive. Strengthen your sense of personal security so that instead of worrying about what might go wrong, you can enjoy yourself in the moment, even amid life's uncertainties.

ACE OF CUPS

TWO OF CUPS

Key Meanings: Pleasure; romantic choices; emotional healing; receptivity to love; turned-on attraction; social or sexual union; yummy conversations

Reversed Meanings: Fear of separation; suspicion; lack of love; shallow romance; disregard of another's needs; a secret exposed; embarrassment

❦ ROMANTIC INTERPRETATION:

Love, a magnetic force, creates attraction in which two hearts come together to create a special bond of oneness. Positive-negative, male-female energies intertwine in balance. Harmonious emotional energies give birth to a powerful force that can attract love, heal emotions, or repel anger. If you're single, this card indicates that you can instigate romance by turning on your social or flirtatious charm, your sensitivity to others' needs and feelings, or both. If you're in a relationship, this two can signify closeness of hearts, and an uplifting of awareness or receptivity to another's hopes, dreams, and feelings. As you radiate qualities of love, new avenues of opportunity and personal growth become visible.

❦ EMOTIONAL INTERPRETATION:

Questions may arise concerning the direction of your emotions. Staying inwardly balanced quickens growth toward fulfillment. From this centered place you'll gain clarity about the decisions you need to make, and find your path even if you're uncertain about your romantic direction. Don't give in to pressure to make decisions until you are sure of the response you want to give. A willingness to communicate openly creates an opportunity to heal old wounds or fix past mistakes. Don't assume that you know what another's feelings and emotional needs are, but ask in an unobtrusive way, while you hold back your own feelings and ideas so you can listen and hear how that person's world is *for them*. Consider whether there's something you can give that this person truly wants.

❦ SEXUAL INTERPRETATION:

Because the Two of Cups expresses the complementary nature of opposites, male-female, positive-negative energies, it symbolizes harmonious sexual relations. People come together, give support, and initiate intimacy. To open oneself to another's penetration either physically or emotionally deepens your bond. The river of emotion flowing to your loved one intensifies and becomes vulnerable to the torrents of desire. The scent of passion evokes excitement and longing for love's consummation. Caressing, stroking, and licking your lover's breasts, burying your head in them, or using your own breasts to caress your lover, may play a role in delicious lovemaking.

❦ Reversed Card Interpretation:

You may feel mistrustful, angry, suspicious, or may worry about catastrophic possibilities. You may be wishing for love or looking for love where it cannot exist. Beware of holding negative expectations that could become self-fulfilling prophecies, for sometimes we unwittingly create the very events we fear. If you're afraid someone will turn away from you, for instance, you may either hold back emotionally or grasp desperately. Behaving in either of these ways might cause the other person to back off (just as you feared). At the same time, be open to hearing others' true feelings so you don't get lost in wishful thinking about someone who doesn't return your interest or affections.

TWO OF CUPS

Key Meanings: Sensuality; the delights of sexual love; giving or receiving emotional commitment; expansion of understanding; joyful festivities

Reversed Meanings: Fears, conflict in a relationship; thwarted desire; unfruitful activities; lack of respect; rejection; loss of freedom

THREE OF CUPS

THREE OF CUPS

৪ ROMANTIC INTERPRETATION:

The excitement of life fills these three cups, energizing the potency of human emotions. Linked with the inspirations of passion, expansiveness, and opportunities for enjoying the pleasure of romance, it indicates that your heart will open to compatible connections and renewed hope for love's success. Perhaps a friend will become your lover or you will find the love you've been hoping to discover. Your confident, flirtatious self may come alive to create temptation in the moment. Celebrations such as a wedding or a child's birth puts fun in your forecast. Exploring the depths of self-knowledge will take you on a journey of which as yet you have only the barest comprehension.

৪ EMOTIONAL INTERPRETATION:

Listening to the wisdom of your emotions invites success and allows you to enjoy the flow of the river of life. Three cups are a recipe for romance, so act with determination and direct your desires with faith in your future. Drinking from these cups nourishes you to grow in mental, emotional, and spiritual consciousness. Loving without fear, being with your family or friends, and being socially gregarious increases opportunities for soul-connecting happiness. A deeper awareness may rise up from seeing more clearly into the world around you—be it the beauty of a flower or the fears or yearnings of another's heart. Unconditional love, transcending emotional limitations, seeking higher consciousness, connecting with a soul mate, and heartfelt values are linked with this three. Radiating love kindles affectionate ties.

৪ SEXUAL INTERPRETATION:

Sex appeal creates a physical magnetism that's hard to ignore. Emotions tipsy with hot sensuality instigate a strong possibility of slipping into the bedroom and saying "Yes!" to heated foreplay. Playful arousal of desire may lead to dancing with temptations that are too delicious to resist. Making each moment count increases sultry pleasures. Lovemaking feeds the body's hunger, but don't forget to pay attention to common sense. The potency of passion increases the need to practice birth control, if you or your partner don't want to become pregnant. Whatever your decisions about lovemaking, personal expansion is almost guaranteed.

℘ REVERSED CARD INTERPRETATION:

Fears may be bigger than your faith. You may struggle with rejection or jealousy, or face the hard task of learning to let go of a romantic desire. You may find yourself called to be a healer of emotional wounds with which those around you are afflicted, or to mediate a problem between others. Increased opportunities for romance, improved communications with loved ones, or healing relations with friends or family are possible results.

THREE OF CUPS

FOUR OF CUPS

FOUR OF CUPS

Key Meanings: Uncertain relations; overanalyzing emotional choices; needing space, changing your mind about love; going too far—too fast.

Reversed Meanings: Unfulfilled desire, unrealistic romantic ideals; infatuation; fear of making a choice; tense family issues; promiscuity

❦ ROMANTIC INTERPRETATION:

Love is the question, the lesson, and the challenge represented by the Four of Cups. Will you give and accept messages of heartfelt caring, or will you overanalyze emotions and let worries make your relationships less than they could be? You may be working too hard to make events turn out exactly as you want them, while fate has a different agenda. Even the most careful and well-organized person (*especially* such a person) can sometimes benefit by letting go and surrendering to whatever the ebb and flow of the river of life may bring. In fact, sometimes there just isn't any other real choice. By letting go of expectations, and opening your heart to spontaneous changes in the moment, life may become easier. In an ongoing relationship, you and your partner need time for your own inner contemplation and your own activities. Don't insist that your partner, who is an independent person, do all things according to your needs or interests.

❦ EMOTIONAL INTERPRETATION:

Emotions are the water of life that nourishes your being. Denying their truth leads to confusion. Contentment results from paying attention to your needs and not allowing your choices to be determined by those who supposedly know what is best for you. Don't worry about others' well-meaning advice. Struggles for emotional well-being may intensify as you pursue options to enrich your romantic life. Contemplation of past relationships can lead to understanding your helpful and less helpful patterns of thought and action that influence your ways of being with yourself and others. Let your imagination play with new ways of handling situations where you're stuck, and take heartfelt steps to fix stressed communications.

❦ SEXUAL INTERPRETATION:

Heighten passion's barometer by getting out of your head and more in touch with your sensuality. Trust is the building block for going deeper into physical ecstasy during sexual relations. Be creative and make your bedroom a sultry delight. Uplift the mood by fashioning a romantic, candlelit environment. However, if you look at the consequences of sexual involvement, and your potential union doesn't feel right, pay attention to what you're sensing. For instance, making precautionary rules or saying "No!" to the temptation of forbidden fruit means you're choosing a less complicated diet to sustain your future well-being. Being promiscuous may not be your ticket to happiness.

☙ REVERSED CARD INTERPRETATION:

Complaining or self-criticism can get in the way of love. Focusing on doubts can stop you from taking action. Affirming your strength to work through challenging emotional situations increases your willingness to do so. Adopt an attitude of courage, optimism, and trust in the choices you're making, but don't pretend you feel good when you don't. Resentment or dissatisfaction may increase if you're not being heard or appreciated. You may need to address your feelings in order to move beyond them.

FOUR OF CUPS

- 165 -

Key Meanings: Looking at the cup as half empty instead of half full; sexual identity crisis; family pressures; conflicting interests; remorse; instability

Reversed Meanings: Drained emotions; feeling isolated; lack of intimacy; extramarital affairs; inner conflict; unreliability; scandal; misconduct

FIVE OF CUPS

FIVE OF CUPS

§ ROMANTIC INTERPRETATION:

You may find yourself juggling the yin and yang of emotion, torn between love and indifference, desire and uncertainty. You may also spend time and energy sorting out truth from fiction—your own, the other person's, or both. Amid this maze of complex emotions, soulful thinking and truthful choices help you find harmony in the moment. Focus on today's realities and possibilities instead of memories of yesterday or wishes for tomorrow. Even if your inner spirit is lost in sorrow, find self-love and appreciation for who you are. You can live the good life now if you don't place demands on your life that cannot be fulfilled, or fret that your romantic situation should be something other than it is. Fears of separation from your present lover or other painful emotions may seem overwhelming, but the steps you take now can help you find resolve. With good intentions and effort based on loving kindness, reconciliation, or better relations are often possible.

§ EMOTIONAL INTERPRETATION:

Accept and bless your experiences, and let go of anxieties—or, if you can't yet do that, notice what you're saying or picturing in your mind that contributes to creating and maintaining those anxieties. Crying over yesterday can interfere with your capacity to enjoy what life offers you today. If your feelings are hurt, it is important that you confront the demons that are preventing you from enjoying your life. Holding on to negative feelings or memories intensifies unhappiness, but in order to be able to let go of them, you must experience your emotions and accept them fully. Pain from past relationships doesn't have to eclipse present hopes and realities. Sweeping emotions under the carpet of pretense creates a lump that will trip you when you're not looking. If you face a difficult situation, use it constructively to help you move toward enlightenment and compassion.

§ SEXUAL INTERPRETATION:

Fears about having sex? Yes, they exist in many forms, and you may come face to face with your own morals or family values that may stop love's juices from flowing. Your fears may be realistic, and create a safety net, or they may be old baggage that needs to discarded. Concern about another's intentions may cause you to be wary, needing more information as to whether the wariness is warranted. This card is partly about learning to trust yourself, and learning when and how much to trust others. With perseverance comes growth, renewal, and opportunities that can improve the quality of your communications and sexual experiences. Look for the magic in the moment, with or without having sex. Your body is a refuge for finding the truth about your emotions and spirit.

⅋ REVERSED CARD INTERPRETATION:

Obsessing over what you "coulda woulda shoulda done" may poison your present. Insecurity or excessive dependency consumes security. Infidelity could sour a relationship. Avoid situations that are emotionally draining, or try new ways of handling them thoughtfully and constructively. As you do, focus on what you gain instead of what you lose and be true to yourself. Increase your focus on what's good in your situation and the pleasing opportunities that life holds out to you.

FIVE OF CUPS

- 167 -

VI

Key Meanings: Pleasure; rediscovery of a childlike quality in oneself; sharing trust; innocence, good impressions, selflessness; a lover's crush

Reversed Meanings: Dwelling in the past; loss of friendship; childish behavior; self-consciousness; rejection; anxiety concerning possible pregnancy

SIX OF CUPS

SIX OF CUPS

 ❧ ROMANTIC INTERPRETATION:

This card indicates happy moments. Take responsibility for making choices that can favorably affect your destiny. If single, be boldly willing to act in ways that may enhance your potential for finding romance. Think about your positive qualities, seek constructive ideas, and look optimistically toward your future. Be open to the playful nature in yourself and in others and give yourself permission to have fun. Throw a small party (perhaps a brunch or small dinner party that doesn't require oodles of preparation), or say "Yes!" to a blind date. Take a chance and reach to fulfill your romantic notions, while keeping your eyes open and your wits about you. Whether you're with your partner, lover, or friends, listen to the sunny spot in your nature that's unselfishly loving and compassionate. Let it brighten this moment in your life and warm the lives of others around you.

 ❧ EMOTIONAL INTERPRETATION:

Inwardly nurture your emotions with a strong voice of appreciation. Confidence in your choices creates a foundation for positive experiences in your evolving world of love. Friends from childhood may reenter your life. Think back on pleasant times in the past to see if you can find almost-forgotten ways of being that can be useful to you in your present. From your place of emotional centeredness, you may see a path to fulfillment that was invisible to you before. As you become more confident of how you can fulfill your longings, unrealistic demands and expectations will fall away. Cultivating inner awareness will help you tell the difference between real needs and unnecessary wants. If you have a partner, make sure you take some quality time to listen to what he or she is feeling. You may learn something new.

 ❧ SEXUAL INTERPRETATION:

Giving a bouquet of roses is a turn on! Lighten up your sexual nature and go naked to lunch. Seriously, what are you willing to do to awaken your life to greater physical, sensory pleasure? The door to a sexual relationship will open wider for you if you're willing to help make it happen. Initiate opportunities for romantic getaways. Have fun with your mind, and your body will follow—and vice versa. Drink from the depths of these six cups of lively emotion, and you'll become intoxicated with the wine of love. If you keep making excuses for not going to bed with someone, then recognize that you're sending yourself a message, at least for the present, and stop worrying or making excuses about it. Your actions show the truth of your desires and inclinations.

❦ REVERSED CARD INTERPRETATION:

Loss of friendship or rejection renders your emotions fragile. Crying eyes show vulnerability. Quarreling with a loved one or holding on to negative emotions left over from past relationships perpetuates pain, and interferes with openheartedness. Blaming triggers a cycle of counterblame; others' blame may cause you to panic or react aggressively. Anxiety over an unwanted pregnancy creates stressful emotions. You just might need an extra hug or two. Strengthen your resolve to find happiness.

SIX OF CUPS

Key Meanings: Love's
fantasies or idealism;
awareness versus confusion
or illusion, search for truth or
clarity; the power of
imagination; dreaminess;
stagnation

Reversed Meanings: Restless
expectations; delusion,
deception, and self-
deception; temptation breeds
distress, misinterpretation of
events, and jealousy;
unfulfilled wishes for
pregnancy

SEVEN OF CUPS

SEVEN OF CUPS

❧ ROMANTIC INTERPRETATION:

Listening to your true thoughts, feelings, and inclinations
destroys ambivalence, lifts the veil of illusion, and illuminates a
path of action. Confusion is replaced with clarity and understanding. Your intuition needs to work in harmony with your
intellect in order to help you move toward greater success.
Energize your romantic nature by letting go of stagnant emotional energy that's related to past situations but not your present. Be alert to—or look for—opportunities for expansion and
growth. This may mean stepping outside your usual habits and
places! With a friend or lover, pay attention to old patterns in
which you act toward *this person now* as you acted toward others in your past, or hear *this person now* as meaning what someone in your past meant; let go of those old, perhaps rigid habits,
and respond spontaneously to *this person in this unique moment
and situation.*

❧ EMOTIONAL INTERPRETATION:

It's a good time to learn more about love, your truth, and your
inner self. Emotions may swing from one extreme to another.
Think about which of your wants are deep and true for you
and which are imitations of what others want or conditioned
responses to society's expectations. Be attentive to your fantasies, looking for what they tell you about sides of yourself
that you're expressing and sides of yourself that you're not.
Don't rush into romantic situations or commitments unless
you have mental clarity. You or your partner may be a dreamer
who faces the step-by-step work needed to give your relationship a realistic foundation. You might find that you've entered
a relationship based on mutual projections and illusions about
each other, and therefore have some work to do to learn to
appreciate each other as you really are. Communications need
to be rooted in heartfelt truths and obtainable realities, not just
idealism or idealization.

❧ SEXUAL INTERPRETATION:

The illusion of love may entangle your emotions and actions in
the bedroom. Your imagination may be playing with a new
vision of a familiar position that can play an important role in
filling your sexual needs. Lust may be hot and tempting, with
sexual attraction hard to resist, even if you have a sense that this

partner or circumstance isn't right for you. Although sex naturally accompanies love and passion, make sure the timing and feelings are right. You don't want to say yes today and regret it tomorrow. Learn from your encounters, be they more or less than what you hoped they might be.

On the other hand, this may be a time to move beyond confusion, doubts, or inhibitions to ignite fiery, emotional alchemy. Reality and dreams are weighed on the scales held by Eros, god of love, but only you can read it to know the truth of your situation. Listen with your heart and body and feel whether your stomach, neck, shoulders, and thighs are tight and telling you not to move forward, or relaxed and open to exploration and expression.

❧ REVERSED CARD INTERPRETATION:

Feelings may be stifled and conflicts buried rather than resolved, leading to anger and resentment. Lovers' quarrels may end by someone walking out the door. Conflicts may put the spotlight on insecurities and the need to make changes. However, if you look closely, there's a lot to be learned. It may be necessary to tone down emotional intensity and go through a step-by-step process of resolving conflict. Perhaps if the people involved hear each other's stories fully, the door to a better relationship will be opened.

SEVEN OF CUPS

- 171 -

EIGHT OF CUPS

Key Meanings:
Misunderstandings; turning away from emotions; shyness; unexpressed feelings; heavy moods; needing to let go of love or to find solitude

Reversed Meanings:
Precarious emotional predicaments; envy, vengeful thinking; pessimism; marital affairs or discord; date rape

EIGHT OF CUPS

❦ Romantic Interpretation:

Frustrations, loneliness, discontent, or unfulfilled desire for love may lead to avoiding open communications by masking true expression of one's thoughts and feelings. Depending on the circumstances, this may stifle needed change or invite it. Opportunities for opening doorways into hitherto unsuspected pleasure may be just around the corner. Courage overcomes fear, strength destroys insecurity, but above all, flexibility and faith can overcome a broken heart. Developing your ability to go up and down and surf waves of joy and sorrow, attraction and repulsion, wisdom and ignorance, dominance and submission makes life a little easier. Don't allow others to persuade you to abandon your dreams, for your imaginings are pathways to new realities. Idealizations or longings based on bringing your past into the present, however, can stop you from making rich connections with people you meet or trying new directions.

❦ Emotional Interpretation:

Miscommunications can bring pain or anger. What one person infers may be different from the message the other intended. You may go through a dark night of the soul in which you must accept the hand of fate or the workings of karma, because there is nothing else you can do. You become, for the moment, a humble servant of the path along which life directs you. The twin dangers are hopelessly railing against fate or adopting a defeatist attitude, as if you can do nothing about anything. External events or your own changing emotions may instigate taking a different direction as you navigate the river of life. Giving up and letting go, whether of a relationship that has gone bad or unrealistic expectations about a person or situation, can draw the veil of illusion from before your eyes and allow you to see a new dawn.

❦ Sexual Interpretation:

Look at yourself naked in the mirror. Find things to appreciate about your body. Self-love is a prerequisite for honoring your body as a vessel befitting love's consummation.

Sometimes, these eight cups indicate intense sexual desire without having a partner, or having a partner who doesn't want to have sex as much as you do. If this is your situation, don't despair. Nourish yourself with extra TLC by giving yourself something special or a treat you've been longing to experience At the right time, sexual love will come into your life. (In the meantime, varieties of vibrating massage toys can bring a new dimension to the art of self-arousal!) Romantic fantasies stimulate passion, but be careful not to get attracted to your friend's mate or any unattainable dream that will cause you and others misery.

✘ REVERSED CARD INTERPRETATION:

Picking forbidden fruit can turn dreams of love into nightmares. Projections of your needs onto another may be so strong that you have major misperceptions of who and how they are. Someone may respond with jealousy, possessiveness, or even revenge. Excessive drug use or alcohol consumption invite the possibility of date rape. Guilt, underlying difficulties, or an unfavorable situation weakens or ends romance. The potential of getting lost in sadness, pessimism, or self-pity can be offset by contact with supportive friends and self-nurturing activities. Emotional strength comes through your efforts to see clearly and make positive attitude changes.

EIGHT OF CUPS

IX

Key Meanings: Energy directed toward positive changes; affection, joy; strong ties; nearing fulfillment; provoking sexual responses; testing limits

Reversed Meanings: Romantic doldrums; obsessing about emotions; unwanted changes; seductive teasing; lies; embarrassment; flattery

NINE OF CUPS

❧ ROMANTIC INTERPRETATION:

Drinking the nectar found in the nine cups awakens a spirit of transformation and the evolution of higher consciousness. Your focus on faith brings good fortune as it helps you find satisfaction within yourself and reinforces your confidence to succeed on the sometimes rocky road of romance. Security issues, tested by love's uncertainties, may be resolved by love and nurturing from those close to you. In a relationship in which selfishness or falsehoods have played a role, tears can give way to forgiveness and acceptance of love's promise. Thus, the card represents movement toward a true psychological and spiritual union as well as a physical one. Strengthen family ties or your bonds to those you love. Call upon your courage to help you fulfill your romantic notions.

❧ EMOTIONAL INTERPRETATION:

Your feelings reflect the movements of lunar, or watery, subconscious currents. Patience and time may be needed to work through emotional questioning, but there will be a breakthrough in understanding what lies beneath the surface of your passions. The Nine of Cups symbolizes fulfillment, or approaching realization of a deep desire, but patience is needed. Let your intuition and your sensitivities guide you toward recognizing your true preferences, as you keep emotions flowing in harmony by steering clear of anger, power struggles, or other conflicts. Decision-making evolves in its own time. Today is just one more step in your life's journey. Infinite potentials for happiness exist as you move toward adventures and realizations yet to come.

❧ SEXUAL INTERPRETATION:

Staying at home wishing for a sexual relationship doesn't make it happen. Give yourself permission to be flirtatious and playful. Buy some go-out-and-play clothes or some sexy lingerie to remind yourself that's it's OK to be turned-on. Look for opportunities to explore the sensory garden of delight. Wanting physical love is a natural part of an emotional nature, so keep your thoughts about your sexuality positive. Let your actions flow from loving kindness and watch your list of admirers grow. Allow hot, sexy, "sun energy" to rise up in you. Next, contact your receptive, sensitive, "moon energy" and let it rise up in you. If you think you already know everything about making love, you can't open new doors to pleasure. Be ready to step out of your inhibitions and habits, and trust your instincts to discover something wonderful in the sexual arena.

⚥ REVERSED CARD INTERPRETATION:

Incompatibility, infidelity, or arrogance can create distance between you and a loved one. If you have to accept or undergo an unwanted change, remember that going through the nadir—the low point—can result in valuable new insights that may not have become available in any other way. Find ways to fix what's broken, if it's important for you to do so. Learning to speak the truth even if it's embarrassing, or giving unselfishly with compassion are vital lessons, even though they may not come easily.

NINE OF CUPS

- 175 -

Key Meanings: Inspiration; family happiness; getting to know someone on deep levels; wholeness; resolving problems; stability; new romance

Reversed Meanings: Releasing tension; ending routine; addiction to love; emotional changes; need for a fresh start; wasting time or energy

TEN OF CUPS

TEN OF CUPS

❀ ROMANTIC INTERPRETATION:

Happiness comes to those who drink the ambrosia from one of these ten cups, which represent hope and happiness. Things may not be perfect, but in your innermost being, you know that life is a dance of dreams where you can awaken possibilities for successfully fulfilling your romantic desires. Take a moment to look beyond mundane reality and find a living spark of the divine in your own consciousness. With your heart open to inspiration in the moment, romance is destined for the time when your invocations to the god of love are caught in reality's web. Within a relationship, peace and well-being evolves into a trusting union or a happy family. Love's fullness can lead to opening your being to sharing a greater sense of connectedness with friends, partners, and all living beings.

❀ EMOTIONAL INTERPRETATION:

Love overcomes conflict. The joys of family life or close friendship bring inspiration and personal expansion. A feeling of optimism and well-being about your own life pervades your experiences. As emotions are clarified, you can move toward feeling more secure or resolving complex issues. Feeling more confident of yourself allows you to take trusting steps to meet people and make new friends. Open communication, combined with tact and consideration of others' feelings, improves your chances for successful connections. Letting go of feeling upset and judgmental and overlooking your partner's minor imperfections fosters good relations. Personal boundaries change when you find the emotional pot of gold at the end of the rainbow.

❀ SEXUAL INTERPRETATION:

Being realistic about sexual desires helps you develop greater clarity about your present situation so that you'll know what's possible and what's just wishful thinking. How open are you to being emotionally and physically loved? What are your ways of keeping closed? Working on trust issues may help you be more receptive to hugs and sexual playfulness. Do you need to do a better job of communicating what you want in the bedroom in order to feel more amorous? Create more opportunities to dance to the music of love. Turn on your mind to being sensually playful. Put sex on the dessert menu after a romantic candlelight dinner, and if you add whipped cream, it can enhance the taste of your pleasure!

৪ Reversed Card Interpretation:

Without trust, loving connections can lead to loneliness and frustration. Hysterical flipouts or emotions wasted on worries drain time and energy. It may be necessary to look for a new direction, inside or outside yourself, where you'll have an opportunity to find greater peace of mind. Nurture both yourself and others by believing in the healing power of love.

TEN OF CUPS

- 177 -

PAGE of CUPS.

Key Meanings: A young or young-minded person, who is learning about courting or pursuing love. Enchantment; love at first sight; innocence; steamy sexual attraction

Reversed Meanings: A young person, perhaps a prankster, with unpredictable emotions; lovesickness; topsy-turvey or manipulated emotions; vanity

PAGE OF CUPS

PAGE OF CUPS

❧ ROMANTIC INTERPRETATION:

This card can represent a love-struck person. Often a student in the romantic realm, this page is only learning about the power, strength, and responsibilities of love. The Page of Cups can also indicate the capacity to love, or the realization that you're worthy of being loved, and that it's time to give yourself permission to be Cupid's next target. Even if you try to escape your feelings, you'll encounter them sooner or later. As you live in the moment, however, be careful about taking actions or making decisions with long-lasting consequences, because you need time to sort out, or find, your best course. The page's romantic journey reflects openness to learning love's lessons with faith in what tomorrow may bring. This card can also refer to the gift of intuition and being sensitive to the emotional undercurrents of others' words and actions.

❧ EMOTIONAL INTERPRETATION:

The Page of Cups is associated with questioning love's direction, an inexperienced lover, the beginning stages of courtship, or the unsure offerings of love one gives to another. Emotions can swirl like currents in a river rushing to the sea, and may feel overwhelming and hard to control. Deep attachments and commitments may be made without serious thought of the consequences. Since long-lasting responsibilities can follow physical expressions of love, make sure your promises and expectations are explicit and not implied. Whatever your age or position in life, there are others from whom you can learn. A sensitivity to understanding what you can gain from these teachers (who may either seem wise or sometimes more like incarnations of "The Devil"), can open psychic vistas that you otherwise might never see.

❧ SEXUAL INTERPRETATION:

Giving love doesn't have to mean giving sexual favors. The page's innocence can be exploited. Be alert to others' attempts to manipulate you for their own gain or pleasure or to tempt you into sexual situations that may not be emotionally healthy for you. If the person and situation are right, this card can signify a green light for moving toward greater sensual exploration. The excitement of sexual attraction may be too enticing to ignore. Make conscious and intuitive awareness your chaperone and don't forget your condoms! Opening the heart accompanies enjoyment of sexual pleasures.

✖ REVERSED CARD INTERPRETATION:

A young-minded man or woman may act foolishly regarding emotional matters. Bumps on the road to love may jolt you away from your heart's center. You might be totally turned-off by a potential liason because the chemistry between you and another is wrong and you know it. You may think you know how to be suave in a romantic situation, when in truth, you're foolish, for there's a whole realm of emotional understanding yet to be fathomed.

PAGE OF CUPS

KNIGHT of CUPS.

Key Meanings: A strong person who can be influential and seductive; connecting with your inner emotional warrior or intuition; multi-amorous relations

Reversed Meanings: An emotionally charged person who may act contrary to your desires; confronting dark or stressful emotions

KNIGHT of CUPS

KNIGHT of CUPS

❦ ROMANTIC INTERPRETATION:

Someone who is strong, yet sensitive, may play the role of the knight in shining armor who sweeps you off your feet with poetic words or even comes to your rescue. It is easy to fall in love with this natural hero with whom you may find yourself caught up in a magnetic web of emotion. He (or she) may be a lifelong romantic who pursues one lover after another. Also, this card can represent your own romanticism or inner warrior of love, which may take either the form of the crusade for the perfect relationship or the ability to say no or good-bye when that's right for you, despite strong pressure to comply with another's demands. A Knight of Cups might even invite you to become a member of an extended family or community of some sort. At the extreme, you might be invited into a polyamorous family—a community that offers a closed circle of lovers to cuddle. Yes, they really do exist, and yes, keeping emotional harmony under such circumstances can be challenging!

❦ EMOTIONAL INTERPRETATION:

Often finding himself surrounded by opportunities for flirtatious relations, this knight has a reverence for romance, and an unusual awareness of how to uplift emotional issues. Sensitive, and perhaps even intuitive, he or she may be inclined to go off on healing or spiritual quests, sometimes to sacred places to commune with the Higher Self and, if the card relates to someone other than yourself, he or she may invite you to come along. This knight may be in your life now, crossing your path soon, or may be a side of your emotional self. In the latter case, it's likely to include owning your strength and confidence in a way that also respects the feelings and needs of others. It's time to talk about your values, needs, desires, and actions.

❦ SEXUAL INTERPRETATION:

This knight symbolizes the calm but intense power of excitement, deep feelings, and sexual impulses. Eager to make love, your passions are aroused and seduction gets serious as heated desires jump to take yes for an answer. Playful, mysterious, and turned-on, this knight is very aware when the chemistry is right for advancing to sexual encounters. This knight may invite you to make love outdoors beneath the trees or stars. Don't be surprised to find yourself feeling your love juices flow and your body wanting more attention. But if your knight doesn't get you aroused, then your friendship may be platonic.

❧ REVERSED CARD INTERPRETATION:

Your knight may prove untrue, or not to be the person you thought was right for you. You may have to confront emotional currents of betrayal, disappointment, jealousy, or a rival who is also attracted to your lover. Frustrations because your demands aren't being met, or fears left over from a past relationship may make it hard to trust. At his worst, this knight can be vindictive and punitive toward those who block his or her intentions.

KNIGHT OF CUPS

QUEEN of CUPS.

Key Meanings: A confident woman who loves courageously; developing intuition; depth; compassion; opening your heart; romantic good fortune; mysticism

Reversed Meanings: An insensitive or overly emotional person; not fulfilling your own expectations; lack of compassion; martyrdom; unhappiness

QUEEN of CUPS

QUEEN of CUPS

❡ ROMANTIC INTERPRETATION:

Luck is often with those who choose this card, for it suggests that your emotional path holds opportunities for good fortune and meetings with remarkable women—or remarkable men who have well-developed intuitive qualities usually associated with women. Trusting your intuition and diving into the soul of your feelings paves the way to success. This queen also symbolizes a good-hearted woman filled with lunar tides of emotion, who touches you deeply and nourishes your sense of self. Unfathomed mysteries hidden within, she gives of herself without selfish motives, and mirrors feelings as the Moon reflects the light of the Sun. She may be your lover, wife, mother, understanding friend, or simply someone who makes your heart smile.

❡ EMOTIONAL INTERPRETATION:

This usually auspicious card can represent someone who likes to touch and be touched, inwardly and outwardly. Intuitive and insightful, affectionate and kind, this queen of hearts can help you be more aware of the truth of your emotions and offer the comfort of nurturing, mothering energy. When you have wronged her, or someone she favors, heartfelt apology is far more likely to bring this queen's forgiveness than trying to defend yourself. She can discern the emotion behind your look or gesture, so it's not easy to conceal your true feelings from her. Or, the card can signify a deepening of your ability to make wise choices that lead you to personal enrichment and fulfillment even while being absorbed by an inner ocean of emotion.

❡ SEXUAL INTERPRETATION:

This queen, voluptuous and alluring, represents powerful, loving women who can be seductive and passionate. Because her muse is Eros, god of love, the Queen of Cups can indicate the boosting of your sexual drive as you get turned-on by your lover's emotional currents. Don't be surprised if the person indicated by this card asks you to take trips to the sea where she'll pull you into deep blue pools and ask you to make love. She enjoys taking playful, sensual baths or showers, and isn't shy about asking for more of your favors while moaning orgasmically. Since she's associated with sexual love, fertility, and conception of children, it is important to make conscious choices about birth control when being intimate.

⅋ REVERSED CARD INTERPRETATION:

Upside down, this card can indicate an unfaithful lover, or a self-centered woman who lacks empathy or doesn't care about others, either due to a personality trait or overpowering situational constraints that are depleting her energy. Her hormones may be surging, creating a rage of emotion. This card can also suggest that you may have the tools and understanding to fix a broken relationship, and increase chances for building stronger inner or outer harmony.

QUEEN OF CUPS

KING of CUPS.

Key Meanings: An attractive man, who is romantic, sensitive, and turned-on emotionally; romantic journeys; perceptiveness; your rendezvous with love's fortune

Reversed Meanings: Someone who may want love but doesn't know how to find it; emotional obliviousness; feeling powerless or victimized

KING OF CUPS

KING OF CUPS

❦ ROMANTIC INTERPRETATION

This regal guardian of the suit of cups represents someone who is strong, charismatic, and intuitive, with a grasp of the great mysteries of the world. Don't be surprised if he affects your emotions or tries to seduce you. He's in touch with his feelings, and is willing to open his heart, for he understands that love is the essence of life, the greatest gift anyone can possess. His wise counsel can be inspirational and may be useful in helping you understand your own situation. But be careful of the potential to depend on his appraisals instead of your own inclinations, for ultimately, you are the one who is responsible for your choices, actions, and outcomes (including your choice of listening to someone's counsel). Since this card also represents gaining emotional wisdom, it can signify being able to control your moods, heal your emotions, improve your romantic fate, or find fulfillment.

❦ EMOTIONAL INTERPRETATION:

The King of Cups has had his emotions both becalmed and driven by winds of change, and has successfully navigated swift and difficult currents in the sea of love. His experiences have made him sensitive to the uncertainties in life, and adept at keeping emotions in balance. A good communicator, he can help others through their trials of life as a result of having gone through them himself. This card also suggests that you may find contentment, commitment, or/and stability in a relationship of mutual attraction, or come to a satisfactory resolution of an old problem. In either case, you may find the key (perhaps outside you, perhaps within you) to opening the doors of your heart and fulfilling your desires. Or, you might meet someone who appears as this king—a perceptive, attractive person who holds the cup of love as if it were a fountain from which you can drink on a hot summer's day.

❦ SEXUAL INTERPRETATION:

Giving and receiving sexual love is a natural part of romance for this king of hearts who weighs his physical desires as he contemplates the rhymes and rhythms of intimacy's commitment. Although he may consider the possible delights of having a harem, he is usually loyal to his mate and the truth of his heart. If his lover wants him to dress in a bunny costume or play the role of Tarzan, he'll amiably agree, for his motto is: "Whatever turns you on!" At the same time, he may hold part of himself back, due to his regal tendency of liking to be in control. If he is a great spirit, however, he may be beyond that, having learned to move gracefully with the winds of time and fate.

꙰ REVERSED CARD INTERPRETATION:

This card can represent someone who is likely to be unfaithful and adulterous, or someone who lacks the wisdom to develop and maintain an intimate relationship. It can also mean that you need to be sure that you aren't giving others excessive power over your emotions. It can alternatively refer to falling from the pedestal of love, being high-strung and emotionally oversensitive, or going to bed with a person who makes you wish you hadn't.

KING OF CUPS

Swords: The Cutting Blade of Truth

*We must dare to think "unthinkable" thoughts . . . because
when things become unthinkable, thinking stops and action
becomes mindless.*
—JAMES W. FULBRIGHT, MARCH 27, 1964

The suit of swords represents the purity and strength of the element air. Without air, you can't breathe, and without breath, you can't live. Yogis meditate on their inhalations and exhalations as air flows into and out of their bodies, to feel the source of life.

The element air and the suit of swords may refer to ideas that liberate us or ideas that bind us. We can easily become caught in mental whirlpools that are often filled with mistaken views and mental habits from which we are hard put to escape. These may be personal ideas, or beliefs or ideologies shared by many. The archetypes of this suit remind us not to become too attached to our concepts or the categories in which we arrange them. Since no one is always right, we need to be alert to when and where we may be mistaken, and work on letting go of useless or destructive ideas. We can look at the real events that underlie our abstractions. Instead of clinging dogmatically to preconceptions, when we find ourselves arguing, we can each stop and listen to the other's personal stories, which can lead us to deeper understandings and appreciations. Now, card by card, we look at the varied forms in which sword energy appears.

ACE OF SWORDS

& ROMANTIC INTERPRETATION:

Inner strength, open-mindedness, and determination to overcome difficulties in love exist within you. Use the sword of discrimination to protect your vulnerabilities, communicate your truth, and move toward new opportunities. Faith in your ideas inspires hopes for tomorrow's success. Living the truth of your inner values helps you find the love you seek. Sharing your feelings expands your awareness, both of yourself and of what's going on in others around you. Plant seeds for future fulfillment by staying centered in the present reality of your feelings. Developing greater sensitivity to your emotional comfort zone will help you take better care of your romantic spirit.

& EMOTIONAL INTERPRETATION:

Using the sharp blade of wisdom, cut emotional cords to the past that limit you now. Prospects for happiness lie in the present, especially when your intellect and emotions are balanced with trust and faith. A tendency to overanalyze your emotions can keep you stuck in your head. Listen to your optimistic voice for inspiration and for learning how to heal your heart and overcome doubt's doldrums. Make or renew a commitment to adopt a healthy attitude about your emotional journey. This may be a good time to network and make fresh contacts that will enlarge your social world. Exploring love's potential can bring priceless rewards.

& SEXUAL INTERPRETATION:

Fun-loving affection and a tender embrace arouses desire. This ace is linked to inspiration, stimulation, and the exploration of the mind and body's pathways to pleasure. Adopting an attitude that will expand instead of limit your experiences, especially when passion is too hot to control, promotes inner harmony. If you're sexually active with multiple partners, overcome concern about STDs by educating yourself and learning to protect your body while honoring your physical desires. Sex, a natural instinct, needs to be nurtured with care and respect while physical expressions of love are enjoyed.

& REVERSED CARD INTERPRETATION:

Reversed, this card symbolizes mental stagnation or emotional anxiety. For healing, confront challenges with your soul's truth

Key Meanings: Entering a new cycle; rebirth of awareness; personal empowerment; forcefulness through ideas; victory's inspiration; faith.

Reversed Meanings: Refusing to accept new ideas; needing a fresh outlook or brighter attitude; worries at the start of a cycle; regrets; bitter emotions.

as your guide. You can always learn something from a difficult situation if you keep your mind open to the messages that experience offers. Meditating on your heart center may help you transcend negativity. If physical love is offered, but is not what you want, be firm in your refusal of others' invitations or pressure.

ACE OF SWORDS

TWO OF SWORDS

ROMANTIC INTERPRETATION:

Give yourself permission to be a student who doesn't know all the answers. The polarities of the mind—right and left brain hemispheres, logic and intuition, activity and stillness—are represented by these two swords which can help you slice through confusion of objective dilemmas and ambiguous emotions.

Balance mind and emotions and use your intuition as your guide to break the hold of indecision. Your decision-making process is leading you toward a greater understanding of your true path in romance. Reflect on the whole spectrum of your desires to discern your best stance in love. Dating or trying out relationships with people who are quite different from previous partners can open up new realms of experience. Some wonderful lifelong partnerships have begun through dating services or online matchmaking.

EMOTIONAL INTERPRETATION:

The two swords represent attraction/repulsion, love/hate, want/don't want, so it is important to be flexible, to let go of the feeling that you need quick answers, and to allow yourself time and space to feel ambivalent when that's your reality.

Giving yourself more time to look within and contemplate your emotional needs or commitments removes the pressure of feeling like you must make a decision immediately or have certainty right now. Listen to sensations of tension or relaxation in your body; these are messages that can help you lift veils of illusion or confusion, so that your mind and body work together rather than being isolated from each other. The sharp sword of your intellect can help you find clarity and find peace within yourself or make peace with your partner.

SEXUAL INTERPRETATION:

This card reflects the power of the mind to attract what you seek. It embodies the idea that once you make a decision, you are halfway to plucking the fruits of your desires. Precisely what do you want in the world of sexuality? If it's feasible, be prepared to find it. You're not the only one looking for love's enjoyment. You can find like-minded people by sending out the right nonverbal signals and finding environments where you can meet interesting people. Look for partners in places connected to your interests. For instance, you might connect with

Key Meanings: Blind love; applying new ideas; balancing mind and heart; serious contemplation; self-discovery; learning about life the hard way

Reversed Meanings: Indecisiveness; failure to make appropriate discriminations; difficulty seeing reality; waiting for love; a need for organization, clarification of priorities

TWO OF SWORDS

a potential playmate while browsing in a bookstore or taking a dance class. Trying new techniques to express your passion ignites the spirit of adventure.

❧ REVERSED CARD INTERPRETATION:
Unexpressed emotions unexpectedly rise to the surface. Words may be spoken without sensitivity to your feelings. To improve communications, let go of relationship dynamics in which you try to "win" in ways that mean the other person has to lose. Overanalyzing your situation may create undue stress. Silence your voice of doubt or anxiety with appreciation of your emotional journey. Thinking about your priorities helps you develop a better sense of direction.

TWO OF SWORDS

THREE OF SWORDS

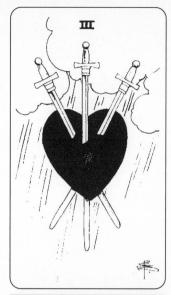

& ROMANTIC INTERPRETATION:

These three swords, symbol of the mind's penetrating power, pierce the depths of your psyche, cutting through self-deception or mistaken ideas about how you ought to think and feel. Quietly listening to your inner voice reveals your own truths, insecurities, fears, hopes, and desires. By boldly facing your concerns, and joining knowledge with faith in your future, you can find strength to overcome challenges. If you're facing a time of romantic conflict, or mourning for love lost, look for ways to carry out self-healing to reduce stress and anxiety. Criticism and blame—toward your lover, your friends, or yourself—don't help anything, but they do interfere with finding happiness. Noticing when and how you're judging and blaming (which we often do almost automatically) is the first step toward letting go of doing so.

& EMOTIONAL INTERPRETATION:

Emotions need special attention. Discussing your concerns with an understanding friend can help you let go of your tears or fears. If you feel blue as a result of some downturn, then let yourself be blue. You might listen to someone sing the blues and get down and dirty in those feelings so you can go through them, rather than trying to push them away. If you're bogged down with problems, take a mini-vacation to a place where you feel soothed and renewed, with a friend or by yourself, even if just for a few hours or a few days. Ingenuity in working through a problem or jumping a romantic hurdle adds a new twist to future prospects. Everyone sometimes has to overcome problems. Despite upsets, be strong, for being stuck in negative thoughts prevents you from finding a rich, new world waiting for you. Whether your situation is bright or dark, come out of your thoughts to enjoy the flowers, sunshine, or whatever source of beauty you find around you.

& SEXUAL INTERPRETATION:

Sexual friction may be created by a lack of trust or breakdown of communications. Broken commitments or violated confidence can often best be handled by discussing them, either with the person involved or a trusted friend, rather than by pretending that they didn't happen. Words have the power to enhance, repair, or break the magic of love, so speak with

Key Meanings: Emotional struggle; a triangular affair; changes unfolding; uncertainty; absence of a commitment; seeing through love's deception

Reversed Meanings: Over-analysis and worry; wasted efforts; separation; violations of boundaries or trust; clinging to mistaken ideas or false hopes

THREE OF SWORDS

passion and awareness. Your physical desires need to be balanced with verbal foreplay and sensitivity to your partner. Can you be like a belly dancer who dances provocatively while balancing a sword on her head, and use your charm for the art of seduction? Build trust with a potential lover by spending time together doing things that he or she enjoys before making a move. A turned-on mind inspires a kaleidoscope of lovemaking possibilities.

❦ REVERSED CARD INTERPRETATION:
Overanalyzing hardship, lack of love or respect, or perhaps longing for love creates sadness. The dark side of love may need to be confronted. Being in denial or clinging to mistaken ideas about a relationship upsets emotions. Negative forces may drive the mind into despair. The pain of these piercing swords forces you to work through your grief so that you can emerge whole, and in time, let go of your pain and find a path to greater happiness.

THREE OF SWORDS

FOUR OF SWORDS

❦ ROMANTIC INTERPRETATION:

The Four of Swords can represent being dragged down by heavy moods, insecurities, or self-pity instead of doing what you need to improve your well-being. This is a time to meditate, not hibernate. Prepare a strategy for your success. Discuss interests with friends and share social times. You may need to trade in some seriousness for efforts to lighten up your life. Willingness to persevere through challenging communications paves the path for building better relations. Contemplation on romantic possibilities needs to be fortified with optimism. Your confidence is a prerequisite to finding or creating experiences that will lead you toward the fulfillment of your desires.

❦ EMOTIONAL INTERPRETATION:

Whether you're with or without a partner, liberate your mind from overanalyzing your situation and concerns about being loved or not. Think on the *I Ching's* comment that, "Everything comes of itself at the appointed time," and balance the sword of your intellect with trust in your emotional direction. Your present path has been built out of choices you previously made. If you're not happy, start examining and trying out different choices that can change your situation. Because this card is associated with deep contemplation, you may also need to balance your energy by being gregarious, open, and flirtatious. Thinking obsessively about your own emotional needs or those of your partner can cause you to miss out on the richness of the moment.

❦ SEXUAL INTERPRETATION:

Think before you give the green light to move forward at full speed to consummate your sexual interest. When your passions are fueled by temptation to go beyond your comfort zone, you may need to listen to common sense instead of getting lost in the intensity of lustful moments. This card indicates using your head and building a foundation of inner security and confidence so that when you decide to be sexual, the experience will be right. Talking can be part of the fun of foreplay. If this is not the right time to say yes to sex, then it might be right for developing friendship and learning to tune in to the truth of your feelings.

Key Meanings: Seriousness; seeking answers to a problem; not taking advantage of romantic opportunities; using contemplation to cut through difficulties

Reversed Meanings: Disturbance; condescending friends; sensing betrayal; need for solitude; taking someone for granted; impotence

FOUR OF SWORDS

- 193 -

❣ REVERSED CARD INTERPRETATION:

Emotions may be disrupted by family problems or love's uncertainty. It's a time to be careful not to let others upset your inner harmony or drain your energy with their problems. Draw on the wisdom of your own mind and heart for guidance and take some time off from worrying about love.

FOUR OF SWORDS

FIVE OF SWORDS

✧ ROMANTIC INTERPRETATION:

A romance may start to wane or change in unpredictable or uncontrollable ways. You may have to face an antagonistic person, deal with changes in your or another's needs and interests, or discuss complex intimate issues. Responsibility for resolution needs to be shared with friends or lovers. Communication blocks can be broken by saying you want to openly discuss your concerns. You may be attracted to someone who doesn't return your feelings, or lay be attracted but are fearful of taking the initiative to reveal your feelings—or vice versa. Or there may be mutual attraction in the context of a situation that makes proceeding further unwise. Whatever the circumstances, while you can't control the future, by taking responsibility for your actions, you just might make things better.

✧ EMOTIONAL INTERPRETATION:

Deceptive forces may present potential or real conflict. Problems in a relationship or lack of love can cause upset or fear. You may need to learn to express what you feel and want in a way that's clear, yet tactful and considerate. Resolving power or control issues in a humorous way may help you both step out of an attachment to "winning." By saying "I can't," you deny your ability to make change. Persevere, focus on your desires, and future fulfillment is likely. Instead of sitting around waiting for love, find something wonderful to do instead. You may discover pleasure treasures and people connections where you least expect to find them. If you look on the sunny side, the Five of Swords can point you toward fascinating experiences that embody both emotional and intellectual learning. You may develop a better ear for hearing what your body and intuition are telling you.

✧ SEXUAL INTERPRETATION:

Sooner or later, you or your partner are going to say what is important for you to say in the bedroom. Secrets may be exposed. Hurts or reluctance due to painful experiences may be revealed and healed with gentle acceptance. Communication is of paramount importance for getting through an impasse. If already-defensive emotional reactions are violated, blocks to physical lovemaking will intensify. Beware, however, of thinking in ways that make matters worse than they really are. It's better

Key Meanings: Expanding perceptions through confrontation; power struggles, competitive stress; unexpected upset; gossip; self-serving love;

Reversed Meanings: Facing aggression; the need to overcome conflict or mental blocks; harassment; bitter turn of an affair; judgmental attacks

to ask for what you want and say what you don't want than to feel violated because you didn't communicate and your needs or feelings weren't addressed. Similarly, communicate your receptiveness to tacit messages that the other person may be anxious about putting into words. This card indicates the importance of getting away from hassles and nurturing the spirit of caring, sensual love.

⚥ REVERSED CARD INTERPRETATION:

You could experience emotional distress, quarrels with a loved one, or betrayal. A clandestine love affair could be discovered, leaving the betrayed one feeling depressed. Good-natured flirting might be interpreted as sexual harassment. Conflicts come to a head, opening the door for changes in decision-making, and lessons in love abound. Combine thoughtfulness and intuition to resolve complex emotional issues.

FIVE OF SWORDS

SIX OF SWORDS

** ROMANTIC INTERPRETATION:**

The receptive mind opens to subconscious murmurings and the ability to communicate intuitively increases. Be careful, however, not to taint this communication with your projections. Unless you have evidence to the contrary, be willing to accept what another says about what's going on with them, for clear, explicit communication also helps improve nonverbal communication. Thoughts traveling through time and space unite lovers regardless of their distance apart. If you're not presently with a partner, your heart will magnetically attract a lover—or at least a good companion. Sharing romance, partners join in greater trust, and gain a better understanding of one another. A truce conveys good news.

** EMOTIONAL INTERPRETATION:**

This six can mean good decisions in love, inward or outward improvement, inspired hope, or greater clarity. Conditions are ripe for your emotions and ideas to influence each other in positive ways. It's time for you to set out on a physical, mental, or emotional journey of some kind that will take you to a depth of understanding that you've not previously experienced. With enhanced awareness, you'll leave behind you habitual or fruitless ways of reacting. Emotional upsets or quarrels will be settled with balanced reasoning or compromise. A partnership may be strengthened as two people work toward the same goal. Spirited talks with a friend who has similar interests brings a closer bond. Happy people attract good times and interesting experiences.

** SEXUAL INTERPRETATION**

Talking directly, acknowledging, and honoring your sexual desires gives you permission to enjoy the musings of Venus. Use of both your logic and your intuitive sensing gives you an edge in knowing the best choices to make to heighten and prolong sensual pleasures. Romantic antics bring happiness to the love-struck. Opening your mind to erotic love brings you to a new level of sexual playfulness, even if it doesn't go any further than your inclinations, or those of your lover, allow. Enjoy and appreciate whatever the moment brings. Sexual satisfaction is felt in the soul, not in multiple orgasms.

Key Meanings: Intuitive sensing balances logic; sensuality; meaningful connections; clarity; explaining yourself; beneficial change; coming out of the closet

Reversed Meanings: Interruptions; disturbing dreams; anxieties surface; grueling communications; unhealthy attitudes; patience required

SIX OF SWORDS

- 197 -

❧ REVERSED CARD INTERPRETATION:

An imbalance of emotional give-and-take tips the scales of love, causing tears, tensions, or conflict. Delays, interruptions, or other obstacles create challenges. A loose mouth that utters thoughtless words shatters harmony. Patience is needed to sort out problems, reach agreement, or allow a progression of events enough time to unfold.

SIX OF SWORDS

SEVEN OF SWORDS

VII

❧ ROMANTIC INTERPRETATION:

There may be an inner struggle or a confrontation with "the shadow" or demonic forces hiding beneath the surface of awareness. Troubles may seem overwhelming. However, using one of these seven swords wisely can cut through negative energy and empower the evolution of consciousness. Strength of the mind turns the wheel of life either forward or backward, up or down, depending on direction of the sword's thrust. You may want to invoke your guardian angel, spiritual guides, or trusted friends to help you overcome any unpleasantness you may be encountering. Hope and faith help you find surer footing as you climb the ladder of your dreams.

❧ EMOTIONAL INTERPRETATION:

While riding the roller coaster called romance, a spectrum of emotions is evoked. This card can mean heavy moods, frustrated dreams, and unrewarding experiences, so it's a warning to protect your vulnerability and fortify your efforts with your mental strength. Through your own challenging experiences, you become more sensitive to the effects others have on your emotions and the effects you have on theirs. Be willing to broaden your understanding of fate's design, and find value in the lessons your situation provides. Sometimes love is difficult, but don't be disheartened by the negative. Rainstorms can bring rainbows, and they're usually followed by sunnier skies.

❧ SEXUAL INTERPRETATION:

Forbidden fruit hangs from the vine, tempting you. Carl Jung, father of depth psychology, claims we each have a "shadow" consisting of those parts of ourselves that we do not recognize or allow expression, and that we need to integrate into our conscious selves. These swords may have the purpose of dueling with that force within you, which may be uncomfortable on one hand and a rich source of aliveness on the other. The trick is to channel it in ways that allow constructive rather than destructive self-expression. Don't expect easy answers. You may have some challenging work to do to figure out what's right for you. Repressed memories may surface from subconscious depths and influence your actions and reactions in the bedroom.

Key Meanings: Negative ideas or attitudes, weighted words, incorrect reasoning, hostility; challenging desires; canceling a date or engagement

Reversed Meanings: Quick exit after lovemaking; breaking contracts; being stood up; lies; seeking wise counsel; trying to correct mistakes

SEVEN OF SWORDS

- 199 -

❦ Reversed Card Interpretation:

An irresponsible person or a negative situation may upset your emotional balance. Misrepresentation of loving intent may inspire an unfortunate turn of events. On the other hand, coping with difficulty can cause you to seek wise counsel or counseling that has lasting value that you might never think about when everything goes smoothly. Focus on your core commitments and move toward success.

SEVEN OF SWORDS

EIGHT OF SWORDS

❧ ROMANTIC INTERPRETATION:

As a snake sheds its skin, so must you be willing to change and let go of useless beliefs that no longer suit your romantic reality. It's time to clean out your psychic closet and get rid of ideas that no longer suit the person whom you or your partner has become. Staying locked in rigid expectations about how previous commitments need to be fulfilled allows no room for growth and change. Feeling trapped can suck the life and joy right out of romance. Since intense communications may be difficult to avoid, focus on protecting your inner state of mind so that negative perceptions won't drain your energy. Channel your strength toward maintaining emotional balance, expanding your perspectives, and developing the perseverance to succeed. Opportunities for betterment may come with lightening speed, so be ready to move fast to fulfill your aspirations.

❧ EMOTIONAL INTERPRETATION:

Intense emotional experiences may be stormy or unpredictable. They may be a response to a difficult situation in which you feel imprisoned, and from which you can escape only with persistent effort. On the other hand, the difficulty may be a temporary one that will pass on its own. Holding on to a memory can block options for contentment in the present. Use your mind to develop mutual trust and focus on current possibilities, and be alert for the opportunities that often lie hidden in love's difficulties. Experiences may be rough, but the ultimate reality is what you make of it. Envision future success and think about what you can do now to move in your desired directions. Seek out friends for insight, support, and laughter. A surprise may change your mood.

❧ SEXUAL INTERPRETATION

The mind may create a defensive wall that limits physical pleasures or says "No!" to making love, even when circumstances for doing so are favorable. Insensitivity by one partner can trigger the other's fear and a whole-body response of tightening up that interferes with the pleasure and satisfaction of both. Being trapped in someone else's ideas about what's appropriate can cause feelings of distance and being out of contact. These swords point to the importance of not going against your feelings and convictions, of making peace with your insecurities or

Key Meanings: Being tied to unwanted commitments; feeling stuck, not finding resolution; challenges with a loved one; obstacles create delay; bad news

Reversed Meanings: Rejection; pessimism; self-pity; denial; guilt; inappropriate advances; impending bad consequence; need for love

fears, and of being sensitive to what's happening with your partner so you don't trigger his or her insecurities or fears. By facing anxieties, your sensual path is evolving toward greater opportunities for happiness. Do something fun to make your sex life a delight!

⚸ REVERSED CARD INTERPRETATION:

You may be feeling rejected, rejecting someone else, or feeling burdened by your commitments or past decisions. Holding on tightly to negative feelings or a negative situation blocks options for improvement. Notice how you hold yourself back and tie yourself up, and think about how you can do the opposite. Breathe deeply and let go of tensions that you're holding in your body. Invest time and mental energy in looking for inviting opportunities that you might otherwise miss while lost in negative rumination. Cheerful perceptions may bring new solutions to old problems. Seeing a good comedy brings healing laughter.

EIGHT OF SWORDS

NINE ⚍F SW⚍RDS

❧ Romantic Interpretation:

The winds of change blow life into annoying situations. Get ready to assert your needs, mentally grow to unfamiliar heights, and encourage your romantic nature to blossom with or without your parents' or best friends' approval. While your emotions may be tested by destiny's demands, being flexible will allow you to adjust to unpredictable situations, expand your consciousness, and open your mind and heart. Even if circumstances aren't ideal and distractions interrupt your plans, problems will be resolved in time. Negative patterns of thinking can cause you unnecessary grief or torment. If you're thinking about sweet revenge, look inward, tap into your inner beauty, and work on letting go. That will do more to set the mood for finding love. Surrender to allowing, accepting, and learning from the hand of fate.

❧ Emotional Interpretation:

An unexpected effect of emotional provocation may push you into new dimensions of clarity and personal understanding. Doing yoga, tai chi, or martial arts to develop inner balance can help you overcome fears associated with change and the unknown. Your mind holds the key to overcoming painful events and heartfelt difficulties. Concentration on your strength and your ideas for creating success brings relief from tension and stress caused by the blues. The card suggests that at this point, thinking carefully about your situation and how you are acting or reacting in it is more valuable than being absorbed in your feelings. Be alert to situations that trigger your emotional buttons and meet them with calmness, centeredness, forthrightness, and consideration.

❧ Sexual Interpretation:

Invitations to try out something new may heighten your sexual experience. You might be invited to try a *ménage à trois,* or to make love in an airplane and become a new member of the mile high club. Dominant and submissive roles may need to change. Uncertainties or anxieties need to be addressed before you leap into uncharted seas of sensual euphoria. Miscommunication, frustration, overanalyzing, or quarreling may get in the way of making love. On the other hand, sometimes when your mind is discontented, sex can become a pleasing distraction. If

Key Meanings: The importance of change; disappointments; self-condemnation; aggression; lust without fruition; revenge; black magic.

Reversed Meanings: Overcoming toxic emotions or disappointment; cynicism; perversion, obsession with sex; worry about STD's; hangovers

your partner wants a quickie, but you're not in the mood, you don't have to, unless you truly don't mind. Just make it clear that the reason has to do with your own state of mind and body.

❦ REVERSED CARD INTERPRETATION:

Misunderstandings, disappointments, cynicism, or worries may upset emotional equilibrium or even destroy a relationship. Quarreling puts distance between you and a loved one. Perhaps you can find a harmonious solution if you assess what each of you wants and search for a course of action that satisfies you both. When someone's self-esteem is threatened, even constructive suggestions may be perceived as judgmental criticism and evoke defensiveness. Even in difficult situations, find ways to be centered and productive. In time, obstacles will disappear and issues will be transformed.

NINE OF SWORDS

TEN OF SWORDS

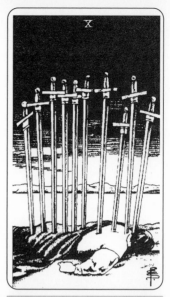

X

℘ ROMANTIC INTERPRETATION:

Out with the old, in with the new! Taking an alternative direction can transform stagnant or frustrating romantic habits. Focus your awareness on noticing how you're going through the same old motions or patterns, and be spontaneous in trying out or responding to new possibilities. Mentally stimulating conversations can bring about changes. Tasting failure can intensify appreciation of success and the desire to try different experiences. Paradoxically, haste or impatience may delay rather than help you find what you're hoping to discover. Instead of over-analyzing possibilities, use the tarot as a vehicle to explore different pathways that might be valuable to you. These ten swords represent the importance of trusting your mind power to make the best decisions concerning your future.

℘ EMOTIONAL INTERPRETATION:

Wisdom may be gained through pain suffered. You may be obsessed with fears or frustrations about the direction your emotions are heading. Let these ten swords cut through darkness so that you can see the light of love. The dawning light of a new day is visible in the eastern sky. Higher consciousness is attained by parting the veil of *Maya,* or life's illusions. Try not to put so much attention on your partner, or on not having a partner, on what other people will do or not do, or think or not think. Have faith that you'll do what's right for you and those around you when you need to do it. If you're willing to take a break from routine and take new steps to discover your own path, you'll find ways to make needed changes or improve the dynamics of your relationship(s). Get out of your head and get busy finding ways to have fun or do something of value for others whose problems are greater than yours.

℘ SEXUAL INTERPRETATION:

You may experience a sexual identity crisis or may be invited to join in something that is beyond your normal boundaries. Even if you give your wild and crazy side a chance to come out, don't do something that feels wrong to you in response to social pressures. You don't have to be kinky just because someone else wants you to. Make choices that are in accord with your sexual temperament. Stop running head trips, get out the grapes and feed the playful spirit. If the time is right, honor your lover with

Key Meanings: Stifling tides of emotion; being drained; drowning in fears; sorrow, remorse; the need to change lovers or go in a new direction

Reversed Meanings: Lack of love; seeking emotional support; mental anguish; liability; skepticism; coming to terms with deceit; obscenity

sweet embraces and warm caresses. When events turn into lovemaking, turn off your mind and turn on the passion. Sex can lighten the weight of holding heavy swords.

§ REVERSED CARD INTERPRETATION:

You may be at an impasse, caught between an urge to move forward into new ways of acting and fears that hold you back. What's actually happening now may require you to respond in new ways in order to break ties with counterproductive habits and bring about needed change. Focusing on deceit or liabilities intensifies their strength. Seek emotional support and don't let anxieties distract you from taking your next important step. Be alert to changes that can enhance your life.

TEN OF SWORDS

PAGE OF SWORDS

PAGE of SWORDS.

❧ ROMANTIC INTERPRETATION:

An immature or irresponsible person may link up with you romantically and affect your life, perhaps in an unexpected way. Usually bright, this person is keen at perceiving his or her intellectual goals, but is not necessarily smart in making romantic decisions. Understanding emotions does not come easily to this page, whose need to ask questions can seem endless, but for that very reason, it's an essential path of learning.

Alternatively, the card may refer to a particular side of yourself that has remained less developed, like the thinker who forgets his intuitive or emotional side. In that case, your own personal development is an important step in mastering the world of courtship and sensual consummation. Learning is the key, so don't be afraid to make mistakes or try new possibilities.

❧ EMOTIONAL INTERPRETATION:

Logic plays a strong role in making emotional decisions. Symbolic of a youthful spirit, this page is a warning not to expect adult behavior out of yourself or those around you (regardless of their ages) at all times. Let your mind help you to be present in, and learn from, your senses, feelings, and intuition as well as your reason. Put your thoughts into action to seek your fortune in love, for overanalyzing possibilities won't answer questions about your direction. In due time, the answers will become clear through experiencing destiny's decree. Look for ways to be helpful to those around you, because learning how to perceive and meet others' emotional needs is a central lesson on the page's path toward love. At the same time, be alert for ways you can learn from others who are more knowledgeable in matters important to you. There is always something more to learn.

❧ SEXUAL INTERPRETATION:

Is it hot enough for you? Your mind may sizzle with the heat of desire and your body may be tingling with the anticipation of consummation. Nonetheless, the page may face a period of waiting and further personal development before sexual opportunities arise. However, if you do have an opportunity for intimacy, you'll need to find ways to ask for what you want, to communicate your limits, to listen to what the other person wants, or even to be helpful to your partner in matters that have

Key Meanings: A versatile young person, with strong beliefs, seeking his or her direction; focused thought; inspiration; testing ideas; new openings

Reversed Meanings: An intolerant or hypocritical person; foolish beliefs; self-righteousness; avoiding emotion; sexual frustration or exploitation

nothing at all to do with sex. Open-mindedness and a willing-ness to learn and serve are this page's hallmarks.

§ REVERSED CARD INTERPRETATION:

Emotional energy may be directed with too much intensity. Playful romantic communications may be misleading and intentions exaggerated when love or passion is aroused. Someone may be a tease and not come through, or suggest commitment where none exists in order to get between the sheets with you. Dogmatic commitment to borrowed beliefs or self-righteous positions may crowd out open-mindedness at the moment when it's needed most.

PAGE OF SWORDS

KNIGHT OF SWORDS

KNIGHT of SWORDS.

❧ ROMANTIC INTERPRETATION:

Get out of the slow lane! This energetic knight charges forth using the mind to overcome romantic dilemmas, and intellectual or competitive swordplay. Contemplation increases awareness and mental strength dominates. There's a good chance that you'll either be meeting a romantic who likes to travel, examine ideas, and go beyond normal limits, or you'll be assuming a knightlike stance and going after the bounty of emotional crusades. The next steps you need to take for successful endeavors will soon become clear. Sometimes this knight represents taking an unconventional path to find romantic fulfillment and sensory pleasure. You may want to explore friendship possibilities and expand your normal social boundaries.

❧ EMOTIONAL INTERPRETATION:

Emotions duel with the sword of logic to pursue inner truth and peace of mind. Decisions may be wrong for the right reasons or right for the wrong reasons. Being in too much of a hurry to find answers to love's dilemmas may keep you from listening to your own intuitive wisdom, or cause you to overlook opportunities as you charge forward. Slow your fast pace to make time to know your heart's reality so that you can be certain of the choices you need to make. The path to your highest good and to finding resolutions to your conflicts are in the crystal ball of self-knowledge. This knight is on a crusade for soul inspiration and is pursuing a path of fortune that cannot be measured by the success or failure of dating or mating rituals.

❧ SEXUAL INTERPRETATION:

The mind is in motion, searching for sexual stimulation and playful hot spots. Passion is turned up high by an active imagination. Once aroused, the knight who has a tendency to charge forth and dominate situations is hard to turn off. Confidence increases by adopting a positive attitude and being willing to explore the treasures of sacred sexuality. You can make choices that turn your erotic notions into potent opportunities to pursue pleasure and make the right love connections. Enjoyment is doubled when you remember that the other person's pleasure and satisfaction are as important as your own. Because knights are not always good at making long-term commitments, enjoy what the

Key Meanings: An intellectual person who is assertive in the world of romance; your power to analyze emotions or conquer love; liberation from dogmatism

Reversed Meanings: A cunning person who may step on others; over-analyzing emotions to the point of dysfunction; incompetence; dogmatism

moment holds without expecting it to endure, although only destiny knows for certain what tomorrow will bring.

ɤ REVERSED CARD INTERPRETATION:
Overanalyzing change or the inevitable future may keep you stuck in your head where turmoil or restlessness keeps you from advancing toward emotional or sexual happiness. Also, this reversed knight can symbolize a competitive or insensitive person who will stop at nothing to succeed. Although often lost in ambitions and out of touch with much of his or her emotional world, if this person likes you, he or she will gladly agree to being your sex slave.

KNIGHT OF SWORDS

QUEEN OF SWORDS

QUEEN OF SWORDS.

❦ ROMANTIC INTERPRETATION:

Powerful and vigilant, this queen dominates the realm of the element air as she exerts her influence in the world of ideas, mental inspiration, and logical understanding. She may represent a mature-minded woman in your life, a lofty thinker who uses her wits to ensure love, laughter, and success in her endeavors. She is at home with both life's simple pleasures and its complicated challenges, but don't mistake her good nature for vulnerability, for she can also be shrewd, calculating, or, when angry, even vengeful. This card can also signify your own inner feminine nature centered in intellectual strength as you radiate personal power, self-control, and far-reaching intellectual curiosity. Goals can be reached.

❦ EMOTIONAL INTERPRETATION:

Emotions and intellect equally balanced resolve dilemmas. Being confident allows inspiration to take the lead in healing painful memories and opening the doorway of trust. Recognize that you have the knowledge and capacity for direct awareness to make the right choices and achieve success in your personal relationships. You may meet or be attracted to an intelligent woman who offers you counsel or helps you understand yourself. Usually she carefully thinks through her emotions before she expresses them. This queen's sword of justice cuts through the chaos of the mind to liberate truth and illuminate the path of wisdom. With luck, her lessons, learned through the joys and wounds of love, have made her perceptive and evenhanded. Without luck, painful experiences may make her closed and mistrustful, so that she detaches from emotions and stops seeking romantic involvement.

❦ SEXUAL INTERPRETATION:

This card represents a woman who has had enough sexual relations to know what she likes and doesn't like in bed. Often preoccupied with ideas, she loves playful meetings in the hot tub or shower where she can relax her mind and enjoy her body. Because she demands more than a physical connection, in most cases she will not commit to having sex for the sake of temporary gratification. She seeks a lover who can offer the potential for a deep emotional bond before she allows her spirited seductive nature to come unleashed. If you're lucky enough to

Key Meanings: A powerful, intelligent woman who is perceptive, reflective, direct, and willful; using your mental power effectively

Reversed Meanings: A woman who is cunning, calculating, or antagonistic; frigidity; indecisiveness; needing to compromise or rethink ideas

become her playmate, her tongue is incomparable as a vehicle of sultry, aphrodisiac delight.

§ REVERSED CARD INTERPRETATION:

This reversed queen represents a nagging, prudish, or overly analytical woman who feels compelled to be in control and dominate situations. Often she has had a difficult time with some of life's challenging lessons. If betrayed, she can be a fierce opponent who is deceitful or vague about what's going on in her mind. Alternatively, this card can represent your own irrational fears, jealousy, or other sources of emotional imbalance whirling through your mind and polluting your romantic vista.

QUEEN OF SWORDS

KING OF SWORDS

KING of SWORDS.

& ROMANTIC INTERPRETATION:

Symbolic of the element air, this king represents an intelligent man who is adept at logical analysis but sometimes clumsy when expressing emotions. Bearing the sword of keen perception, he can see into the truth of your spirit, and when turned-on, he can touch you deeply with heart-stealing words. As a leader, he is charming and suave, but he can be a powerful verbal opponent if you challenge his beliefs or actions. Because he's a thinker, he doesn't like being told what to do. Also, this card can represent your own assertive, mental strength at the ready like a sharpened blade, able to strike and take control. Decisions are made. Sharing ideas brings recognition or improved relations.

& EMOTIONAL INTERPRETATION:

This king represents a mentally alluring man who enjoys confident, strong women. His ingenuity sets him apart, often as an individualist or free thinker. He can be flirtatious and play the field, but is willing to make a commitment when the emotional chemistry is right. A strong-willed decision-maker, he loves intensely and may try to dominate his partner. A leader in the world of ideas, this king rules with the piercing and swift sword of justice and honors fairness and loyalty in the dominion of love. If this card does not represent a powerful masculine influence in your life, it can indicate using your own mind to correctly analyze the demands of a romantic involvement and its probable, logical progression or outcome.

& SEXUAL INTERPRETATION:

Sex may be hard to resist when this regal man tempts you with passionate words that get you on his wavelength and push your thermostat up high. In the bedroom, he likes to let go of his leadership qualities and let his lover take the dominant role or top position. Lovemaking is a realm of pleasure where he can be playful and forget his responsibilities for a time. Bondage games allow him to let his hair down and become subservient to his partner's amorous needs. He can get kinky at times, for he has a large sexual appetite and thrives on excitement in bed, especially when oral sex is involved.

Key Meanings: An intelligent man who is confident in leadership roles; virility; optimal execution of ideas; effective mediation; piercing insight

Reversed Meanings: An overlyanalytical, controlling, or socially inept man; inaccurate perceptions; detaching from love; or lack of libido

8 Reversed Card Interpretation:

A bossy, or overlyanalytical man may try to control your situation, your life, or your perceptions. When reversed, intelligence becomes ignorance in this card that can represent someone who is unhappily divorced, socially inept, or lacking in emotional maturity or sexual savvy. Or the card may refer to struggles with decision-making, lack of emotional understanding, distancing yourself from love, or deception and the problems that go with it.

KING OF SWORDS

Pentacles: The Material Plane

*All love is capable of energizing wishes into reality, but love
between two people whose personal auras have thus harmoniously blended creates the kind of vibration poets write
about, and can manifest marvelous magic.*
—LINDA GOODMAN, *LOVE SIGNS*

Pentacles invoke all the archetypes that are connected with the
earth and the material world. They refer to practical work, prosperity, house and home, and a playful zest for life. They also remind
us of the dangers of getting caught up in materialism, and drama-
tize how all these dimensions are intertwined with our relationships. Now, on to the cards.

ACE OF PENTACLES

Key Meanings: Seeds of material desires are planted with love's interest; sex appeal; dating someone new; financial gain; creative expression

Reversed Meanings: Not being grounded; a disagreeable date; lack of fun; being overly conscious of your weight or physical appearance

ACE OF PENTACLES

ACE OF PENTACLES

❧ ROMANTIC INTERPRETATION:

This pentacle represents the essence of the power of the element earth and the tangible foundation of new beginnings on the material plane. Sparks from close contact set the stage for a lover's rendezvous, while soulful discussions intensify feelings. A tender touch may lead to intimacy. Your zest for life is your winning ticket to advancing toward greater self-expression and confidence in both romantic and worldly pursuits. Love of animals, children, and Mother Nature brings happiness and new friends. Be open to expressing your romantic dreams and your unique form of physical vitality, for the future offers rewards for your efforts.

❧ EMOTIONAL INTERPRETATION:

This card is auspicious for beginning a new adventure, courtship, or enterprise. Opportunities for success increase as you plant the seeds of good fortune with down-to-earth determination and effort. Concerns about money or material needs may affect a relationship or the direction in which it moves. The time is not yet ripe for answers to some emotional questions. Doing nothing is sometimes the best thing to do until it becomes obvious what steps need to be taken to create greater possibilities of fulfillment. Something of value may appear from an unexpected source. A lover from your past may cross your path, and trigger old emotions.

❧ SEXUAL INTERPRETATION:

New ideas and impulses emerge, creating a cornucopia of potential erotic delights, as passion's force erupts like a sexual volcano. The sun shines on the moment, as the vibrational chemistry of mutual sex appeal spreads through the door of doubt and inspires hope for intimacy. Touching, affection, titillation, and erection go hand in hand with the forces of nature. Making love in a secluded spot in a field or forest may be an event remembered for a lifetime. Be conscious of using (or not using) birth control, as this ace represents the fertile soil of love where children may be conceived. Decisions are made concerning the direction the dating game is going, as you and your partner ground love's ideals in the world of reality. Dancing together or doing couples yoga adds spice to your lovemaking.

Physical compatibility lays a foundation for building a secure love nest.

❦ REVERSED CARD INTERPRETATION:

Not being emotionally grounded causes upset. There may be problems in the early stages of dating or courtship. A shaky start to a relationship creates waves of anxiety about what the future will bring. Being self-absorbed or obsessed with physical appearances gets in the way of having fun.

ACE OF PENTACLES

Key Meanings: Juggling opportunities, finances, or direction; seeking the best opportunity, becoming wiser or more worldly, receiving material gifts.

Reversed Meanings: Lack of finances; uncertainty; the need to balance romance and career directions; wrong choices; trust issues; lewd conduct

TWO OF PENTACLES

TWO OF PENTACLES

& ROMANTIC INTERPRETATION:

Becoming more aware of your childhood conditioning and habitual responses gives your heart freedom to follow its own truth. Don't let others' expectations distort your reality. You may connect with someone who seems externally your opposite— or at least very different from you—but who, on an inner level, suits you well. Today's situation highlights choices you need to make to create tomorrow's successes. You may have to choose between two lovers, between staying in or ending a relationship, or between changing or not changing some other aspect of your life. Listen to and talk about your feelings rather than ignoring them, in order to make decisions that will suit your nature and move you forward on your path. In a new relationship, take things one step at a time, and don't expect all your hopes to be met right at the start. Time may be required to discover who another person really is, or how you can work together well.

& EMOTIONAL INTERPRETATION:

Maintaining mutually nourishing relationships takes work. Be down-to-earth and honest with yourself about your feelings and inclinations. You can't hide your truth from yourself. Its message is your path to happiness. Involvement in enjoyable activities or career interests can open up the possibility of sharing them with others. Be willing to give and receive the kinds of friendship or love that the moment and circumstances offer. Thoughtful and careful efforts are needed to give newly planted seeds of intimacy a start toward their maturity. It will take time to see what fruits ripen from the vine of your endeavors. This card can also suggest an incipient struggle between the desire for emotional or sexual fulfillment and having worldly success, or conflict about how to balance family and career responsibilities.

& SEXUAL INTERPRETATION:

Do you say yes or no to physical involvement? You may feel ambivalent about love or having sex, and question what direction is best for you. Pretending that either your inclinations or reservations don't matter can break the cookie jar of sensual pleasure. Be sensitive to your personal issues so you can be clear about your preferences. Rejoicing in your sexuality gives you a connection with the strength of your spirit to do or say what your body thinks is right for you, but once you've accepted an invitation to play, the heat of the moment may take precedence over rational decision-making. If your head and heart need to have a dialogue, a conversation with a wise and trusted friend or friends may help you achieve clarity. On the other hand, this deuce may point to an unhesitating and unequivocal yes to coupling, and if so, enjoy!

𝔤 Reversed Card Interpretation:

Indecision or anxiety due to trust issues, past wounds, or relationship problems may get in the way of emotional confidence. Love may get lost in places where you're rigid, or stuck. Small first steps in trustworthiness and trusting by both you and whoever else is involved can lead to larger steps and greater confidence. If love is violated or not reciprocated, you'll need to make some kind of a change, either inwardly or in your actions.

THREE OF PENTACLES

Key Meanings: Establishing deeper connections with people; growth; making romantic or artistic dreams tangible; gaining material possessions

Reversed Meanings: Limited resources; withdrawing emotions; financial restrictions; sexual stereotyping; not developing your talents

  ℬ ROMANTIC INTERPRETATION:

This three points toward fulfillment of your desires in the material world. Finding what you want in love can emerge from the process of living with passion and listening to heartfelt preferences. Someone you're attracted to may reach out to you, or you may have to make the first move. Set your mind to fully exploring the possibilities in your current situation and make the very best of them. Responding to your partner's financial concerns helps your relationship develop a secure foundation. Tilling the fertile soil of your mind with prosperous thoughts inspires your growth and success. Seeds of desires planted in the past may yet bear fruit, such as a relationship growing in depth and richness. An investment or other money-making opportunity may come into your life. (If so, examine it with great care and be wary of "hot tips" from questionable sources. Check on the references and connections of those who offer the opportunities.)

  ℬ EMOTIONAL INTERPRETATION:

Saying yes to occasions and opportunities for meeting people deepens your emotional awareness. Socialize, exchange feelings, and step into interesting activities to heighten your social skills, confidence, and chances for improving connections with friends, family, or lovers. Continue to develop skills involved in worldly or creative pursuits, for they may become the basis for enriching your present relationship or finding a new one, or become deeply rewarding in their own right. Money may be the deciding factor in moving in with your lover, getting married, having a child, or continuing your education. Romance may combine with a business or creative adventure, especially if you and your husband, wife, or lover try working together.

  ℬ SEXUAL INTERPRETATION:

Think about what you want in the sexual arena. This card is auspicious for lovemaking, the expansion of passion in your life, and for having experiences that make your physical senses blossom. Sharing your sexual feelings in an amicable way and listening to those of your lover can help your relations grow in depth, richness, and commitment. Exchanging emotional energy opens the sensual gates of earthly paradise where you may find unexpected rewards or even an opportunity for a *ménage-à-trois,* if that sort of thing appeals to you. Making love in unusual places, such as on a billiard table, kitchen counter, in a telephone booth, or someone else's bedroom, can intensify excitement. Physical compatibility lays a foundation for building a secure love nest.

✌ Reversed Card Interpretation:

In its reversed aspect, this pentacle signifies being restricted by external circumstances that may be hard to control. You may suffer from the shock of finding that someone has lied for the purpose of having sex with you or to take advantage of you financially. Use setbacks to sharpen your awareness and grow in wisdom, and look for a way to turn adversity to your present or future advantage. When a problem runs deep, find a real solution instead of settling for an inadequate quick fix. In time, you'll master the challenges that are facing you.

THREE OF PENTACLES

IV

FOUR OF PENTACLES

FOUR OF PENTACLES

Key Meanings: Building strong foundations; security; trust; realizing goals; putting your heart in your work; love's aspirations; initiating sexual play

Reversed Meanings: Being unrealistic; insecurity; losing yourself in a relationship; emotional distraction from financial goals; procrastination

❧ ROMANTIC INTERPRETATION:

Strong desires for love create increased circulation in your social world and opportunities for being with friends, having fun, and initiating romance. On the other hand, building a solid foundation at hearth and home stabilizes roots of inner security and provides a basis for meaningful relations. Whatever your situation, steady and predictable events are likely to alternate with sudden and unexpected ones. Keeping centered in what you know is right for you unearths richness of inner spirit that appears outwardly as romantic or career potential. Determination and persistence bring you closer to completing your goals or starting consequential undertakings that can endure through the years. Times of silence shared with friends amid Mother Nature increase inner peace and reduce anxieties about the future.

❧ EMOTIONAL INTERPRETATION:

Love of home, family, and physical security inspires making a responsible choice for your emotional direction. Your efforts to balance dreams of the perfect relationship with reality are tested by situations that will make you laugh and cry, curse and pray. Commitments need to be discussed openly (not assumed) so that you know what they are and are not. Creating the emotional security you desire comes from within yourself, not from listening to words from another, although tender assurance usually brings comfort. To break the chains of the past and live consciously in the present, respond flexibly and spontaneously to emotional situations that arise. Being solidly in tune with what feels right for you and watering aspirations with practical efforts will bear fruit in times to come.

❧ SEXUAL INTERPRETATION:

Gaining clarity about your compatibility with a partner before expressing yourself sexually reduces anger or regrets. Focus on the present and honor your true sexual inclinations, within the context of what's possible, appropriate, and considerate. Flirtatiousness can be an exciting prelude to foreplay. What's important to you in the bedroom will emerge when the time and mood are right. Candlelight, massage, and incense can help create an enchanting atmosphere (unless one of you is allergic to incense). Be willing to relax your expectations about the other's behavior in the bedroom as you distinguish between limits that are truly important to you and those that are merely habitual, and take responsibility for helping your sexual fantasies become playful reality.

❦ REVERSED CARD INTERPRETATION:

Being unrealistic or in denial about your personal situation generates confusion. Be honest about what makes or doesn't make you feel secure within yourself and give yourself time before jumping to conclusions about the direction your involvements are going. Notice when you're worrying, and then involve yourself in an engaging, present activity that gives you something better to think about. Reversed, this card can also be a warning against being obsessed with a partner's financial situation or so concerned about money, material matters, or appearances that you miss out on the joy life can offer.

FOUR OF PENTACLES

Key Meanings: Rethinking worldly values or responsibility; money or power issues; unwise investing; excessive dependence; compromise; modesty

Reversed Meanings: Sexual blocks; coldhearted relations; draining communications; distance from a loved one; lack of family support

FIVE OF PENTACLES

§ ROMANTIC INTERPRETATION:

Five pentacles point to the importance of not letting money or power issues distract you from enjoying the richness in your life. Compromise may be your passage to harmonious agreements. Stress can rise and effective communication decline unless you do more than usual to keep conversations open, clear, and loving. Be willing to hear the other's deep feelings and to take off your mask and share your own, being careful to do so in a way that will not cause the other person to feel negatively judged. Rethinking your worldly needs or your anxiety about future possibilities may cause you to plant seeds of change. Taking concrete steps to sharpen your listening skills and improve your ability to hear what others want and feel will help you succeed in life and love. If you have no partner, broaden your circle of friends and activities, or try a dating service.

§ EMOTIONAL INTERPRETATION:

This five represents a point on your journey: neither a beginning nor an end, but a place where work must be done to harmonize emotions. Balancing your ability to think logically with your direct awareness of what's happening in and around you and your ability to sense intuitively is an important key to meeting your challenges successfully. Work on listening to your body's messages about how you're reacting, including your heart rate, breathing, and muscle tension. Too much focus on problems drains emotional energy, depletes resources, narrows your horizons, and blocks the emergence of sensitive, heartfelt expression. Comments may be heard differently than the speaker intended, so be willing to ask for clarification or provide it by saying something like, "I think you're saying . . . Is that right?" or, "I guess I was unclear there. What I intended to say is . . . " or even, "That's what I meant, but if it affects you that way, I'm willing to change my mind. Let's work together to find a course of action we can both agree on." Exchange massages as a means to reduce stress and get away from the blahs. Emotional renewal that brings together mind, body, spirit, and improved relations is within your reach.

§ SEXUAL INTERPRETATION:

Passion for life is your ticket for adventure and sexual fulfillment. Listen to your intuition: Are you "turned-on" or "turned-off?" Do you have sexual stress, feel coldhearted, or desire change? Be true to your feelings and act accordingly. If your partner is not satisfying you, don't complain! Instead, do something to improve your situation. If you're struggling too much, you and your partner might take a weekend workshop, or talk with a professional sex therapist about improving the quality of your sex life. Be alert to when conditioned negative associations from the past are getting in the way of making contact or enjoying yourself now. If yesterday's unfinished business is interfering with being comfortable with your present partner, draw your attention into being fully present in this moment, and work through old hang-ups in counseling or conversation with a trusted friend.

8 REVERSED CARD INTERPRETATION:

Reversed, this card highlights the importance of learning communication skills that will put love matters in order and empower you to have enriching intimate experiences. An affair may trigger jealousy, distance, or separation. Lack of good judgment may cause worry about consequences. Family members may not be supportive of you or have expectations opposite your needs. Time helps heal emotional wounds and solve the riddles of conflicting romantic experiences.

SIX OF PENTACLES

❧ ROMANTIC INTERPRETATION:

This six is linked with the richness of love and the raw power of the element earth to manifest the dual qualities of human nature—giving and receiving, crying and laughing, loving and resenting. Take steps to align fantasy with actuality and work to enrich your life. You may unexpectedly meet an interesting and uplifting person. When you seek romantic perfection, don't forget that people snore, fart, and have bad breath when they wake up in the morning. (*C'est la vie!*) If your partner seems less than perfect, remember that almost all people show their best side in early encounters, and once you get to know them well, you see their imperfections, too. A realistic approach to love increases your ability to get close to others. When paradox is present, listen to your gut instincts. Your sensitivity is your Geiger counter for recognizing truth. With many paradoxes, we have a choice between becoming indignant or finding humor in an all-too-human situation. Look on the light side when you can!

❧ EMOTIONAL INTERPRETATION:

Emotions may swing back and forth like a pendulum, but self-knowledge and inner strength evolve as you think through your experiences and gain a broader view of your situation. Letting go of old wounds, or masks of self-deception, can open doors to appreciation of your deeper self. Money or other material matters may be affected by emotional decisions or by relations with family or loved ones. You may need to come to some kind of resolution regarding your financial world to help strengthen your sense of your life's direction. Finding a path that allows you to feel secure in the world helps you attune your emotional efforts to bring about both your well-being and the highest good. Likewise, by helping others find ways to meet their financial and material needs, your life becomes enriched. Flowers or gifts of love solidify bonds of appreciation.

❧ SEXUAL INTERPRETATION:

Look intently into the eyes of someone you love or admire. You'll know whether feelings are hot or cold, or right or not, for getting physically close. If you feel caught between yes and no, be patient until your indecisiveness fades. By contrast, if things feel right, this card is auspicious for a positive, mutual flow of harmonious energy and for stimulating excitement of

Key Meanings: Positive turn of events; meaningful encounters; balancing income with spending; financial progress or decisions; sensuality

Reversed Meanings: Progress delayed; dreams don't match reality; sexual frustration; emotional neediness; greed; selfishness; health issues

the senses. Obstacles can be removed and intimate connections encouraged. Gentle touching or massage can awaken passionate energy. If you're not skilled in massage, a weekend workshop will give you skills you can use to help your partner or friends let go of stress and feel better. The anima, female-lunar energy, finds its complement, or balance, in the animus, male-solar energy and two souls merge into one.

Reversed Card Interpretation:

Greed may inhibit sensitivity to others' problems and stifle emotional awareness. Expectations may not be met or dreams may be unfulfilled. Feelings may be stuffed or buried rather than resolved, leading to anger and poisonous resentment. Disappointment may create frustration or self-pity. Remember, though, that if nobody ever felt lonely or down, we wouldn't have rhythm and blues (or rock-n-roll, for that matter)! Groan and moan, do whatever you need to do to express your disappointment or sorrow, and then, once you've done that, get busy using your energy constructively to create a brighter tomorrow.

SIX OF PENTACLES

- 227 -

VII

SEVEN OF PENTACLES

Key Meanings: Financial issues affect emotions; lending money; security through marriage; questioning material goals; creativity in lovemaking

Reversed Meanings: Money issues negatively affect romance; facades of affection; double standards; empty promises; love without security; exhaustion or depleted energy

☙ ROMANTIC INTERPRETATION:

"Show me that you care" are words connected with this card, so don't forget the flowers, and/or perhaps a gift for no reason other than to show you care. Financial realities are evaluated in relation to long-term goals. You might be putting your energy into saving money for a house, car, vacation, or some other tangible interest. Relationship concerns may be placed on the back burner as money quests become paramount and ambitions are focused on survival or worldly success. If so, don't leave love behind and expect it to sit there patiently waiting for you. The mind can only spend so much time worrying about money before the desire for the love surfaces to claim your attention. And vice versa: You may reconnect with an old friend or lover who just might ask for a loan.

☙ EMOTIONAL INTERPRETATION:

In a relationship, you may need to adjust to your partner's timetable in order to spend more quality time together. Sharing similar financial goals helps bring compatibility and security into focus. You may want to prioritize earthly desires and question which ones you truly need to fulfill for yourself, and which, if any, you expect others to fulfill for you. If you're looking for a partner, inner confidence and a willingness to smile gives hope to finding opportunities for meeting someone. Choose gathering places or activities where there's a good chance you'll meet someone who shares similar interests. Giving affection through words, body language, or a casual touch clears away the impression of being distant or emotionally unavailable. Take the initiative to create more of what you want in your romantic world.

☙ SEXUAL INTERPRETATION:

Listen to the language your physical body silently speaks. Are you tense, relaxed, or excited? Tuning in to such responses gives you a closer look at your true thoughts and feelings that underlie your surface ideas about what you "should" think and feel, and can clarify what you do or don't want from a given relationship. Your physical response to lovemaking makes a statement about your compatibility in which it's not easy to conceal your deep feelings. If your hearts touch deeply as you laugh and play, you don't need satin sheets for a great roll in the hay.

Sensual caressing calms fears and evokes trust. Sex without sensitivity can be fun for a while, but your lover may soon go looking for greener pastures. The results of your financial decisions register in your romantic lifestyle. Living in the "fast lane," for example, can drain emotional energy or lead to mistaking casual sex for courtship.

☙ REVERSED CARD INTERPRETATION:

Double standards or fear of infidelity creates friction. Repulsion dances with attraction to create ambivalence and confusion about how much to offer, or how to receive another's offerings. Love may be lost or sabotaged—by you or another's empty promises, or by overly suspicious responses to real offerings of the heart. You may be at an impasse or have challenges to overcome in achieving inner or outer security. Financial dilemmas can negatively affect romance.

SEVEN OF PENTACLES

- 229 -

Key Meanings: Financial or creative interests blossom; efforts bear fruit; efficiency; wise choices; practical efforts enhance romantic possibilities

Reversed Meanings: Financial complications; hoarding instincts; being out of touch with feelings; recklessness; wasted time or energy

EIGHT OF PENTACLES

EIGHT OF PENTACLES

৪ ROMANTIC INTERPRETATION:

Career goals and financial aspirations may be higher on your list of priorities than romance, or you may be in a situation where worldly enterprise takes your mind off romantic concerns. Deadlines or other work demands can be a distraction from passion's interest. Even if your focus is love, moneymaking concerns or business responsibilities will need your time and attention. The challenge is to free your mind from mundane duties enough so you can enjoy yourself and create more time for pleasure. One remedy for too many worldly concerns is to treat every day as Valentine's Day. If you do, you'll make people feel special, and are likely to improve romance or find it more readily.

৪ EMOTIONAL INTERPRETATION:

Developing your artistic talents, creativity, or service-based efforts for community or environmental concerns can connect you with a new group of friends. Communicating your visions brings feedback that may help you solidify your ideas and get more in touch with what you can do to make your interests blossom. Meaningful work or an exciting future opportunity inspires high energy and motivation, while lending a helping hand to others who are just learning to do what you already do well can bring deep satisfaction. Go with your heart and let playful energy dance the salsa with your inner spirit. Make a date to do something exciting. If money is an issue, remember that a walk in the park is free.

৪ SEXUAL INTERPRETATION:

Allow yourself to make love like a tantric lover, slowly, carefully, and sacredly. Sexual attraction triggers lustful feelings that may be enticing, but you need to ground your energy in tangible understanding of how to savor the fruit of your desires. For love to be real, the armor of mistrust may need to be removed before ecstasy and communion can be experienced. You may wish to take steps to deepen your contact with others. Aphrodisiacs, pheromones, mood-enhancing drugs, or alcohol may be used to open the permissive door to pleasure if you're into them, but be careful and don't partake beyond the point where you lose your sensitivity and the sharp edge of your awareness. Celebrate the splendor of your physical nature by making lazy love in the warm light of a sunny afternoon.

8 REVERSED CARD INTERPRETATION:

Unpleasant aspects of materialism may drain energy and get in the way of love. Beware of letting money concerns become obstacles that block romantic possibilities. You may struggle with a tendency to spend too much time searching for material possessions instead of making time to find love. Distractions from emotional needs make romance harder to find, rather than easier. Look for the means to get where you want to go. "Where there's a will, there's a way" is an important cliché for healing the worries associated with this reversed card.

EIGHT OF PENTACLES

IX

NINE OF PENTACLES

NINE OF PENTACLES

Key Meanings: Changing careers; financial gains; harvesting fruits of your efforts; tangible evidence of success; passionate physical connections

Reversed Meanings: Detachment; hurtful accusations; projects terminated; money or status attracts romance; need for grounding

✌ ROMANTIC INTERPRETATION:

Walking the path of the romantic opens the heart. These pentacles represent the zest for life that helps you overcome obstacles and find what you need to pursue happiness and make a relationship or a commitment a reality. Staying at home reading a love story won't help you find a companion, but taking action to find romantic fulfillment just might. If events on the material plane go well, as they're likely to, don't try to impress your lover with money, a fancy wardrobe, or expensive doodads. Your mate or playmate needs to connect as much with your inner spirit as with outer appearances if the real you is to be discovered. Listen for the inner theme and needs of the person you're with, and find meaningful ways to connect. You might profit from spending some time on creative projects with your friends or lover or brainstorming about future possibilities.

✌ EMOTIONAL INTERPRETATION:

Open your eyes to the physical world around you! Recreational activities, a workout in a gym, or walks in a pleasant outdoor setting can lift your mood and ground volatile emotions. A deep and profound experience may occur that influences your choices. Jealousy or hanging on to the blues needs to be replaced with hope and concrete action to strengthen your spirit. Taking a personal growth class or retreat can inspire valuable insights about your relationships or moneymaking interests. Speaking or acting from your heart, in an alert, considerate way that expresses your feelings without coming on too strong is likely to help you to bring the best out of your situation. It's time for tangible accomplishments and for harvesting the fruits of past efforts.

✌ SEXUAL INTERPRETATION:

You may need to experiment with different lovemaking positions and approaches to stimulate more satisfying experiences. Not just thinking about possibilities, but acting adventurously with sensitivity will help you find sexual fulfillment. Because these pentacles are linked with tactile, perceptible, touchy-feely situations, this card suggests that communication through your sense of touch can move lovemaking to another dimension of enjoyment. Licking sensitive spots with the tongue entices rapture to flow from passion's vine. Expect consequences from your libido's decisions. Perhaps your physical connection will lead to a commitment such as moving in with your partner, or deciding to have a child.

❧ REVERSED CARD INTERPRETATION:

A roller-coaster relationship may come to a standstill. Practical solutions need to be found to resolve love's dilemmas, even if it involves confrontation. Being nagging or judgmental about your partner's qualities causes arguments. A confrontational or critical comment is likely to be much better received if it is both preceded and followed by praise and appreciation, and expressed with recognition that with most problems in a relationship, in some way both partners are 50 percent responsible. Also, repetitive recitation of accomplishments, or egotistical displays of money, power, or status, can reduce the chances of truly contacting others and touching their hearts.

NINE OF PENTACLES

X

Key Meanings: New beginnings or completion; using resources wisely; effective goal planning; first dates; marriage proposals; steps toward emotional trust; arousal

Reversed Meanings: Obsession with money; remorse; not enough reciprocity; a square peg trying to fit a round hole; voyeurism

TEN OF PENTACLES

TEN OF PENTACLES

❧ ROMANTIC INTERPRETATION:

This is a card of completions, endings, and new beginnings. A catalytic experience may bring you face-to-face with a need for change or making new plans. You may finish a task, come to terms with the need for completing one, initiate a different direction, or begin a new cycle of personal development. In a deepening relationship, marriage may be on the horizon. Destiny holds pleasant surprises and reciprocity creates good relations, as acts from your past bear their fruit in the present. Listen to what's happening with those around you, for a friend, lover, relative, or someone else close to you needs your support. Courage and emotional strength pave the way for meeting your own needs and lending a helping hand to others when they need it. Dare to meet your life situations in creative ways that challenge old boundaries and limits.

❧ EMOTIONAL INTERPRETATION:

Follow intuitive feelings to discover your emotional reality. Your own impressions in matters of the heart create your personal world. Questions about the direction or manifestations of love bubble up from your unconscious to the surface. Seeds of love and caring that you've sown are nearing maturity now and their soulful cultivation will allow them to bear fruit.

Stop worrying about what others say! Jump high with good intentions, and you'll get a better view of where you're going. Look carefully for hidden or unexpected opportunities. If you don't like your situation, look at practical ways you can change it, because this card indicates you're in a position to consciously turn the wheel of fate. Now is a time to make concrete plans for tomorrow's good fortune, in a spirit of enjoyment and optimism. Call or visit a family member who cares about you, or give a bouquet to a deserving friend or lover to brighten his or her day.

❧ SEXUAL INTERPRETATION:

Kissing under the mistletoe can lead to other exciting events. When primary instincts take their turn in your decision-making process, don't forget that your partner has primary instincts, likes, and dislikes, too. Turn your lovemaking into a dialogue in which you both give and receive, and act and listen, to enhance your sexual perceptions. Avoid getting caught up in feeling like you have to do it "your way," "his way," "her way," or "the way." Allow new possibilities to emerge from attentiveness in the moment. Bring playfulness into your lovemaking, when you're both receptive to it, since making love is usually more fun when it has a playful dimension.

§ REVERSED CARD INTERPRETATION:

Financial responsibilities may keep you busy, but it's the development of your deeper self that can carry you through difficult times. An expanded state of awareness evolves from practicing concentration, meditation, or other practical methods to educate your consciousness. If you have to overcome a challenge, trust in your ability to do so. Jealousy, worries, or irritability put a spotlight on hassles. Since laughter helps liberate the mind, look for unexpected moments of humor in trying situations.

TEN OF PENTACLES

PAGE of PENTACLES

Key Meanings: A youthful person; striving for tangible expressions of love; material ambitions; learning about finances; innocent emotions; flirting

Reversed Meanings: A person who isn't grounded or is financially foolish; immaturity, irresponsibility, impermanence, insensitivity; love's folly

PAGE OF PENTACLES

❧ ROMANTIC INTERPRETATION:

Practical actions, adventure, and learning by doing are the key-words for this page. Your dream lover may be unpredictable or unavailable, so it's not a time to sit and wait for your hopes to be fulfilled. If you're single, a buoyant, flirtatious, or seductive role may work to your advantage, since a relationship (or a series of adventurous, exploratory relationships) may be right around the corner. You might try going out with people who open doors to new activities and experiences. A tentative or exploratory stage of a relationship, however, may be mistaken for a more stable commitment, so be realistic in assessing how much the other is ready to give. If you're in a partnership, love can blossom as a result of shared financial efforts. Look for practical, common goals to strengthen unity. In a partnership, discussing material ambitions and concerns about spending or saving money help keep expectations in balance with reality. Plans need to be down-to-earth for progress to ensue.

❧ EMOTIONAL INTERPRETATION:

This page refers to an apprenticeship or introduction to a path of work that helps you take a meaningful career direction where you can earn tangible success or to new learning that will boost your abilities or responsibilities. Also, it can signify the unfolding realization that material well-being alone means little without interpersonal and spiritual sensitivity. It can also refer to coming into prosperity or wealth without having the judgment, experience, or knowledge to handle it well. Ambitious, but foolish at heart, the page's search for love may be postponed until busy career or financial responsibilities are fulfilled. If emotional commitments are made, they need to be grounded in clear perceptions of financial reality, or when bills come due they may be more than you expect because you weren't paying attention to how much you spent.

❧ SEXUAL INTERPRETATION:

Pages typically represent trusting youth, the fancy-free and young minded whose feelings are vulnerable and sometimes volatile. Often novices in love, they may make promises and professions of love that are good only while their pants are being unzipped. On another level, this card refers to standing at the threshold of transforming lovemaking from a merely physical experience to one in which two souls touch. The mysteries and discipline of tantric lovemaking beckon, while the page is torn between the urges of simple lust and the allure of stepping across the threshold into a grander realm of sexual experience. Sexual experimentation helps the budding romantic explore the realities of passion, sensuality, and love.

Reversed Card Interpretation:

Money matters may make you sing the blues. Still learning moneymaking skills, this page can become frustrated when pockets don't hold the dollars his or her dreams deem necessary for success. Fun, rather than responsibility, may be the focus, and you or your partner's checkbook may register a negative balance. The page may need to learn the difference between real needs and flashy toys.

Beware of accepting what others say just because of their position or authority, since the rich and powerful can be emotionally and spiritually bankrupt. Where can you turn for thoughtful counsel that will help you find your goals, directions, and suitable paths when you're uncertain about how to proceed? Remember that in your very choice of advisors, you're affecting the kind of feedback you're likely to get, and remember, too, that wise counsel can come from unexpected sources.

PAGE of PENTACLES

KNIGHT of PENTACLES

Key Meanings: An assertive person who is financially astute; your own inner warrior who is willing to push hard to achieve tangible results

Reversed Meanings: A person, perhaps confrontational, going blindly after success; money issues create warring emotions, power struggles

KNIGHT of PENTACLES

§ ROMANTIC INTERPRETATION:

As a romantic seeker, this knight symbolizes someone on the move who may be challenged to make or keep a commitment. Adept in strategy and tactics, this warrior's energy is usually focused on making money or achieving other victories in the material world. This knight may also mean that you are getting in touch with your own inner crusader and developing or acquiring the resources you need to succeed in your goals. Parts of yourself that you seldom reveal may offer resources for connecting with an interesting person, or for deepening your relations. Disclosing your own struggles or being open to those of another can complement and inform decisive action. Alternatively, this knight can signify that an industrious, willful person may cross your path. Your finances, or matters concerning either physical or emotional security, may be subject to this person's influence.

§ EMOTIONAL INTERPRETATION:

This knight is a symbol of confidence, zestful living, sexual attractiveness, physical strength or stamina, and accomplishment. Love is not always the first priority for this warrior, as actions are directed toward gaining momentum and eliminating obstacles in the physical realm. However, be active in going after the treasures of love. Opportunities for romantic encounters or for deepening your loving relations will emerge as you move forward with the rhythm of time. Becoming a moment-by-moment witness of your thoughts, feelings, and muscular tensions helps you see how you do or don't open your heart. Awareness of how you hold the reins of your emotions—tightly, loosely, or flexibly in response to circumstances—increases understanding of how to win love's battles. In many contests between valiant knights, the winner is often not the one who strikes first or strikes back, but the one who ducks others' arrows and knows when to stand firm, when to admit a mistake, when to reach out, and when to make a move.

§ SEXUAL INTERPRETATION:

Earthy passions can lead to sensual delights, enlivening the world of physical euphoria. Embracing and hugging your sweetheart moves you forward toward the consummation of love. Why not visualize yourself as the knight who loves to touch and be touched? A word or a touch of loving playfulness at appropriate times can brighten your day and relationships. Perhaps someone will take advantage of the bridge you're building toward love in the moment. Put your fears aside; if someone doesn't reciprocate your passion, remember that it takes two to tango, appreciate him or her as a friend, and trust that you'll find the right someone who desires your love! This knight can also symbolize a self-reliant "virgin goddess" like Artemis who enjoys solitude and feels no need for a partner.

❦ Reversed Card Interpretation:

The upside-down knight denotes a person lacking experience or responsibility, who refuses to recognize these limitations, thinks he or she knows more than is the case, and acts rashly or carelessly. Finances may be at risk. Unwanted effects of one's actions may be blamed on others. Physical involvement may prove stressful or confusing. A retreat to an inspiring natural place may provide needed centering and rejuvenation before moving forward, or for deepening your love connection.

KNIGHT OF PENTACLES

QUEEN OF PENTACLES

QUEEN OF PENTACLES

Key Meanings: The archetypal Earth Mother; a powerful woman with earthly resources; prosperity, abundance; achieving status; fertile seduction; living life with passion

Reversed Meanings: A woman who struggles with power or financial issues; unwise attachments; the inability to manifest desires in reality

❦ ROMANTIC INTERPRETATION:

Planting and harvesting a bountiful garden in the material realm is this queen's delight. Feminine ruler of the element earth and the financial plane, she is linked with prosperity, status, and fertility, whether of crops or procreation. She is also connected with growth, regeneration, and being firmly rooted in reality. She typifies the successful woman who understands the concept of mind over matter and can materialize her dreams of success so that love prospers and goals are reached. Be careful what you wish for, because this card indicates the strong possibility that you'll get your wish. Will mixes with determination to achieve positive results. Possibilities for romance are vivid in the woman represented by this card. Most often she doesn't like to be overpowered with words or actions, but prefers taking the initiative to expand the romantic dimensions of her life.

❦ EMOTIONAL INTERPRETATION:

Optimism enhances prospects for success. This card can refer to a straightforward woman who venerates opening her heart, sharing feelings, and giving love. Her actions are decisive, yet subtle, so that often others do as she wishes without realizing it. She is usually conscious of keeping her physical body strong and healthy and acts wisely to further her emotional awareness and well-being. She lets her hair down and her spirit fly when surrounded by nature. Her ability to read people's emotions makes her receptive to their needs. At the same time, being a romantic, she seeks sincere and lasting love. If in a relationship, she is keenly aware of protecting her privacy and is loyal to her partner and family. Also, this queen can symbolize an ambitious woman with career aspirations who directs her energy in practical, enterprising ways to attain success. She hears messages that many others fail to notice, and is adept at handling complex or tricky situations.

❦ SEXUAL INTERPRETATION:

Associated with beautiful women who are irresistibly attractive, this queen personifies passion, desire, and the heat of sexual love. Not that this kind of woman is easy to get into your bed, but once there, she's giving and lovingly spirited. Even though she may be a seductive enchantress who is confident of her sexuality, she's also discriminating as to whom she allows to penetrate her body and heart. Conscious of soul connections, fertility, and the higher purpose of procreation, she's probably not likely to have sex on a first date. During courtship it may help to win her heart if you offer her flowers, a love bird, or a trip to the mountains.

☙ REVERSED CARD INTERPRETATION:

Upside down, this card shows a woman lacking a sense of purpose or her own personal power. She can be pessimistic or emotionally cold, as a learned defense against repetition of past disappointments or others' insensitivities. Seductive flirting, expensive possessions, and fleeting pleasures may substitute for fulfilling relationships. This can also be a warning that there's a crucial need to build better relations with your partner, someone close to you, or even your inner self.

QUEEN OF PENTACLES

KING of PENTACLES.

Key Meanings: A man with moneymaking power; achievement; cleverness; harvest season; sexually stimulating techniques that make you want to come back for more

Reversed Meanings: An impotent, problematic or dumped man; facing challenges; emotional power struggles; rigidity; conventionality; loneliness

KING of PENTACLES

KING OF PENTACLES

§ ROMANTIC INTERPRETATION:

Hold on to your heart, for a mesmerizing man may influence your emotions and affect your life. If by chance he's married, he might flirt and act like he's single, but be forewarned, he's deeply committed and his queen won't let him go. If single, he's a lover by nature, and may like to play the field. It is possible for him to give his heart and settle into one relationship, but it requires a very magnetic partner. If you want an intimate involvement with him, expect it to be on his terms unless you possesses a mental keenness equal to his, or have an abundant reserve of your own power.

§ EMOTIONAL INTERPRETATION:

A natural leader, this king rules the domain of the element earth, material reality, financial concerns, and tangible assets. Frequently, he is assertive, enterprising, and bold. Down-to-earth understanding of emotions and a commonsense approach to life make him a solid pillar in his community, respected for his practical wisdom. Concerned with the body's realities, he's often athletically minded and keeps physically fit. When he plays a significant role in your personal world, you'll have a lot to do to keep up with his high energy. He listens to counsel from every quarter, including wise advisors, court fools, and his queen, and then, having heard all, is confident in his actions and decisions. He has mastered the skills of strategy and tactics that the knight is still learning. Through instinct or experience, he understands the spectrum of human motives and knows how to sway others to follow his lead. Likely to be keenly aware of ecological issues, he may play a vital role in the quest for the expansion of environmental consciousness, with nature's world constituting part of his sense of the sacred. This card can also refer to tapping into your own physical strength, leadership, or personal power, and using your talents to achieve a tangible goal.

§ SEXUAL INTERPRETATION:

Often irresistibly attractive, this king has an easy time meeting women. His commanding, yet considerate manner is a turn on. He loves exploring sensual realities and giving a massage with oil is a frequent part of his foreplay. If you get naked and wrap your legs around him, he'll take you on a ride you won't soon forget. A connoisseur of lovemaking, he likes to hold his staff of power erect for a long, long time. (Some kings, however, have cultivated power instead of sexual maturity, and must be treated as beginners in learning the mutuality and sensitivity of love-making.)

℘ REVERSED CARD INTERPRETATION:

Reversed, this king can represent an impotent man or an immoral person, or someone who is arrogant and lacks compassion. He may be shrewd or egotistical, sacrificing love and caring on the altars of power and wealth. If he lacks sensitivity, he may exhibit a myopic "bulldoze everything in his path" mentality that can apply equally to people and other living beings. This card can also signify that you yourself have to deal with challenges, frustrations, power struggles, or negative earthly issues. Protect yourself by detaching from negative emotions and saying "No!" to controlling people who try to interfere in your life.

KING OF PENTACLES

EPILOGUE

Love in its spiritual essence is an attribute of wisdom. It flows from the vision of the interdependence of all life and the oneness of all existence.
—Sri Aurobindo, *The Mind of Light*

To the degree that you're open to the lessons of the cards, they can help you appreciate the beauty within yourself and others, and cultivate a loving heart. They can open doors to heretofore hidden chambers within you and in your communication and relationships. They can help you develop the strength to persevere in the pursuit of your hopes and dreams, make your way through life's maelstroms, and appreciate simple joys in the present moment.

As a card reader, what you've read and pondered in these pages can help you help others. If you're already reading for others, actively bringing these insights into your work can assist you (or your students) in moving from being a beginning or intermediate reader to being a master of the craft.

When you make the cards your friends, they will provide support and inspiration as you travel along life's path. They will offer many messages—sometimes in a whisper and sometimes in a shout—that can sharpen your thinking and awareness, and draw forth your love and laughter.

BIBLIOGRAPHY

Aurobindo, Sri. *The Mind of Light*. New York: Dutton, 1971.

Bolen, Jean Shinoda. *Goddesses in Everywoman: A New Psychology of Women*. New York: HarperCollins, 1984.

———. *Gods in Everyman: A New Psychology of Men's Lives and Loves*. San Francisco: HarperSanFrancisco, 1989.

Boulet, Susan Seddon, and Michael Babcock. *The Goddess Paintings*. San Francisco: Pomegranate, 1994.

BPC Publishing. *Man, Myth, and Magic*. New York: Marshall Cavendish Corp, 1970.

Crowley, Aleister. *The Book of Thoth*. York Beach, ME: Weiser Books, 2002.

Dening, Sarah. *The Mythology of Sex: An Illustrated Exploration of Sexual Customs and Practices from Ancient Times to the Present*. New York: Macmillan, 1996.

Douglas, Nik and Penny Slinger. *Sexual Secrets: The Alchemy of Ecstasy*. Rochester, VT: Destiny Books, 1979.

Gibran, Kahlil. *The Prophet*. New York: Alfred A. Knopf, 1952.

Goodman, Linda. *Linda Goodman's Love Signs*. New York: Harper & Row, 1999.

Johari, Harish. *Chakras: Energy Centers of Transformation*. Rochester, VT: Destiny Books, 1987.

———. *Numerology, with Tantra, Ayurveda, and Astrology*. Rochester, VT: Destiny Books, 1990.

Jung, Carl Gustave. *Synchronicity: An Acausal Connecting Principle*. Trans. R. F. Hull. Ed. G. Adler. Princeton University Press, 1973.

Knight, Sirona. *Moonflower: Erotic Dreaming with the Goddess*. St. Paul, MN: Llewellyn, 1996.

Lacroix, Nitya. *The Art of Tantric Sex: Ancient Techniques and Rituals That Enhance Sexual Pleasure*. New York: DK Publishing, 1997.

Medici, Marina. *Love Magic*. New York: Fireside, 1994.

Nichols, Sallie. *Jung and Tarot: An Archetypal Journey*. York Beach, Maine: Weiser Books, 1991.

Odier, Daniel. *Tantric Quest: An Encounter with Absolute Love*. Trans. Jody Gladding. Rochester, VT: Inner Traditions, 1997.

Ouspensky, P. D. *The Symbolism of the Tarot: Philosophy of Occultism in Pictures*. Trans. A. L. Pogossky. New York: Dover Publications, 1976.

Perls, Fritz. *Gestalt Therapy Verbatim*. Highland, NY: The Gestalt Journal Press, 1988.

———. *In and Out of the Garbage Pail*. Highland, NY: The Gestalt

Journal Press, 1992.

Rama, Swami. *Living with the Himalayan Masters.* Honesdale, PA: The Himalayan Institute Press, 1999.

Resnick, Stella. *The Pleasure Zone: Why We Resist Good Feelings and How to Let Go and Be Happy.* Berkeley, CA: Conari Press, 1997.

Rogers, Carl. *Freedom to Learn for the 80s.* New York: Macmillan/Merrill, 1983.

Sinah, Indra. *The Great Book of Tantra: Translations and Images from the Classic Indian Text.* Rochester, VT: Destiny Books, 1993.

Vanmali, Nitya. *Yoga.* Rishikesh, India: Vanmali Publications, n.d.

Wilhelm, Richard. *The I Ching, or Book of Changes,* 3rd Edition. Trans. Cary F. Baynes. Princeton: Princeton University Press, 1967.